What a story, what a life!
Big Daddy Graham
Comic~Talk Show Host

Traveling at the Speed of Life is a very provocative book of essays about cycling and of humankind.
Teri Maloughney
Adventure Cycling Association
Missoula, MT

"Travelling at the Speed of Life" contains some vivid and charming descriptions of the people David has met on his very personal journey of discovery. His extra-ordinary determination and self-belief to explore the world and the impact simple personal connections can make is inspiring.
Catriona Kennedy
Edinburgh, Scotland.

Traveling at the Speed of life recounts the exceptional journey of a Black man and his mission to bring this large and diverse world a little closer together through everyday actions of compassion, tolerance, and understanding. In travelling around the world on a bicycle, Sylvester shows the reader exactly what can happen when an ordinary individual acts in extraordinary ways. By showing that all human beings are the same when it comes to such simple things in life as hugs, smiles, and handshakes; David's story teaches us that the key to thwarting stereotypes and bridging gaps of difference is human interaction and getting to know individual people personally. Sylvester is an inspiration to the African/Black community, specifically, and all of humanity, in general, and is doing exactly what we, in the discipline, define as Black Studies.
Dr. Aimee Glocke
Professor, University of Wyoming

'Traveling at the Speed of Life' is an honest success because of David's open heart. It is obvious that he has so much more to give and I cannot wait to read what he will do next.

Tess Orgasan Zwizanski
Philadelphia

Filled with courage, determination, and passion, *Traveling at the Speed of Life* is an inspirational journey of self-discovery. David's telling is honest and emotional, and even humorous at times reminding us that we are part of a world much bigger than our own families and communities. David's heart reminds us that we can all make a difference.

Dr. N. Tamanaha
San Francisco, CA

David's passion and excitement for life is evident when you meet him. But upon reading about his worldwide bike adventures, one can truly appreciate his compassion and understanding for those from all walks of life. *Traveling at the Speed of Life* reminds the reader that sometime's life's richest moments come from enjoying the journey, regardless of the destination. .

Kathryn G. Moore, ESQ
London

Traveling at the Speed of Life and the story of David Sylvester are so special because they are honest. They are real. Dave weaves surprising insights and earnest reflections into each adventure and bike journey, even when it is not pretty. That alone is inspiring, and that is what makes this book so inspiring. By the end, you wonder what you, yourself are waiting for? What is stopping you from making your dreams hap-

pen? And that to me, makes Dave worth knowing, and his story worth reading...
Malini Sekhar
Arlington, VA

The descriptive nature of David's proses are so vivid that you are feeling the raw emotions that David is feeling in that moment as described. In this book David shows you how to live with passion and it will get you through hard times and good times. Sharing that passion can only make it better. I am humbled by many of David's observation about our world and himself and that we are all human. The are open and honest stories that bring you face to face with real stuff - suffering, joy, struggles, achievement. There is a story for everyone in this book.....
Cynthia Kwan
University of Pennsylvania

I've met David and rarely do you meet someone with his sense of confidence, charisma and wisdom. His story/book is, not only inspiring, but also paints a "no bull-shit" picture of who he is- a man all of us should be lucky enough to meet.
Chris Fireoved
Paris, France

Hardly a cushy travel journal, "Travelling" is a how-to live manual for the athlete, the social worker and the next door neighbor. Through genuine humility and brutal honesty, Sylvester takes the reader around the world on rocky trails and through the streets of large cities, to show that, in our vast differences, all humans are exactly the same. The reader will become empowered as they get a first hand look at his tremendous evolution to become the very best version of himself.
Lynne Hernandez

'While writing about his youthful joy of pedaling around the world to connect with the people, Dave captures the emotions and epiphanies many bicyclists have experienced and inspires us all to take our passions to their limits.

Joe Wentzell -Breakaway Bikes

"Love = [Forward Movement + Physical Power of My Body/ Wind] + [Human Interaction (Smiles+Hugs) / Exploration] x Passion."This is David Sylvester's formula for life. If you're ready to shed the cynical fear that is so prevalent in this 21st century; if you're ready for huge passion, huge honesty and huge integrity, then buy this book. Traveling at the Speed of Life is part travelogue, part man-meets-humankind and part bildungsroman, but mostly it's a lesson in courage. Traveling at the Speed of Life + A Few Quiet Hours = a Life Changing Experience.

Sheryl Leonard
Writer, Editor
Ventura, CA

David Sylvester draws us in with his charm and sincerity. His essays on cycling, service and personal growth are sometimes irreverent but his willingness to bear his own human foibles make his message come across as genuine and not preachy. His travels in Africa and a visit to a battered women's center in the US made this a very memorable read and I'm already looking forward to reading his next books.

Deidre Woods
Philadelphia

David Sylvester has done the unachievable and written the great American novel....and it's about his life.

Maurice Baynard MS PhD
Lecturer Biology

I met David in Austin on his '08 bike trip. Wearing a large white cowboy hat, you couldn't help but notice him. David is larger than life and his tangible and inspiring enthusiasm and compassion comes across loud and clear in Traveling at the Speed of Life.
Melissa Bernstein
Austin, Texas

"Travelling at the Speed of Life" is like a bike trip. The first time around is filled with surprise. Each repeat trip reveals some new detail in the old familiar scenes. Yet like different bike routes there is always the favorite – for me it's "Faceless Angels".
Anne B (Mother and Physician)
Ireland

Big Dave. That was his original moniker. But as his Lycra loosened and weary seatpost relaxed under his shrinking girth, it became obvious that he was really Big-Hearted Dave. To me, my wife Traci Lynne, and the other "leisure" participants of the Cairo to Cape Town adventure, it was always a delight to ride with David for a few minutes or for hours. His unique perspectives on life and this crazy world are refreshing and interesting. He would frequently appear with a smile, a cold drink, or a great story. My personal favorite was when he went splat in a dusty road in southern Tanzania and a Catholic priest picked him up, bandaged him, and fed him--ice cream if I greedily recall. That is a quintessential Big Dave moment....he seems to find a way to get lemonade out of that lemon.
Dr. John Brewer & Dr. Traci Lynne Brewer.
Alabama

I met David through the pages of this book, first as an article, sent to my sister Stephanie, whom David met in the Santa Barbara

Airport, then as chapter after chapter, sent to me rough and then gently polished and shaped into the work that you find in your hands now. Upon facing challenge after challenge, David reveals a way of living through love, a path of trust and willingness that we don't often see in our modern world. David uses his bike to connect to the people of the world, but he also uses his voice; eloquent, honest and like a best friend sharing his experiences with you so that you may travel the world with him, one pedal stroke, hug, tear at a time. When I grow up, I want to be just like David.

Shelley Meaney
Creator, Terra Celeste Productions
Santa Barbara, CA

Traveling at the Speed of Life

DAVID HALE SYLVESTER

Dedication

To my friend, my mother: Thank you for leaning on me, re-grading my papers downward, making me use my brain, challenging me, giving me a lifetime of memories, and just being there. You made me better.

To Peter, the Tanzanian: We only met once but had one very dynamic conversation that broadened my outlook on life. You reminded me that I had "power" and cautioned that I "better find a way to use it." This book is the full use of my power, as of this moment. I hope you like it.

Contents

Foreword

Lance Armstrong recovered from cancer in his brain to win the Tour de France seven times, turn a generation of Americans onto cycling and make a plastic yellow wristband into a true fashion statement. But for me, America's most inspiring cyclist is David Sylvester.

If you've never heard of Big Dave you're in for a treat because you are about to meet an amazing man in the following pages.

So Lance has won seven races around France? Big deal. Big Dave has ridden across the width of the United States (twice), down the entire length of Africa and across Asia from Turkey to Beijing. Lance may have powered up Alpe d'Huez but try riding though the Himalayas when the weather is so cold ice is literally forming on your frame. And surely even winning the world's most famous and demanding bike race is made somewhat easier when you have a multi-million dollar support crew of riders and mechanics tending to your bike, breaking the wind resistance for you and bringing you food and water. Dave once called me from somewhere in Arizona after having to repair his punctured tires 10 times in one lonely, 100-plus-degree day.

And no matter how hard, how far or how fast Lance rode, he never had to pitch his own tent at the end of a stage.

I first met Big Dave one afternoon a couple summers ago when he agreed to ride with me through Pennsylvania's Amish country. He gave me a hug at the end of the ride and I think my ribs are still healing. Big Dave is a powerful man and when he hugs you, you feel it. He literally lifts you off the ground. Which is fitting because he also figuratively lifts you up to see beyond your horizon. Funny, friendly and a force of nature, Dave started talking to me that afternoon and I don't think he stopped more than a dozen times before evening. Consider this book a Cliff's Notes version of his story.

Be forewarned though: whether you experience Big Dave's stories in print, through his documentary or in person they will be as gripping as one of hugs.

Dave's stories are funny- ask him about the wedding reception he crashed in Azerbaijan if you ever meet him. Dave's stories are entertaining- listen to his descriptions of the various toilets he incurred along his travels in his movie. Dave's stories are sad- read his chapter 'Shut up and drink your coffee,' about him stumbling upon an Ethiopian funeral march. Dave's stories can be very simple and emotionally wrenching at the same time -like when he came across a man doing very well with a roadside coffin business in an AIDS-stricken country in Africa. But as compelling as those cycling stories are, it is his other stories that will strike you the hardest. His thoughtful observations about life, about friends, about family, about attitudes, about strangers from foreign lands will force you to set down the book and reflect at the same time they drive you to read onto the next chapter.

I guarantee you will think hard and long when you read Dave's chapter about the guys who opened a clothing store called Niggers in Malawi. Or when a couple cycling companions voted him out of the group and onto his own shadow ride through the mountains of China, saying they feared him simply because he was big and black.

That last story is particularly disturbing because Big Dave's overriding message from his biking adventures is precisely the opposite: Don't be afraid. Don't be afraid to go somewhere you've never gone. Don't be afraid to try something you've never done. Don't be afraid to take a chance. Don't be afraid to get lost. Don't be afraid to find yourself.

But I'm getting in his way. It's time for me to peel off and let him take his pull at the front of the peloton.

Read his stories and be entertained. Read his stories and be appalled. Read his stories and be inspired. Mostly, read his stories and learn how far you can take yourself and how much you can accomplish one little revolution of the pedals at a time.

Jim Caple, ESPN

A word, before we start...

On September 11, 2001, I couldn't move.

From what I saw in my hometown of Philadelphia, all of us were immobile that day. In the blink of an eye, our once-familiar world had gone mad and left us waiting by jammed phone lines for word from our loved ones, or looking skyward, wondering if we would be next.

While the images that we are now all too familiar with flashed across the TV screen, I sat riveted to my chair, too stunned to cry, too stunted to move and too insignificant to grasp the totality of what was going on. On that day, the problems of the world seemed too immense. I was left holding my breath and thinking of the four friends who worked at the World Trade Center. So many reports, updates, and perspectives made time crawl by as if the dust would never settle. But slowly, very slowly, word filtered out:

"David, I'm okay. I was on a lower floor."

"Dave, I was out of town that day."

"Dave, I overslept, and I am alive..."

I exhaled with great relief after each call, but I kept wondering about Kevin Bowser. I needed to know where he was.

Strictly speaking, Kevin Bowser was only my neighbor, but because I had known him, his twin brother, Kelvin, and the rest of his family my whole life, he was much more. Kevin Bowser was family—my family. Each viewing of the plane smashing into the very floor where Kevin worked made me wince and stoked my fears.

For days I waited with Kevin's family in his childhood home, an address that held a lifetime's worth of memories. I stood in solidarity with his family, but as time agonizingly trickled by, we bowed, one by one, to the obvious: Kevin Leah Bowser—the husband, father, brother, twin, son, friend, and loving human—was gone.

When I concluded that Kevin was not coming back, I did what I did a lot in those days: I just stood.

I stood leery of what might loom on the on the horizon for my nation. I stood and wept while Kevin's wife received a folded American flag from a senator's aide. I stood with teary eyes at Kevin's memorial service. I stood helplessly everywhere.

Maybe that was why the messages from U.S. leaders to "go out and shop," in order to boost the American economy and to assert our American virtue stirred me so much. Frivolous spending had never defined life for me prior to 9/11, and I had stood idly by for far too long to waste time just purchasing things afterward. With sorrow and loss in my heart, I started thinking, more than any other time in my life, about what I really treasured and what my role could be in making the world a more sensible place.

It didn't take long to realize that the only things that really held any value for me were the smiles and hugs from those who were left in my life. That unique warmth was my life's only real currency and the only thing that I wanted to acquire. It also didn't take long to realize that I was done standing around.

I am a person who can go a long way on just one emotion, so once I came to these conclusions, the next decision was a snap.

I would ride a bicycle across North America to raise funds and awareness for a scholarship that had been started in Kevin's name, and to try to acquire as many hugs as possible.

Now, in a life filled with skips of conviction, the endeavor to bicycle a few thousand miles across the USA was my biggest leap of faith yet. Even though I had the initial idea soon after the tragedy of 9/11, it wasn't until the summer of 2002 that I actually packed up my bicycle and boarded my flight to Astoria, Oregon. I was excited about what I was about to do and possibly see, but I would be lying if I said that I wasn't a bit nervous about the whole thing.

Truth be told, by the time I put my bike back together, I was *real* nervous.

The whole thing left me so uncertain that I pedaled in the wrong direction at first and rode west into Washington State. But once I righted myself and started giving and receiving smiles, hugs and high-fives, I became more at ease.

I became so at ease that, believe it or not, bicycling across the continent — through Washington, Oregon, Idaho, Wyoming, South Dakota, Wisconsin, Minnesota, Michigan, Canada, Vermont, New Hampshire, Massachusetts, Connecticut, and into New York City to leave a picture of Kevin at the World Trade Center site didn't seem like work.

Now don't get me wrong, none of what I did was easy and yes, it was effort to pay for the trip, buy another bike and take leave from my job but… by the time I finished honoring a special friendship by pedaling on through New Jersey and finally back into Philadelphia- all of the smiles and many heartwarming gestures made all that I did *feel so damn right.*

My trip ended at the address where I had spent much of my youth and where just months earlier had waited for a call that never came. But after seeing the nation through a lens of genuine human warmth, Kevin's childhood home is where my journey began.

My journey didn't start right away, though, because I didn't know what could possibly rival my American experience. But once I heard about a bicycle race across Africa and saw the route, my mind reeled as it contemplated the possibilities.

I worked as hard as I ever have to go on that trip, and any time I felt tired or like I was going astray, I pulled out the route map. Just seeing the bike route — through Egypt, Sudan, Ethiopia, Kenya, Tanzania, Malawi, Zambia, Namibia, Botswana, and South Africa - immediately refocused me.

Bicycling North America took me right to the limit of what I thought I could achieve, but Africa pushed me right over the edge. Bicycling Africa freed me from what I thought was possible and revealed to me that I was more capable than I ever believed. Once I saw that I could achieve even more, I wanted to do even more.

It didn't matter that I wasn't a professional filmmaker, professional writer, professional speaker or professional anything. I was unfettered and worked tirelessly at pushing my own boundaries. In a year, I made a film, got published, and earned enough to make plans to ride South America, too— across Columbia, Ecuador, Peru, Chile, and Argentina.

Those plans ended when a drunk driver hit me.

The injuries sustained left me limping around and unable to ride a bicycle, but the trips across North America and Africa had left me with a strong will.

And will always triumphs.

I rehabbed like mad to get rid of my limp and get my act together to ride across another continent: Asia.

Bicycling across Turkey, the Republic of Georgia, Azerbaijan, Turkmenistan, Uzbekistan, Tajikistan, Kyrgyzstan, and China was tougher than North America and Africa. It required even more focus and drive, but I emerged from this journey even more resilient and with a definitive voice.

ESPN contacted me about writing an article on my travels, and in order to possibly connect with readers, I decided to use my resilience to channel that voice. The response to my voice, writing, and experiences revealed a worldwide network of people who believed in me and wanted me do more.

I had already gone a long way on emotion, but the calls, emails, and letters that I received from people made me want to go even further. I decided to make another cross-continental bike trip as a way to show my gratitude, but merely riding through the communities wasn't nearly enough. From July 4 to September 11, I pedaled solo across North America again — through California, Arizona, New Mexico, Texas, Louisiana, Mississippi, Alabama, Tennessee, Virginia, DC, Maryland, Delaware, Pennsylvania, New Jersey, and New York, doing stints of service at local charities once a week.

And that, my friend, is my story, short and sweet.

Now let me tell you about this book.

Upon returning from my last cross-continental bicycle trip—my fourth— in September of 2008, I felt that I finally had enough nerve, powerful encounters, life experiences, and, most importantly, perspective to write my story in the way I wanted it to be told. Since then, I have sat down daily and used every bit of maturity, discipline, will, and passion within me to write, self-edit, rewrite, grow up, and allow my work to be edited and honed. All of this has led to something that I hope is a compelling and motivating book.

Traveling at the Speed of Life is a book of independent essays that are about a journey that began after my friend's death on September 11, 2001 but which focuses on the powerful, opportunity-filled and living moments that comprised September 12th, 13th, and every other day that we live.

It is a book where people who never met me will get a good idea of who I am and my longtime friends will understand my drive even more.

I am aware that people don't have a lot of time to read a whole book these days so I chose to treat each essay as a lengthy postcard and, like any postcard, the essays are about everyday occurrences: drinking coffee, meeting people, finding love, losing love, getting lost, and getting in fights. But unlike other postcards that may have frivolous messages scrawled on them, these postcards are about how these common occurrences have profoundly changed my life and broadened my perspectives.

Almost all of the stories in this book happened on a bicycle, but I am not a great bicyclist, so this book is not about bike gears, terrain, metal alloys or weight grams. I am just a big, regular guy who likes riding bikes (yet always seems to break them, maybe it's my size) and loves meeting people. Thus, this book is about the people one can possibly meet while riding a bike and the emotional and spiritual journeys that those encounters can set in motion.

But let me get to what I believe is the coolest part of this book. The coolest part *of Traveling at the Speed of Life* is that, hopefully, while reading this, you will think, "If that big, regular guy can do all of this, then I certainly can do _____."

That's the coolest part because it's true.

I am living proof. There are many reasons why I should not have been able to do what I have done: too big, too broke, too slow, too black, too this, too that, too unknown, too unprofessional, too foulmouthed, too something or too other. The list is long, but there is only one reason why I have been able to do what I have done: *Because I wanted* to.

So know that everything I've done and have written about, and anything that you want to do, is attainable if you truly want it.

It doesn't matter if you are up, down, or have just been standing around in life; *Traveling at the Speed of Life* is for you because it is predicated on the beliefs that any given moment can change your life, and that passion is the key ingredient to make every one of your moments successful.

Sit down and read an essay or two. Allow my stories to mix with the fertile soil of your own imagination and personal experiences. Let it all ferment and then go somewhere out in the world and attempt something that you believed was beyond your grasp. Go do something to lead a fuller life.

And then get ready to meet the most fascinating, most textured, most complex and most powerful person you can ever meet: yourself.

This book is not some deep or complicated tome.

This is just me, David Hale Sylvester, traveling at the speed of life.

Read on.

NORTH AMERICA

Eulogy

Any story about my life after 9/11, or any attempt to explain who I am, has to start on the day I buried my father. No excursion, trip, or expedition to any county, country, or continent can compare to the day I traveled from pew to podium to eulogize my father.

I was 28 years old on that day and openly acknowledged to my friends, my father's colleagues, my family, and even perfect strangers that I was alone and unaware of where I was going. I was adrift, and knew that I was going to need my father but more than needing him, I was going to want my father—all of them.

You see, while your average person may get *one* father per lifetime, I've had the luxury and blessing of having three.

First, there was Daddy.

Daddy had three things with him at all times: admirable charisma, a perspective-giving life lesson for every person he encountered, and a cigarette dangling from his mouth. All of that combined to give him something that all truly great men have: presence. His presence made him much, much larger than life and seem like he could do anything. This made me want to study him in every way, from how he spoke down to his signature fist pump and the words he used to end every conversation: "Be good."

A great basketball player in his day, Daddy was more excited than I was when I told him that I made my seventh grade team. His face lit up as he put on a dribbling display around the house, using the furniture as defenders. There was a magic and exuberance about him that the walls of the house could not contain.

"Let's go outside," he said. Once outside, he performed a few more tricks and started doing a drill he called taps, where you shoot the ball onto a spot about ten feet high and then jump up and tip it back to the same spot with the same hand. He did all of this with his ever-present lit cigarette dangling from his lip.

As an adult, I can look back on this memory and clearly hear the huffing and puffing as he talked about how his jump shot could never be taken away from him. But when I was a kid, his display left me amazed and wondering if any of Daddy's spark, athleticism, and charisma might be in me.

It wasn't—at least not at that point.

After this demonstration and a few weeks of riding the bench, I was excited to finally get in a game. Maybe I was *too* excited. My heart pounded furiously as every sentence of sports advice I had ever been given screamed in my head all at once. My mouth dried up and my legs felt heavy, but the longer I played, the more everything settled down. I started to feel more in control, and that's when I saw my opportunity.

My opponent mistook my anxiety for lack of skill and got sloppy with his handling of the ball. I stole the ball from him, ran down the court and beautifully laid the ball up for two points. I then pumped my fist—just like Daddy—and felt like I was on top of the world.

I turned to look at him in the stands, only to find an expressionless stare on his face. I then wheeled around to look at my bench of teammates and coaches, each of whom sat with the same glass-eyed gaze. Even the referee stood silent for a moment.

Apparently, in my eagerness to make the play and be Daddy-like, I didn't dribble the ball once, except for the single bounce I did before the lay-up.

And if that wasn't bad enough, I argued the call.

Daddy and the rest of my family were natural competitors at everything, from debates to cards. He would tell me that once you got in an opponent's head, the competition would soon be over. So, in an effort to try to ignite the same competitive fire in me, he was merciless while beating me in any game we played.

"All day," was just one of the things that he would say while wearing a wry smile and trash-talking nonstop. He did all of this with a glint in his eye, only stopping to tell me, "Think. Remember everything and do different." He would then repeat the same move in the same way, over and over, until I learned to defend it. During every game we watched or played, he would remind me that all great competitors remained focused, at all times, on what was going on in the game. But I was an underachieving schoolboy at the time, and the concept of paying attention to anything all the time — let alone paying attention to everything, all of the time — seemed a Herculean task.

I never really got what he was saying until much later in life.

How a person thought and what they thought about was a big deal to my entire family. Each day, as a part of my parents' "home-work" (not my regular schoolwork), I had to read a newspaper and be prepared to weigh in on any local, national, or social issue with my mother, father and sister at dinner. Being the youngest afforded me no breaks.

Neither did my position at the kitchen table. My beautiful, willful, caring, and driven mother sat to my right. My sister, who embodied intellectual excellence, sat across from me. My father sat to my left. Each conversation slowly (though for me, much too quickly) made its way around the dinner table, eventually putting me in the crosshairs.

I said that I didn't have an opinion once, but that didn't get me a break, because I then had to be able to express why I didn't have an opinion. I quickly learned that trying to defend my own apathy was much harder than learning all the sides of an issue, so I developed an ability to grasp the broadest concepts of an issue.

As a kid, I was obsessed with action heroes — but Daddy appreciated men who thought while taking action and always pointed out the huge differences between the two. Whether talking about an athlete, activist, or artist, my father would say, "Talent's not enough in this world," and then give glowing words only to those who leveraged their talent to do something more. "You can't just take. You have to give something back," he once told me.

Daddy was a thoughtful and thought-provoking man.

He was my daddy, but to everyone else he was Mr. Sam.

Though I saw Daddy every day, I never got to truly appreciate Mr. Sam, the esteemed professor at the University of Pennsylvania's School of Social Work, until I saw him through the recollections of others. Mr. Sam would stroll the grounds of the Ivy League campus acknowledging everyone, from the president of the university down to the custodial workers, and was always willing to share a smile or a bit of wisdom with either.

At seventeen, I was in two different summer basketball leagues and barely knew when one of my teams was practicing and the other one was playing a game. During one game, after I committed a dumb foul, I was surprised to hear "Think. Think. Think," resonating through the grandstands. As I watched my opponent take his second foul shot, I was convinced that I was hearing voices in my head.

But then I glanced up in the bleachers to see my father, holding a rolled-up newspaper and talking to the gym manager. Cigarette dangling from his mouth, he shouted the word "Think" once more.

As play resumed, I stood there with a puzzled look, silently asking him how he knew when and where I was playing when I had barely made it to the game myself. "I've told you," he yelled across the court, "you don't know who I know. Now get your head in the game."

Mr. Sam was as relentless at engaging and debating my friends as he was with me, and they gravitated toward him because they rightly saw a man that gave a damn.

While many fathers would cheer and encourage only their sons, Mr. Sam yelled for all of us to play our best, and to always keep thinking.

After a football game during my senior year of high school, Daddy hugged and kissed me, but believing myself too old for such displays of affection, and flush with teenage bravado, I pushed him away.

My friend Ray hit me in the head with his football helmet and said, "Don't do that to Sam!"

I was embarrassed and told Ray that he didn't understand.

Ray retorted, "Nah, Beef [my nickname at the time]. You don't understand. Some of us have no one coming to our games."

Everyone found Mr. Sam funny, but he always reminded us that he was no joke. When he thought that we were bordering on being disrespectful, he would remind us it would not be pretty if he decided to "go back home" to his roots on the tough corners of South Philly in order to put us back in line. "I can go there in a second," he would say with a sly wink.

When I was in high school, a friend of mine came over to the house to speak with my father. I had no idea what they were talking about, but I could tell from their body language that it was serious. It was only as an adult, when my friend told me, that I found out that he had been sexually abused. At an age when most young men wouldn't speak to anyone, especially another male, this boy sought out and talked to Mr. Sam. I still run into this friend from time to time. Before we part, he always hugs me and says, "Thank God for Mr. Sam."

Mr. Sam was a father and friend to many. Even those who never met him appreciated and admired him. A college classmate who was raised by a single mother only knew my father through my countless stories. One day she tearfully told me that I naturally smiled when I spoke of him, and that she felt she had missed something essential in her life. Even when not physically present, Mr. Sam had a way of leaving an indelible mark on lives.

Most got an opportunity to enjoy Daddy and benefit from Mr. Sam, but I alone met Samuel.

Samuel Sylvester in any incarnation always deserved my full respect and admiration, but another level of understanding developed between us when he was diagnosed with cancer. Each conversation we had during his battle was like no other. Our talks were a spontaneous mix of hugs and memories during which we shed tears and I learned even more life lessons. Though a lot of the lessons he communicated were hard to grasp at the time, they were impossible for me to forget. I knew that he was trying to tell me as much as he could during our last moments together.

Our relationship evolved beyond the limits of father and son, or even of friendship. I'm not going to imply that this evolution in our relationship was due to any action on my part; this change between us was all due to Samuel. I did nothing but stand there and let his love and perspective on life steep within my being.

During his illness, Samuel displayed the most basic and best qualities that a man can display. He exhibited bravery, because he continued to move forward even though he was scared. He projected intelligence, because he didn't fake anything and admitted what he didn't know about life when it mattered most. He showed strength, because even in a weakened state, he did everything he could to strengthen my resolve in life and living. He was thoughtful, because during our private conversations, he let me in on what he was thinking. He was beneficent, because he gave me what I would need in life before his own life ended. He was a visionary, because he knew that in order to be successful, his son would have to see the world through the eyes of someone who wasn't going to be alive much longer. Doing all of this solidified his presence as my enduring hero, because, above all of this, Samuel was beautifully human.

During his final days, Samuel called me to his room to tell me that over the course of his life, he had been holding onto years of unexpressed feelings. He went back over some of the less-than-stellar events of my life.

He said in his professor's voice, "Now that I am at the end, [the negative emotion] I held onto was worthless. David, whatever you feel, express it and get it out of you." I gave him a droll smile, which he immediately (and correctly) read and responded to: "Don't be a butt."

Then he addressed one of my biggest weaknesses, and urged me not to say the first thing that entered my mouth. He admonished me to really try to learn how to clearly communicate my feelings properly. He told me that whether it was love, disappointment, sadness, happiness, or whatever, I should struggle to find a way to communicate it. He explained that people could then walk toward me, walk away from me, or work with me, but once the sentiment was outside of me, I was free to move. He told me that doing this wouldn't stop the hurt of living, but it would help with the healing of life.

Daddy, Mr. Sam and Samuel were my three fathers.

My family and I stayed with my father in shifts toward the end of his illness. After what would be my last shift with him, I drove home, exhausted. My only thoughts were of him and getting some rest. My whole being groaned when I approached my house and saw two figures standing on my doorstep. I had absolutely no energy to be hospitable.

A great sense of relief came over me, though, when I recognized one of the people standing on my porch. I knew that he was well aware of the gravity of my father's situation. We didn't say much. We didn't have to.

"Get some sleep. I'll answer the phone and take care of things," Kevin Bowser said.

I told him that would be a great load off my mind. We started to enter the house, but he stopped right at the threshold and said, "Wait a sec, you still have cable, right?"

"Yeah, we got cable," I said.

"Cool. We're going to be here all night."

Kevin and his twin brother Kelvin were the sons of my father's good friend and grew up one block away from me. Even though I was ten years younger, with no brothers of my own, and without any boys my age living on my block, I was relentless about turning them into the brothers that I wanted.

Kevin and Kelvin had very distinct personality traits. Kelvin was more effusive and cocky, and Kevin was more deliberate. But both men were very driven toward their own pursuits, and also driven to help guide me through life. I could say so much more about my relationship with the twins collectively, and specifically about my friendship with Kevin, but the bottom line was that this was no ordinary man joking about cable TV at my door. He was family. He was my brother.

Worrying whether I had crammed as much life into each remaining moment I had with my father made me feel trapped—ensnared in the present, unable to run back into the past when my dad was healthy, and very fearful of a future without him. Feeling emotionally and physically drawn and quartered I fought sleep during those days.

I was beyond tired, but with Kevin manning the house, it was different; I could comfortably turn off the lights and relent to the darkness that eventually ushered in peace along with a few hours of sleep.

Later that night, light filled the room. Kevin stood in front of me with the phone in his hand. Because I trusted that Kevin would not wake me for anything minor, I knew who was on the phone and what was going to be said.

"I don't want it," I said.

Holding back tears, Kevin said, "You have to take it."

All I clearly remember was my mother saying two words: "It's time."

Frenetically, I moved everywhere but went nowhere. Thoughts of my father's final moments, his last breaths, and what he would see before he closed his eyes seized me.

Kevin's hug centered me. He wept with me as I broke down crying at my doorway. "I know," he said, "I know."

Kevin wasn't reiterating empty platitudes; he knew how time and a life could slip away, even when you are holding tight. His mother had passed away from cancer two years earlier. His words and his brotherhood made me very conscious of what was going on—so conscious and aware that I still remember running two lights while speeding to the hospital. I remember my mother's and sister's faces in the hallway. I remember entering my father's room. I remember him being gone, but still strongly feeling his presence as I sat alone with him one last time.

Daddy was dead.

Mr. Sam was gone.

I was already sorely missing Samuel.

I am extremely fortunate to have known each of these men all wrapped up into one marvelous man. They each imparted nuggets of wisdom that continually challenge me, to this day, to struggle toward my greater potential.

In his eulogy, I spoke about my father's ubiquitous presence, his attending basketball games that that I never had told him about, and I jokingly imitated the way he yelled my name. I acknowledged my fortune at having such an excellent father when others had none and I admitted to everyone in the church that, now that my father was gone, I was going to have to grow up.

My parents and their friends valued a person who gave and honored their word, so I made a vow in front of them to be a walking, breathing, thinking monument to my father. I pledged to be smarter, more helpful, more healthful, and more passionate about life. I pledged to be more compassionate to those in my life who have not been as fortunate as I have been to have received as great a gift as my father. I knew that when I made this pledge, my family and friends would hold me accountable. I also knew if I made such a weighty promise, that they would guide me should I ever stray. The day I stood up to make this speech was the day that I started my journey of becoming a man.

Both Kevin and Kelvin were pallbearers at my father's funeral, and both helped me get through those initial days by simply being there to listen to me cry.

My relationship with and respect for Kevin had grown a great deal during my father's last months. Kevin lived in Philadelphia, but worked ninety miles away in New York City at the World Trade Center. His daily commute called for him to catch a train by 6:45 a.m. Despite this, after working a full day, he opted to come straight to our home to visit my father at least three times a week. The radiation treatments my father received had depleted his energy to the point where some of Kevin's visits consisted of him just sitting next to my father or doing small things that we were too busy to do. But regardless of what Kevin did, he would always find me before leaving the house to urge me to talk about how I was feeling.

Even though our fathers were contemporaries, and in spite of the fact that I found Kevin's care and concern vital, I was also intrigued by his attention to my father and to our family. When I asked him why he came over so much, he told me that my father would be the first friend that he knew he was going to lose. He said, "Until I figure out where to be, I would just like to be here." After he said this, he took off his suit jacket and tie and started sweeping the floor.

My father may have been the first friend that Kevin knew he was going to lose, but because he was familiar with the unique pain and anguish of losing a parent to cancer, our conversations on my father's treatment became spirited. Each discussion Kevin and I had about my father's cancer treatment immediately brought forth a passionate response on his part about alternative healing methods, macrobiotic diets and the quality of my father's life.

Those talks were tangential strands of discussions that began around 1979, when Kevin decided to become vegan. At the time, I was a meaty, meat-eating, high school freshman who was highly influenced by stimulating conversation and the willpower of others. Kevin's sudden switch intrigued me to no end. While Kevin ate tofu, I ate cheese steaks. A typical exchange involved me asking "Why are you eating that?" and Kevin countering with "Why are you eating *that?*"

Since Kevin was older and much more insightful than I, he always had more answers. When I would say that I didn't know something, he would stop talking and tell me to go look it up so we could finish the conversation.

Most people I knew back then liked to remind me that no one likes a person who is dumb or lazy. Kevin was no different. He bluntly reminded me that if I was either, I could not hang around him anymore. So because I didn't want to seem stupid or lazy, wanted to hang around my "big brother," and had the competitive drive my parents had bred into me, I always looked up whatever Kevin and I spoke about.

No matter how long it took for me to look up the answer for something, Kevin was willing to pick up the conversation right where we left off. Even if I didn't find the right answer and only found just a bit more information, Kevin was there to have another conversation—a higher, intellectually-informed conversation that always went well beyond what one ate and onto how one thought, acted, voted, trained, and lived.

Looking back on it, I am amazed at just how much information I learned about different thought processes surrounding varying disciplines while trying to only learn about Kevin's strong self-discipline toward veganism. The sheer volume of knowledge exchanged between us was priceless to me.

Whenever something weighs on my mind, I like to get up when it's still dark out and ride my bicycle into the rising sun. On one of those morning rides, I saw Kevin running across the street toward the train station and rode up to him. He knew me well, and from the look on my face understood that something was bothering me.

The more I talked, the more he heard, and the more he heard, the more he slowed down. We sat down as the first call for his train was announced on the PA. He smiled and said, "Screw that train; you're more important. Just relax … but talk fast, because another train is coming in 45 minutes." Nothing was solved in those minutes, and I can't even recall what was so pressing, but Kevin's smile and attention to my small drama made me remember the moment.

The last time that I spoke to Kevin was Friday, September 7, 2001. While standing in a market, I heard a familiar voice behind me saying, "Wheat grass juice, salad, and water? Man, you are really doing it!" I turned to see Kevin peering appreciatively into my basket. When we started talking about our lives, he told me that he needed my help in getting back in shape.

"What can I tell you?" I said. "All I learned was because of you." I was incredulous. What could I ever really say to Kevin? It was the casual conversations we had had throughout my first two decades of life that had spurred my interest in health, fitness and wellness, and what finally made me decide to become a personal trainer.

He said, "You're training a friend of mine. You spoke at the church of another friend. You're bodybuilding. I'm hearing some real good things about you. You are beyond me now, brother."

These were essentially Kevin's last words to me. He chatted more and invited me to a barbecue that he was having that Sunday, but I didn't really hear it. All I heard was that "You are beyond me now, brother."

It wasn't 1979 anymore. I wasn't fourteen years old and he was no longer 24. We weren't even really mentor and mentee anymore. We were grown men.

Hearing such a strong statement casually come out of this grown man's mouth was truly a gift. He had a lot to do with my maturation, and I never thought I had, could, or even wanted to

be "beyond" him. That moment was worth extending, and that comment was deserving of a lot of acknowledgment. I wanted to hug him. I wanted to express so much but all that came out was a stuttering, stammering, and bravado-fueled, "Thanks, dude." I left the market telling Kevin that I would see him at his party, but I wanted to do so much more; I wanted to say so much more.

As I drove out of the parking lot, Kevin was leaving the market. I can still see him walking through the door, smiling at everyone and no one, wearing sandals, olive green shorts, and a crisp white tucked in T-shirt. I stopped the car, wanting to get out and say "Thank you." But I didn't, and drove off figuring that I would see him later and just say it then.

I can still see it all, as clear as day.

Saturday September 8, 2001. I never made it to see him because I got caught up in my day and planned to talk to him later.

Sunday, September 9, 2001. This was the day of his party, but I opted to go watch football at a sports bar instead.

Monday, September 10, 2001. Kevin took the day off and I went for a bike ride. I rode right past his house but didn't go in, thinking that I was much too sweaty to visit.

Tuesday, September 11, 2001. Kevin went to work on the 98th floor at the World Trade Center. I was in Philadelphia and decided that the warm, cloudless day was perfect, certainly too perfect to be trapped in a gym. I canceled all my personal training appointments for the day and decided to go ride my bicycle.

There is no need to go into the details. We all have our own deeply personal memories of that day, and mine are no greater than yours. All that I will say is that I had a chance and blew it. My opportunity to do and say something so simple, so appropriate, so human, so necessary, and so natural was taken away in an instant.

Kevin's memorial service was so packed that I stood outside ready to resign myself to the fact that I wasn't going to get in. it was then, when one of Kevin's friends called my name and said, "You belong in there. Take my spot."

The scene inside was surreal. Experiencing the death of a friend is enough to shake anyone, but when that friend dies while working at his desk 95-plus floors above the ground, and a plane, purposely, flies into his office and instantly incinerates him, leaving you with nothing, not a trace to even say goodbye to, it leaves you more than shaken. It leaves you broken.

Before I sat in that pew, I took in the sight of Kevin's friends, many of whom I had looked up to my whole life. The sight of these men standing there lifeless, like marionettes with lax strings, pained and captivated me. During Kevin's service, many of his friends, coworkers, and family members stepped up to the podium to speak about Kevin's many genuine acts of kindness.

Listening to their words and thinking of my own experience with Kevin made me redefine the word "extraordinary." Being extraordinary is not the performance of superhuman acts; it is the action of one person performing very human acts on a highly consistent and caring level.

Kevin was one extraordinary individual.

"How can this be the way it is supposed to happen? How the hell can this be right?" These were the questions that were in my head when Kevin's wife came to me and whispered in my ear "Oh, David, I feel so sorry for you."

I walked away from the service feeling dazed and weeping for the Bowser family. I wept as well for the huge loss that the black community of Philadelphia was being dealt. I felt that something had to be done, and because I had the extreme honor of knowing such men as my father, Kevin's father, Kelvin, Kevin, and others, it was up to me to do it.

Little did I know that the something I came up with was going to change my life.

I Go Where My Love Takes Me

Bike

It was late December when she first rolled into my life. I was just a shy kid at the time and was captivated by her beauty at my initial glance. With nowhere else to go, my family allowed her to stay in the living room of our house, and the first few months of having her near were torturous. I wanted to be with her, badly, but my own youth, innocence, and shyness intimidated me from even approaching her.

Even though she was my only desire, I didn't understand her at all. Every touch of my hand turned into clumsy fumbling. Too forceful, she would toss me off of her. Too delicate, and our relationship would quickly hit a wall. And if I stared at her too much, I became mesmerized and stumbled. Nothing my inexperienced mind could think of worked.

I thought that if I voyeuristically watched while others skillfully handled her that it would teach me something. It didn't. The image of others on top of her consumed my days with anxious thoughts and filled my nights with tantalizing dreams of us together. Overall, my plan left me feeling confused, conflicted, mocked, and still very unaware as to how to even touch her.

What does she want? I wondered.

Someone suggested that I relax, stop listening to others, and be myself. But the back and forth of my yearning, attempting and then failing, left my young and naïve self twisted with no idea as to how to relax, or even a clue as to how to "be myself."

But everyone has his limitations, even a young boy.

One Saturday morning in early spring, I woke up with one thought in mind: Today is going to be the day. I got cleaned up, brushed my teeth, and scampered downstairs. I had blocked everyone else's ideas out of my head; all of my thoughts were devoted to her. I didn't watch cartoons; all I wanted to see was her. I didn't even eat breakfast; all I needed was her. I went straight to her, escorted her outside of the house, took a deep breath, and touched her. Everything about the experience was the same as it ever was, but just slightly different.

I had been through all of the trials and tribulations of attempting and failing before, so I was no longer intimidated.

I was willing to endure more failed attempts to gain whatever glory there was to be had with her, so my spirit was strong.

She was still as gorgeous as ever, but I wasn't blinded anymore and now only focused on *our* horizons.

I wasn't afraid anymore.

The lack of tension cooled my approach, eased my breath, and steadied my hand. My next touches were smooth and respectful, not fumbling and not forced. It took us a few strokes to get in sync and to gain confidence, but soon, she and I connected.

She and I rolled.

We rode.

I could finally ride a bike.

It was only a few yards, and I don't remember actually yelling, "I can ride a *bike*!" but I probably did. You see, I was the last person on my block, and felt like the last person in Philadelphia, to learn how to ride a bicycle so I naturally wanted to shout this to the world.

I was so overcome with excitement that I didn't even ride my bicycle back up the block. I just hit the brakes and let it drop to the ground. I ran as fast my nine-year-old body could move my Converse sneakers and burst into my house. Looking back on it, my running into the house with a huge afro and thick glasses, yelling about riding a bike, must have looked crazy as hell.

Because everybody in my family was busy, the only accolade I received was a cursory pat on the back. Oh, wait a second: my mother did stop to ask if I left the bike in the street, where it could be stolen.

"Uh, yeah mom."

Because my world had just opened up, I had to tell someone. I tore out of the house and ran next door to my friend Stephanie's house. Not even bothering to knock or ring the bell, I just pressed my hands and face against their screen door and screamed, "I can ride a bike!" into a darkened house. When nothing stirred, I screamed again: "I can ride a bike!"

Stephanie wasn't home, but her father, Mr. Alvin, was. Now Mr. Alvin was classic '70s cool. Wearing loud colored pants, a pair of open-heeled slippers, and an undershirt with a pack of cigarettes rolled into the left sleeve, he strolled to the door, glaring as if a kid's manic screaming had just awakened him.

I stood there fearless—someone was going to acknowledge my achievement.

He blew out a puff of cigarette smoke as he stopped at the door, looked down at my beaming face, glanced at my bike lying on the sidewalk, and said two words before he strolled away: "'bout time."

Mr. Alvin's flippancy after my months-long ordeal was one of the best things that ever happened to me. By the time I walked down the seven steps from his porch and across the few feet of concrete to grab my bicycle with my young hands, so much had changed. On my left, I saw my home. On my right, I could see the end of the block. Being alone with my bike meant that the rush of triumph and achievement was all mine, and that made me smile.

In the days that followed, pedal strokes and happiness were one. Each time I rode down the street, I noticed something different, everything from the cracks in the sidewalk down to how my tires sounded on the dirt as compared to the grass. I had discovered a whole new world, and it was all outside my door.

Time may have dulled some of the details of those days, but one thing that remains etched in my memory is the feeling of the wind pressing against my body. It wasn't the breeze in the air, but the wind created through my own power. When I pedaled hard, a stiff breeze leaned into me; if I pedaled slower, a soothing whisper blew over my skin. The feeling was so intoxicating that I often rode shirtless, just to have the wind touch as much of my skin as possible. One day while riding, I became so distracted by the inebriating feeling of the wind that I crashed and cut myself up pretty badly. But within hours and in spite of the pain, I sucked up my tears and was back on my bike—bandaged, shirtless, and smiling.

I became so attached to the intense feelings on a bike that my first flat tire left me crestfallen, because I wouldn't be able to ride for a while. I begged a friend to ride his bike, which wasn't as nice as mine, and I got on it thinking that it was going to be different. It was, but not as much as I thought. As I rode around, sprinting here and climbing there but smiling the whole time, I was surprised to feel much of the same spark that happened on my bike.

As I returned the bike, I made the connection that any magic that may have existed was not due to the bike at all, but within me. At nine years old, the connections between my not being afraid to fail, my will, my achievement, and my happiness weren't as defined as they are now, but I knew that I was onto something. This was so much more than a bike ride. This was my first taste of my own self-confidence. This was my first taste of love.

My first bicycle expedition was in fourth grade when my family and I had literally just moved to Starkville, Mississippi from Philadelphia. Within hours of our arrival, my restless energy was driving everyone crazy. So, to ease tensions, my mother said something that gave me the ultimate green light.

"Just go out and ride."

Without a care in the world, I grabbed my bike with its purple banana seat and pedaled out into the surrounding farmland with only my tremendous thirst for exploring to guide me. I ripped through Starkville's rural streets, screaming "Hellooooo" as loudly as I could to anyone or anything that could hear me, until it started to get dark.

Starkville, Mississippi is not Philadelphia, Pennsylvania. Without nearly as many streetlights, night falls hard. My little heart pounded furiously as I pedaled through the unfamiliar graveled streets with one eye on the darkening horizon and the other on the road. As the encroaching night amplified my fear, along with every sound I heard, I remember thinking that what I felt must be the exact feeling that the vampire hunters in the movies must feel. Frightened by my own thoughts, I raced through the streets and eventually barreled through the doorway of our new home. Once inside, I looked out the window and across the blackened acres that surrounded me and smiled. The ride was not that far, but it was a big stepping stone for me, because I had made it through a vast territory: my own fear. 1ˢᵗ expedition

My life's second expedition was two years later, and much had changed for me in the interim. I was now a 6th grader, back in Philadelphia, and my time riding through the endless miles of Mississippi farmland made me consider myself worldly. My sleek, well-oiled machine was now a rusted shadow of its former self that squeaked with every turn of the wheel. The two working handbrakes were down to just one, and a towel taped to the seat post had taken the place of the banana seat. The cool, easy, and carefree cruising posture I had now bordered on reckless with me standing up all the time, except for an occasional butt-cheek rest on the towel. The only thing that remained the same was the feeling of the wind and my never-ending thirst to get a handlebar's view of the world.

My new air of "worldliness" made my parents' rule of not venturing beyond our city block seem inane. Eager to quench my thirst for adventure, I decided to ride across town to a classmate's house. Truth be told, more important and thrilling than biking the few miles of city streets to see my friend was biking to the sign near his home. My friend lived just one block away from

Philadelphia's city limit, and the vision of me biking up to that sign and touching it fueled me—I wasn't going to be stopped.

I was so driven that I rode with even more reckless abandon than usual and unknowingly cut off one of my father's colleagues in traffic. When he informed my father, I was in huge trouble. My father was furious, but while angrily droning on and on about everything from disobeying him and my mother to not properly caring for my bike and more, I just sat there in front of my dad thinking, "This city cannot contain me."

Because I had achieved my goal, the punishment I received—no TV, no bike riding, and more chores—was harsh, but worth it. I had touched that "You are now leaving the Philadelphia city limits" sign. I must have been sitting there with a bit of a self-satisfied smirk on my face, because it was one of the few times in my life that my father ever lost his train of thought, mid-rant. Taking his cigarette from his mouth, he looked me in the eye, and asked, "Did you really bike *all* that way standing up?"

"Sure did," I said with a huge smile.

I wasn't into girls yet, organized athletics were still a few years off, and I was barred from TV shows and movies, so all punishment did was give me time to think about my own achievements of riding a bicycle to my chosen destination and my burgeoning thirst for adventure. Though it wasn't an overt thought, it was around that time that I began to formulate my very raw and very personal equation for love:

Love = My forward movement x the wind my body could generate + my freedom to explore.

As a boy, the pursuit of this love urged me to pedal and explore Philadelphia's neighborhoods and thus brought new friends, opportunities, and smiles into my life. At the time, that was enough for me, and I never looked deeper within my pursuit. But as I lived more and incurred some bad times—like bad report cards, which came often—I discovered that no matter how bad things were, a simple bike ride could always make me smile. I continued to ride and mature, and as I did, a few more components to my love formula became evident. Passion was the one crucial variable that I could not articulate as a kid, but was the essential ingredient to everything. It was a passion to experience things that got me out of bed early the first Saturday I ever rode, and which made me comfortable enough with my past failings and fears to understand that I would fall and then move beyond it to get back on that bicycle. To this day, passion is the lightning bolt that gives my love life.

That said, my current formula is:

Love = Forward Movement + Physical Power of My Body/ Wind + Human Interaction (Smiles+Hugs) /Exploration x Passion.

When times were especially bad, like the days after the World Trade Center tragedy when I was grappling with whether to hold on or let go of my hope of seeing Kevin Bowser again, love was with me. Each component of my formula was there, as if it were a caring friend. The passion to always move forward made me ride until the wind dried my tears. The warmth within each human interaction and the hugs I gave and received cooled my vindictive impulses. The smiles I came across slowed me down just enough to refocus and hold onto the amazing power that is contained within one human being's laughter. More than ever, love came through, and in the process, sparked the idea of bicycling across North America in order to share some of the components with others and possibly make the world a better place.

John Lennon wrote, "All you need is love," and that may be true, but for my 55-day trip across North America in 2002, I packed a lot more. I was so nervous about what I may possibly need between Washington State and Philadelphia that I took enough cycling clothes, regular clothes, balm, toiletries, and other stuff to live for three times that long. The cycling was tough at first, but soon I became comfortable with the routine, and the ninety miles a day wasn't grueling or even daunting anymore – it was just what I had to do.

But as much as the pursuit of love makes me smile, the offer of free food brings an even bigger ear-to-ear grin, and explains the start of my next adventure.

With my riding for the day completed, I sat on a park bench admiring the beauty of Fond du Lac, Wisconsin's Lake Winnebago, when a guy wearing a suit and tie and sipping a beer sauntered over and introduced himself. His name was Ron, and his opening question was if I was crazy for riding in this heat. When I jokingly said that I *was* crazy, but gave my reasons for being on the road, he sat down and started chatting away.

After a short while, he said, "Hey man, do you want something to eat?"

I said "yes" before he could finish the question. What can I say, I'm greedy.

Now the free meal that Ron was leading me to was not going to be easy to get. That's because it was being served in a hall, in the middle of the park, and was the venue for a 20th wedding anniversary party. With my cycling tights, sleeveless bike jersey, and skin color sharply contrasting with the attire and tone of the guests, I was *so* not going to fit in. But my greediness for free food made me look past that fact.

I boldly walked behind Ron right up to the doorway, propped my bike up at the entrance, and thought about some of the things that I had learned while living my life before I entered:

1. Being a guest of a guest does not always mean that you will be welcomed into a party.

2. If you are uninvited, you have, at best, five to ten minutes of people whispering, "Who invited him?" before someone approaches you.

3. Regardless of who is in the room, you should always enter like you belong there.

4. Once you get through any door, always make good use of your time.

With these tenets in mind, I took a deep breath, smiled, and entered as smoothly as a lone, uninvited black male wearing Lycra tights could. Using the stunned silence, the stoppage of movement, and the questioning stares to my advantage, I headed straight for the buffet table. Assuming that I had only minutes before someone said something to me, I piled food high on my plate and stuffed rolls and a beer in my back cycling jersey pocket. I figured that even if I got kicked out, no one was going to ask for the food back. With a full plate, full pockets, and my eyes straight ahead, I was steps from being back outside when the music stopped.

Oh shit, I thought.

I heard a knocking on the microphone, and Ron's voice making a rambling but very sweet speech about the endurance of love and the virtues of staying married.

"But," he paused, "only a special person can bike all the way across the U.S. to honor a fallen friend. Everyone meet my new friend, David Sylvester."

There was a period of silence, and again I thought, *Oh shiiiit.*

Then a pat on my back, accompanied by the word, "Welcome" made me smile, sit, stay a while, share a few laughs, sip some cocktails, and even sign the guest book. After imbibing, eating more, and enjoying the company of a lot of fine folks, I biked to my hotel and told my roommate, Steve Ebersole, what had happened.

Steve and I had met on the first day of this tour and would often swap life stories, to which he often skeptically responded with, "No shit?" This time was no different.

I knew that he doubted my story, but I didn't have any proof, so I leaned back in my chair to chill out for the rest of the day. When I did, I suddenly broke out with a huge smile. Reaching behind to my jersey's back pocket I took out a bratwurst, wrapped in a decorative anniversary napkin, and a body-temperature beer.

I took a bite of the sausage, handed the beer to Steve and said, "No shit!"

The components of my love formula had always felt good throughout my life, but somehow, each component felt even better during my fifteen-state, cross-continental journey that overflowed with encounters like the one I had with Ron. In addition to putting a smile on my face, the feelings of the wind, forward movement, hugs, and simple human encounters started to fill the void in my life that my friend's sudden and senseless death had created. I returned home wanting to do anything I could to further enhance what I was feeling, but was at a loss as to what. That is, until I heard about a bicycle race across Africa.

I can honestly say that just seeing the map of Africa with a route line going through Egypt, Sudan, Ethiopia, Kenya, Tanzania, Malawi, Zambia, Botswana, Namibia, and South Africa was enough to hook me. It didn't matter that I hadn't been off the North American continent before, hadn't camped before, or wasn't even a professional bike racer. All that mattered was that I had extended myself for love in the past and felt that I had become a better man for it. Pedaling through Africa was the step that I needed to take.

Even though the Africa trip was going to be three times as far in mileage, and would last twice as many days as North America, I didn't have nearly the same amount of anxiety during the packing process. My self-confidence grew and left me feeling that as long as my love was strongly present, I would be all right.

So, amidst an amazing bicycle love affair, I set off to Africa. However, it was hard for me (and for the other cyclists who rode with me from Cairo to Cape Town) to smile in the face of the searing Sudanese sun. The 112-degree, sauna-like air combined with each peak of the undulating sandy and rutted roads we biked on drained and splintered our group of cyclists more and more to the point where we were nothing more than a few individuals on bikes scattered across the East-African countryside. The few Sudanese citizens we passed just stood in whatever shade they could find and looked at us quizzically as we whizzed past.

Once alone, I unconsciously found myself cranking hard up the hills in search of the soothing wind of my youth on the other side. But as the day wore on, the minutes of work for only a few seconds of a slight breeze became an exercise in diminishing returns that slowed my pace dramatically.

I rode down the next craggy hill as fast and reckless as my legs could pedal just for about three seconds of grin-enabling wind. The slight breeze was worth it, but while I careened down the hill, both water bottles shot like rockets from my bottle cages. I could have stopped to retrieve them from the sides of the rocky road where they landed, but again, the breeze felt too good. Instead, I sailed to the base of the hill and stopped. Eager to be off my bike for a minute or so, I walked back up the hill, only to find the bottles gashed and leaking their cherished contents onto the rocks. With no water, I looked into the cloudless, burnished sky and let out a loud and long yell. I then headed back down the hill, consumed with my own problems, unleashing an expletive-laden tirade for the ages. I was so preoccupied with indulging my frustrations that I was stunned to find a couple silently standing a few feet from my bicycle. I abruptly stopped hollering.

The man, who was holding a staff and dressed in traditional Sudanese garb, quietly spoke in an Arabic dialect to a woman. She wore a wrap that acted as a skirt as well as padding for a huge bag perched on her head. My presence on the hill, my strange outburst, and my sudden look of surprise must have been an amusing sight for them, because when we made eye contact, they both snickered and then quieted themselves. For moments, there was nothing but a few feet of silence and the stifling air between us.

The man broke through it by saying, "Too hot," with such a thick accent that it was only by repeating himself a few more times and gesturing in a pedaling motion with his hands that I was able to understand what he was saying.

"Yeah, too hot to be pedaling a damn bicycle," I shouted across the road.

"Yes, yes, bi-bi bicsy..." he said, trying to utter the word with the emphasis on the right syllable.

"Bi-cycle," I said, finishing his sentence.

We stepped toward each other and began crudely communicating via his few words of English, my very few words of Arabic, a few giggles from the woman, and a whole lot of body language. Specific details were lost on both of us, but he was able to convey that the woman was family but not his wife, probably his sister, and that he was interested in examining my bicycle.

The two of them spoke Arabic as he picked up my bike and remarked, using the high arch of his eyebrows, that it was much lighter than the heavy bicycles that he was used to. All of a sudden he smacked the seat as hard as he could a few times. *Wham, wham, wham!* When no pieces fell off of my bike, he and his sister seemed impressed and let out a hearty, approving laugh. After figuring that we had milked the moment for all that we could, I attempted to straddle my bike and continue my ride.

The man grabbed the handlebars firmly and said, "Too hot," a few times and motioned for me to follow. When I said "no," made the pedaling motion with my hands and pointed into the distance, the man grabbed my bike even more firmly and yelled more loudly, "No!"

Well, since you put it that way, I thought.

Figuring that I would get a break from riding for a few more minutes, at the least, or, have an adventure at best, I shrugged my shoulders and released my bike into his care. I walked with

them up and down a few hills, cobbling together a conversation, until we came to a clearing and a hut made of thatched straw.

When the hut was just meters away, the man's behavior changed. He rushed past me, disappearing inside, but once at the doorway, everything became evident. This hut, which was one sparsely-adorned big room, was this man's home, and he

31

was tidying up because he had an unexpected guest. Within minutes, he had darted around the dim room and his sister (who stood giggling) enough to make his place hospitable. He signified this by smoothing out the only place that was available for anyone to sit: his bed.

Now this was an awkward moment for me, because I did not want to insult his hospitality, but I also didn't want to place my sweaty, dirty body on his bed. I sat on the very edge of his bed, clasping my hands against my cheek and tilting my head to the side, to say that if I got too comfortable, then I would surely go to sleep. But he countered my mime by laughing and mimicking my motion and adding a snoring sound, as if to say, "Relax, dude. It's okay, take a nap."

I don't know why people always speak louder to foreigners, as if yelling will make them understand things any better, but I yelled the word "sleep" a few times, to which my host nodded his head approvingly and then made an even louder snoring sound. Again, there was a brief, awkward moment of silence between us. Again, he broke the silence.

"Chai?" he said while making an eating motion.

By this point, my cycling buddies and I had been in Sudan long enough to know that when someone said a word that sounded like "chai" they meant for you to sit down, relax, and drink tea. I obliged my host. I remember enjoying the shade and being surprised by how cool the air was. I remember leaning on my elbow. I remember wanting to close my eyes. I remember....

Sometimes you don't know just how tired you are until you actually go to sleep.

The hospitality I received in this home put me at ease and permitted my drained body to go into a deep sleep. I woke up feeling like Rip Van Winkle; I don't know how long I slept, but a lot had changed during that time. The sister and brother who welcomed me into the hut had gone and there were now two tittering boys standing over me, staring. I sat up to clear my head. I also noticed that the air in the hut seemed breezier and there was also the aroma of food wafting through that had not been there before.

Before I could make any more observations or ask the boys their names, my host entered with a tray of food and shooed them out of my face. He then set the tray down in front of me and stepped behind the boys, placing his hands on their shoulders. After noticing the man's prideful grin, it didn't take a genius to see that these boys were his sons.

With bags slung over their shoulders and one of the boys holding a weathered notebook, they looked like they had just gotten home from school. At the father's prodding, each boy stepped forward and greeted me in Arabic. I smiled at the thought of the boys telling their teacher and classmates, "Hey, you aren't going to believe who we found sleeping in our bed yesterday."

For me, the difference between eating and dining lies solely in the conversation and the company who shares your food. That being said, despite our language differences, we dined over a meat and gravy dish and some tea. After dining, I made it clear that I had to push on and shook hands and shared hugs with the men. As I biked off into the sun, I noticed that, after basking in the family's warmth, the heat didn't seem so oppressive anymore.

Whether it was Egypt's majesty, Sudan's warmth, Ethiopia's mountain ranges, Kenya's equatorial heat, Tanzania's lushness, Malawi's reenergizing lake waters, or Zambia's hospitality, Africa touched me in the way that I wanted and needed to be touched. By the time I biked onto Botswana's flat, well-paved roads and into sunny skies, I felt like I was in a wonderland and more in love with life than ever before. In addition to all of that, along with the cool breezes and beautiful cloud formations, there was always a very strong chance that I would see wild elephants crossing the countryside. How awesome is that?

One day, I actually was fortunate enough to take a picture of five elephants crossing the road and didn't think that any day in Botswana could top that until I woke up the next morning. That morning in particular was so special because everything was just golden.

I woke up that morning after camping in some dense brush and did the usual routine of changing into my cycling tights, eating

breakfast, talking with the other riders about nothing in particular, and breaking down my tent. I did all of this half asleep and emotionally unengaged, until I walked my bike up to the road.

The road was flat, straight, and went on that way for miles in either direction, as was usual for the country, but tall grass lining both sides of the road made things special. The grass filtered the wind to the point that it was almost chilly as it brushed over my skin and diffused the sunlight perfectly so that every blade of grass and every bush glowed. I took a step into the middle of the street to get a better vantage point of the world, and when I did, I could see with breathtaking clarity that everything on the horizon was gilded. It was amazing.

Other cyclists must have felt the magic of this particular morning, too, because a few of them abandoned their normal cycling routine of getting off to a fast start. On this particular day, we cyclists pedaled into the horizon at a nice easy pace. Botswana is a sparsely populated country with little traffic, so it was easy for those mesmerized by the moment to form a convoy and ride eight abreast on the road. The group could have easily fallen into the normal pattern of one person trying to outperform the other, but I think that we all stayed together that morning because someone asked one question about a common experience that had led each of us to the most uncommon of trips: "Tell me about your first bike."

That question kept us together and made the day's next miles compelling.

Cross-cultural bridging stories were told with a crackle of excitement, whether the rider's native tongue was English, Japanese, or Dutch; whether their demeanor was loud or shy. Nuances like brand names, special dates, colored spokes, streamers, and other details were said with such emphasis that each story was the same but different. But no tale was complete until each rider searched their vocabulary sufficiently enough to find the right words to fully paint the picture and say, "You should have seen me! I could ride a bike!"

Under any other circumstance, I would not have noticed any of this, but this conversation was unlike any other I'd had before because I had to work so hard to hear it. The indefinable spirit woven into each rider's story made each increase his or her cycling pace while speaking. So we had to practically sprint in order to stay within earshot of each rider's fervent voice.

By the time the eighth story was started, the sun was over the horizon line and we were well beyond the tall grass. The increase/decrease of our pace had become a strain.

Our gilded hue was gone.

But for a beautiful moment, we raced into the glowing horizon while sharing the memories of our first loves.

The pursuit of love through Africa left me fulfilled, energized and more enlightened. I boarded my flight back to Philadelphia with wide eyes, wondering, "Where else can love take me?"

I got off the plane, burning to do another cross-continental ride. I talked less, read more, listened better, and eventually, did enough to plan a bicycle trip across South America going through Colombia, Ecuador, Peru, and Argentina in 2006. But that trip was never meant to be. A drunk driver struck me and seriously injured me days before I was to leave.

Now my trip was ruined.

My body was battered.

My emotional state was dark.

Everything about me was so weak that I doubt that I would've made it through that time and recuperative process but for two components of my love formula: human interaction and will.

The friends that I'd known all of my life, as well as the friends that I'd made while cycling, all came through and reignited my personal will to always move forward. I felt so indebted to my friends, so reengaged with my will, that I wanted to do something to acknowledge both – if I could ever ride another trip.

My opportunity came later that year when I registered for a bike race across Asia, from Istanbul to Beijing. To honor 122 of my friends, I taped their photos all over my bicycle. To recognize and demonstrate what can be done on sheer will alone, I didn't physically train for the ride. But that was not my brightest idea ever.

The first week of that four-month tour was hell. Turkey's hazy skies, hot temperatures and dense humid air were energy-sapping and forced me to pedal more hours than I slept. I lay in my tent at night wondering if I was going to be able to get through Turkey, Georgia, Azerbaijan, Turkmenistan, Uzbekistan, Tajikistan, Kyrgyzstan, and China. Even wondering hurt. This was going to be a long trip.

I was only about 15 kilometers into a 140-kilometer day and already looking for places to sit for a while. I pedaled along for another hour or so until I spotted a stool outside a crudely constructed shack on the right side of a desolate rural road. Waddling over, I wondered whether this shack, built of splintered planks and surrounded by huge bags of onions and dried brush, would tip over when I sat down. It didn't, but I wasn't going to stay long anyway because the onions gave the surrounding air a foul stench.

Just then, a man stuck his head out of the doorway and excitedly walked out to greet me. I was so exhausted that I didn't want to be bothered by anyone and actually groaned when this grizzled, mustached man, smelling of onions and hard labor, extended his hand. The man started talking immediately, but, being only literate in English, I had no idea what to say in response. I just sat slumped on the chair and repeating the words "hello" and "English" over and over again. To this onion farmer's credit, he tried to speak with me in at least two other languages, but when that didn't register with me, he gave up.

Now, he didn't give up talking – he just gave up talking *to* me.

Seemingly happy with the company regardless, he talked and talked and talked at me some more, even when I nodded off for a second. When I woke back up, he was still talking, but this time his breath smelled of strong coffee. He seemed eager to say something, but without a translator, there was no effective communication happening between us.

Finally, his face brightened and he raised his hands as if to say, "Don't say another word."

I didn't, and, for that matter, I hadn't.

He stood, entered the shack and started yelling something that in any language sounded like "Wake up."

While he did this, I took in a big, deep breath in an effort to wake myself up and was shocked at just how foul the air was. Apparently one can nap through a whole lot of stink when tired.

The man came out of the shack with a groggy, pre-teen boy. I assumed the boy was the man's son by the way he kept pointing to the boy's nose and then pointed to his own nose.

The boy, who spoke very limited English, was to be the interpreter for his father, who was now examining my bike, trying to figure out the significance of the pictures taped on it. Winking, the grizzled man pointed to the pictures, gyrated his hips and let out a moan as a way of asking if these were sexual conquests. When I pointed to some of the pictures of males and frowned, shaking my head "no," the farmer then looked at me, laughing, and punched my arm as if to say, "Hey, fun is fun."

He went back to closely examining the photos, snickering the entire time, but kept coming back to one picture in particular. As he pointed to one woman's picture he spoke to his son, placed his hands on his heart and did all of this while looking me in the eye. His son asked, "Your lover?"

Maybe it was the confusion of not knowing whether to answer the son or the father, or that I was really tired, or that I had unresolved feelings about the pictured female, but for whatever reason, I lied and said "No."

The onion farmer saw through my deception right away and turned up his lip. He then hit me with a look that said "Dude, I know what you are going through." He put his hands up again to signal me to be quiet, which amused me greatly because I had said a grand total of five words. He muttered something to himself and entered his shack. While he rummaged around his home, I asked the boy, who looked just as confused as I, what his dad was doing. He just shrugged.

The father stepped out, producing some simple colored beads. He then pointed to me, back to the picture of the woman, said something in Turkish and winked. Before the son could say, "These are for her," I knew what was going to be said and took the gift.

I had taped my friends' pictures to my bike as a tribute to those who helped me through the previous year's trials, but never imagined that those same images would or even could establish a gift-giving connection with a man I could not even understand. I tried resting longer but the farmer wasn't having that. He continued talking my ear off. It wasn't until I stood up to go that he even took a breath, but that didn't even really stop him—he yapped and yapped and yapped some more. I hugged him good-bye, straddled my bike, and took my hefty ass and my 122 friends up the road.

By the time we bicycled through Turkey, Georgia, Azerbaijan, Turkmenistan, Uzbekistan, and Tajikistan and were about ninety kilometers from the Kyrgyzstan border, I was feeling better conditioned and used to border crossings. Now border crossings between small countries can be tricky, bureaucratic nightmares, so the bike tour officials decided that all of the cyclists would cross together at 3:00 p.m. With all of us in much better condition than when we'd first started, cycling ninety kilometers on a flat terrain gave us more than enough time to reach the border.

About ten kilometers from the Tajikistan-Kyrgyzstan border, all of the cyclists stopped in a nameless town to spend their last few Tajikistani somonis like a bunch of drunken sailors on bottled water, cookies, soda, candy, and ice cream. Now, one foreign cyclist bicycling into a small Central Asian town will create a scene, but thirty sweaty, money-blowing cyclists in that same town practically guarantees a riot. Even though we all were surrounded, I probably received a lot more attention from the town's citizens than the others.

Throughout my time in that region, there was a fascination surrounding the hue of my skin that caused me to believe that I was the first black male to step foot in these parts. Overall, it was an honor to be that guy, but sometimes the gawking, occasional rubbing of my skin to see if the color would wipe off, and even the random woman handing me her baby so we could be photographed together was overwhelming. This time, I encountered all of that and more and after holding enough babies, having my skin rubbed and spending the last of my money, it was time to make a run for the border.

I didn't cover more than a few blocks when a car with shiny rims and a blaring sound system drove up beside me. I gave a cursory wave and smile and kept pedaling, but the driver was persistent. He kept speeding, honking, and swerving so manically that he almost caused an accident. For his safety, and especially mine, I pulled over. The driver stepped out of his car and started to stroll toward me with his arms open for a hug. Tall, well-built, with a tattoo on his shoulder and wearing a tank top and a camouflage New York Yankees cap, this guy was not like the other men that I'd seen in this region.

Our whole exchange was brief, but, from the outset had a different feel to it than the others I'd had around the world. Initially, I attributed it to the fact that we were both disappointed. His disappointment was due to the fact that I was from Philadelphia and mine was due to his wearing something from New York, Philadelphia's rival city. But that wasn't quite it. He just hugged me as we both laughingly shrugged it off.

Then I attributed the vibe I was feeling to the fact that the same Kool G. Rap song that was blaring from his sound system was also on my MP3 player. But, after bobbing our heads back and forth to the beat; I figured that wasn't it either. I couldn't help but feel something was different about this moment, but it was getting close to my three o'clock border crossing time, and I didn't give it any more thought. I pointed to my watch, posed for a few pictures taken with the driver's camera phone, hugged the man goodbye, and pedaled into the rolling farmland that stood between me and the Kyrgyzstan border.

I was enjoying the countryside until I heard a distant boom, boom, boom. Then the sound became louder and much closer. It was my friend again, and this time the volume was so amplified it was as if Kool G. Rap himself were giving me a personal concert. With the border within sight, I really wasn't interested in stopping. I just pedaled faster while holding up my left arm to flash my wristwatch. But my friend was unrelenting and drove even more erratically making me once again fear for my safety. I skidded to a stop and did nothing to mask the exasperation in my face. My friend must have noticed this because when he got out of the car, he wore an apologetic look. He stepped toward me, handed me some papers, and said, "We are brothers now," and hugged me.

Annoyed and still eager to get to the border, I began to mindlessly shuffle through what he'd given me. But as I began to take note of what was on the pages – his name and email address and the pictures taken from his camera phone – I slowed down and became more aware.

Focusing on our smiling faces and his name, written in Tajik, made me acknowledge the effort it took to quickly print out these pages and then race to deliver them to me before I left his country. Thinking of his effort made me really stare at the pictures and observe that he was the one initiating every hug between us, which is something that I normally am the one to initiate. Seeing the spontaneous embrace made me take note of his choice to use the word "brothers" made me see that this man was offering me the mantle of his "brotherhood" throughout our whole meeting.

Overall, there were many moments of brotherhood on my Asia trip, but at the same time there was an overshadowing edge about that trip that challenged me in a way my African and North American trips never did. That edge had me limping back home a bit detached from love, looking inward for answers that weren't there, and outward for support that didn't seem to be coming fast enough. I got off the plane thinking: ~~love is beautiful,~~ but it is not always easy. I was ever faithful that I could and would figure things out in due time, but when ESPN contacted me about writing an article with a very tight deadline, time wasn't a luxury I had anymore.

From ESPN's perspective, all they were asking for was a comprehensive article about my trips. But, from my vantage point, they were asking for something deeper and more personal. They were really asking me to explain my love.

Trying to explain my love was an intense, soul-searching, therapeutic process. Sixty-five different times I started the article. Sixty-five times, I picked different sets of pictures. Sixty-five different times, I channeled what I could to effectively communicate the warmth, presence, and power of love in my life to anyone who happened to read my words. The response I received back was overwhelming, global and very loving.

I was so touched and in such need of the reaffirming emails that poured in from around the world, that I found myself reconnected and inspired to find a creative way to lovingly shout, "Thank you!"

My best idea was my 2008 "Let This Be the Moment" tour, where I rode my bike from San Diego to New York City while stopping weekly to give service at various charities. As much as making a helpful pest of myself across the country was a celebration of my love, it was also a test of it. Riding solo, with no support vehicle, meant that my gear was scaled down to only what I could carry, which boiled to two changes of cycling gear, a change of regular gear, and a lot of heart.

The southern leg of the trip took me through California, Arizona, New Mexico, Texas, Louisiana, and Alabama. When

I stopped to grab a bite to eat at a restaurant just outside of Birmingham, I stood at the counter and started wondering: Is this muffaletta going to taste as good as the one I had in New Orleans, the birthplace of the famed sandwich? *question!* :)

Before I could finish weighing out the pros and cons of that burning issue, the server asked what I was doing there on a bicycle. Sweaty, very tired, and very hungry, I rushed through my whole story, naming each country and giving my order in less than ninety seconds.

"We'll buy his lunch," a voice said from behind me.

When I turned to thank my benefactor, I saw two smiling women sitting in a booth. I told them that their offer was nice, but I would only accept it if they would dine with me. "Wouldn't have it any other way," they said with a bit of southern pluck that exuded genuine warmth and hospitality.

The conversation we had over my muffaletta — which, by the way, was nowhere near as good as the original — centered around the feelings I had about my travels rather than any where I traveled. When the conversation turned from my life to theirs, one of the women told me that her mother had just been taken off a ventilator within the last 24 hours and wasn't expected to live much longer. She said that her girlfriend was accompanying her to shop for that one last dress her mother would wear.

Once this was disclosed, our conversation quickly went to a new depth. As we discussed our personal losses, I felt that simply saying "Thank you" for the sandwich and taking precious time from their day was not enough.

I told the woman that I was done cycling for the day and willing to do anything to ease her burden and pain. She kindly refused my offer to go to her mother's house and move any furniture around for her so that she could accommodate visitors after the funeral and suggested that I go get some rest. But she did ask me to pray with her before we parted, and though I am not overtly religious, I complied.

We clasped our hands, bowed our heads, and I closed my eyes. The woman whose mother was dying started the prayer with a familiar refrain that I had heard many times in my life, but I literally and figuratively opened my eyes when she deviated from the prayer. That's because this woman, who was going through the death of a parent, prayed for my continued safety and the strength of my being. That experience was truly a blessing.

I completed that trip on September 11, 2008 by riding into New York City and returned home not only reevaluating the events of my recent trip, but also the events of my whole life. So much about me had changed. The more I thought about it, I couldn't help but think that a lot of who I am and how I look at life goes back to that day when I was young and felt that the act of riding a bike was my defining benchmark. The succession of events that started that day taught me much about life and helped me discover an attitude that isn't necessarily perfect for everyone, but one that has been perfect for me.

Sitting by myself on my steps and watching my friends and neighbors ride bikes everywhere gave me a keener eye and appreciation for the human body's ability to move. I have since applied that ability to train myself for various events, as well as effectively train others as a personal trainer. Now the first thing I do with every new client is to watch them just walk around, because their body's movement tells me more than their mouth ever will.

Asking others to describe their ways of cycling gave me an overall appreciation of others' voices and stories that I have gone on to use while writing this book. And developing the ability to block their voices and focus on my own was another step toward being at peace with who I am.

Trying and failing gave me a sense of personal resilience and confidence that I channel every time that I dust myself off and try something again...and again...and again.

This chapter has not been about the bike rides that I have taken around the world. This chapter is about my motivation *for staying* on these bike rides around the world: it's all about the love. My love's components aren't rooted in a specific language, culture, custom, color, or religious faith, but they have combined to enhance my faith in life and my fellow man, and I would be a different and lost man without them.

Love is what makes me feel something deeper when the wind touches my skin. Love is why I get more than a boost when someone hugs me. Love is why my travels can comfortably go off course to have me eating at an anniversary party in Wisconsin or dining with a family in a Sudanese hut.

But I am certainly not alone in harboring this compelling and forceful belief: love exists within us all.

Love was what compelled every cyclist to race into Botswana's rising sun. Love was what drove the young Tajik man to call me his brother and drove the Turkish man to give a gift to a woman pictured on my bike. Love was what coerced the Alabama woman to pray for my safety before praying for her mother, and, in turn, led me to pray for her and her mother later that night. Love was what my mother unknowingly sent me off to find when she said, "Just go out and ride," and probably what my father saw in my eye when he stopped mid-tirade and asked if I rode "all the way standing up?" Love is what has enabled me to ride across continents with a smile on my face.

Love is waiting there within your own abundant being. You just have to overcome the fear of it, unshackle it, and trust where it will take you.

For those who are still unable to envision what I am conceptualizing, I suggest that you close your eyes. Picture a quiet, tree-lined neighborhood sidewalk in Philadelphia, circa 1974. Feel a peaceful, cool breeze waft over your skin and then see a fireball of energy in the form of a big-headed kid with glasses with an even bigger uncombed afro, screaming past you on a purple bicycle yelling, "I can ride a bike!"

If you can picture that dimpled face and feel that particular moment, then you have just seen, felt, and heard love in its most raw form.

If you are still having trouble imagining this, then just find me. I am easy to spot. I am the large, big-headed man wearing glasses, with a lot less hair, who is still smiling, still riding his bike and still following his love to the ends of the earth.

What I Was Thinking When

I have always loved listening to people's stories. It doesn't matter if they are funny, sad, dramatic, or otherwise. It doesn't matter if someone young, old, black, white, or otherwise is telling the stories. It doesn't even matter if the story is being told to me—I just love listening. My favorite stories are the ones about achievement. You know the ones: the stories where someone describes going without something but really wanting that something and then mentally focusing themselves to go out and get that something.

By the time I reached high school, I had listened to so many stories of adventure, attempt, and achievement from so many different people, that I began to hear something else resonate through each tale. Listening to that resonance led me to compare and contrast all of what I heard and eventually deduce that size, strength, race, religion, orientation, age, nationality, wealth, and even circumstance can, at best, only classify individuals, but it is an individual's thought process that separates and eventually defines them.

Basically, how we think is the most special part of who we are.

Believing this made me further realize that any achievement is possible, if you want it bad enough. More importantly and more personally, I came to understand that any achievement was possible by *me*, if I wanted it bad enough.

From that point I found a person's thought process as interesting as a person's actions, and started listening to stories of individual achievement differently. I would dissect each word of an article, book, or narrative searching for anything that would clue me in to how people were thinking. If what I read or heard didn't reveal or touch upon that defining thought process, I would be left wanting more and walk away, feeling incapable.

That is not how I want you to feel after reading this book.

I didn't write this book for you to think that I am a great bicyclist or writer, because I am not. Also, I don't want you to read my story and feel incapable of anything. I wrote *Traveling at the Speed of Life* for you to put this book down afterward and then go out do something. So, with that purpose in mind and being the protagonist as well as writer of an achieving story, I am going to try and break down everything I have done to its most basic thoughts. Here goes...

My defining ethos came to me soon after my father died. I was the first one among my core group of friends to lose his father. During the first year, especially, I felt like a living conundrum: too young to really know who I was, too unsure of myself to know who I could become, and the one person that I felt could help me the most through this painful predicament was the man who had just died.

This overwhelmed me and left me uncomfortable in my own skin, unable to express the depth of my anxiety, which led me to be reluctant to express much of anything at all. I resorted to trying to satiate my anguish by eating every comfort food available. All this did was make me grow edgy as well as just … grow.

My constant eating of comfort foods fattened me up.

My unhealthy state made me edgy and argumentative, which got me fired.

My girlfriend dumped me.

In short, I was a hot mess.

My normal behavior during stressful times was to go to the gym and lift heavy weights. But this time, my maximal bench presses, squats, dead lifts, grunts, and groans no longer gave me the same emotional release and had me exiting the gym tired and an even bigger, stronger, edgier, and hotter mess. No matter how much stronger I became, my life's issues seemed to weigh -just one ounce- more than I could lift.

I realized that I had to do something very different, because this routine was certainly not cutting it any longer.

At this time, I recalled my days at Temple University when a classmate and weightlifting buddy of mine was trying to balance his schoolwork and life with the grief from his grandmother's recent death. One day while working out, he tearfully broke down in the middle of the gym and confided in me that he was not coping well. Even though we were close, I was totally unaware of the depth of his feelings and sat listening to him describe being at his wits' end, and his willingness to try anything to feel better.

Between the two of us, and a lot of repetitions of a lot weights, the idea of doing everything differently came up. He was going to study at different times, hang out in new places, and even lift at a different gym, all in order to stimulate his mind more so that he wasn't preoccupied with his grief.

My friend apparently really bought into this pattern-change theory, because I didn't see him much over that semester. When I did hang out with him after the semester break, he looked totally different. His weight hadn't changed and his style was the same, but he was smiling and looked emotionally unencumbered. He looked free.

I never got too many details about what exactly my friend was thinking, but I think that I found out all I needed to know when he told me that he was so busy concentrating on the new sensations that surrounded the new experiences in his life that he didn't have much time to stress about the past — and when he did think about things, they weren't as bad as he made them out to be.

So with my wanting to be out of my current rut and my mind focused on wanting to feel free and eventually smile again, I started doing things differently.

Normally an afternoon weightlifter, I was up, out and on my bicycle early enough to be at the gym when it opened at 6:00 a.m. My plan was to run a preprogrammed thirty-minute hill workout on the treadmill, lift weights, and then grab a shower and go look for work.

Stern-faced, I was a man on a mission. I stepped on the treadmill, pushed the "hill workout" button, and thought, *today is going to begin a week that will be different than the rest.*

Prepared to go the distance, my pace increased to match the machine's. I thought *I am going to experience the famed runner's high, and it's going to be sweet.* In anticipation of the euphoria, I let my mind wander and thought, *When that high hits me, it will be just like the commercials I see, and my problems will melt away like so much sweat off my body. I am going to figure it all out. My dad's death, my aimlessness, my newfound singleness, and my joblessness won't hurt anymore.*

The treadmill's speed leveled off, and the incline increased a bit. I kept striding, waiting for the exhilaration. I waited for the hill to crest and for the relief of the descent. It didn't happen. I became alarmed, because the incline wasn't budging and I was not doing so well. I thought, *Shit, I can't catch my breath.*

Strained, because time was passing and I couldn't breathe, I thought, *Jesus, I can't go on any more.*

Spent, I jumped off the treadmill.

Gasping as the treadmill belt kept whirring on, I caught a glimpse of the timer. It read 8:03.

Ego aflame, I knelt down and thought, *You've got to be kidding me. I had this grand idea of running for thirty minutes and I couldn't go eight?*

Lungs burning, my whole being screamed, "Dammit!"

Muscles ablaze, I thought, *This was supposed to be the day that started off the week that was going be the start to a better me.*

With the losses of my father, girlfriend, and job already weighing on my mind, my inability to control my own body for eight lousy minutes led me to kneel on the floor. As the other early morning gym-goers walked by doing their thing, the embarrassment of it all reduced me from kneeling to sitting on the gym floor, quietly weeping. *There is no denying it*, I thought, *my life is out of control.*

I picked myself up and sulked off to lift weights, but my eight-minute performance ate away at me the whole time. The thought of having a rut-busting plan and then getting stymied on the first step put my mind in overdrive thinking of some way out of this mess. This was beyond a want. I had to figure this out, because I *needed* to smile again. For the rest of the day, I thought of the other times that I had been at a crossroads and what had been said to me then.

Once, when I had been down, rather than do anything for me my mother just looked at me and told me I was smart enough, willful enough, and strong enough to think my way out of any dilemma, and walked away.

My father told me that no one should beat me the same way twice.

One of my football coaches told me that I had a million-dollar body that was worthless because I thought with a two-cent mind.

I had a lot of recollections of things that helped me endure, but each time I was on the verge of a good idea, the blinking treadmill numbers of 8:03 erased it. It was not until late that night when I figured something out.

The next day, I was up, out and in the gym by 6:00 a.m. I listened to the same song on the tape, on the same Walkman, and even wore the same clothes as the day prior. I stepped on the same treadmill and keyed up the same hill program. I started running.

My lungs burned.

My legs ached.

My heart raced.

Everything was just as it was 24 hours earlier but my mindset was completely different. I knew that I wasn't going to run for only thirty minutes that day. I believed that I could push myself to last at least one second longer.

So that morning I got on the treadmill, not worried about competing with a program or any other inanimate object. I stepped on that machine only concerned about being in competition with myself. That day, I had an unflinching focus on *being better than I was yesterday.*

It all hurt like hell, but I stared at that clock until it read 8:04. Only then did I allow myself to relent to what I physically felt and stop. The blinking numbers on the treadmill dashboard weren't damning anymore. If anything, they were emotionally freeing. Going for thirty minutes wasn't going happen, so I was free, at least for eight minutes and four seconds, to mentally slow everything down and focus only on what I was feeling inside of my body at that moment.

The next day I was able to eke an extra second out of my body. I gasped out a few additional seconds the day after that. But on that first day when I could not go one more second than my previous day's time on the treadmill, I had to do something more.

I dropped to the floor and did pushups until I could not do any more. This meant that the next day's goal was to run on the treadmill for one more second than before and *then* do pushups.

Treadmill running and pushups were the goal until I couldn't run as long and/or didn't do as many pushups as the previous day. That meant I added another exercise to my next day's goals. This meant that the following day, I had even more to do.

Because my daily goal was nothing grander than being better than I was the day before, I had over 23 hours free to focus and strategize as to how to accomplish my overall goal. Soon, I didn't think about the treadmill time at all, I only focused on being better than I was the day before.

In order to push myself to be better, I had to start changing my behavior. There was no other way. I started reading more about how to eat, because I didn't want to lose any strength or to gain any excess weight. The ideas I got from exposing myself to alternative foods led to my exposure to alternative training methods and exercises. I next started reading about the life stories of the different trainers who came up with these exercises. All of this constant exposure to new things stimulated every area of my life.

For the first few weeks, I felt bad when I could not do more work and looked at the additional exercises as punishments. But once I saw that I had increased my endurance, improved my physique, and was more learned, I got over that quickly. By comparing myself to and competing with the "me" of yesterday, I became a much broader and stronger individual.

This "being better than I was yesterday" thought process that I stumbled onto soon grew to well beyond beating a treadmill. It lessened my perceived barriers of entry toward attempting new things, giving me an almost overwhelming hunger and duty to attempt everything, in and out of the gym.

Without a care in the world, I started entering stair-climbing races, bodybuilding shows, triathlons, attending poetry workshops, reading about other faiths, and things that I'd never thought of before.

Entering into new endeavors was never about winning or doing anything to anyone else's limits. What I was doing and how I was thinking was about giving myself more boundaries to push and allowing myself the freedom to push those boundaries. I mean, winning felt great, but it was really rare when that occurrence happened. But now I was feeling excited about everything - even just the experience of attempting stuff. Even if I performed poorly at something, like the poetry writing, so what? I found that I was succeeding on some other level, like biking faster to actually get to the poetry workshop. Overall, I felt as if I couldn't lose.

Each time I turned what I had previously perceived as impossible into possible, turned the "improbable" things in my life into "likely, replaced the words "I'm scared" with "I already tried it," and changed the "whys" of my life into "why nots?", I became more comfortable and secure with myself and more confident about what I could achieve.

Losing could only happen if I failed to challenge myself to be better and to move forward, and, since not moving forward felt horrible, I felt like I was going to be winning for a long time.

I still cried about the loss of my father, but now it was tears of happiness for the time that he and I had rather than anything else. I conceded that my girlfriend and I weren't really that compatible after all, and soon I even found a job that I was happy at. It was an amazing time of discovery for me but more important than anything, I was smiling again. A lot.

My thought process even changed how a few of my friends viewed me. "You can still be an ass, but I like you a lot more now," one friend noted.

Some may read this essay and wonder about how much weight I lost, how long it took to get from eight to thirty minutes, or if I ever found that runner's high I was looking for. I really wish that I could answer that for you, but somehow, after thinking differently, none of those benchmarks that I strove for held much significance anymore.

During a speech at a school recently, a fifth grader asked me a great question that stumped me. She asked me what I would have done in my life if my friend Kevin had not passed away on September 11.

I said that I didn't know and, for the record, I still don't know. But, I do believe that if I hadn't faltered on a treadmill back in 1995 and started to think only about being better, that my behavior would have been very different. I will also say that I don't know what will happen tomorrow, but I do know that whatever it is, I will handle it better than I ever could have handled it yesterday.

Above The Fold

It was July 2002, ten months since *that* Tuesday in September, and the country was still reeling. *Philadelphia Inquirer* columnist Mike Vitez was driving east-to-west across North America, looking for interesting but unknown Americans to write about in order to restore our spirit a bit.

In Philadelphia, the Bowser family was still reeling as well. When the airliner slammed into Kevin's floor, the jet-fueled explosive force and fire incinerated his body as well as disintegrated the hopes of his family and friends to have something to say goodbye to in order to obtain closure. This surreal experience had me bicycling west-to-east across North America, looking for something within the nation to restore my spirit.

With our somewhat shared mission objective and Philly connection, Mike was intrigued by my story but there was no guarantee that our paths would cross for an interview- North America is a huge continent. But I was relentless at trying to connect with him, because I needed this interview, badly.

Officially, the purpose of my ride across the United States was to drum up publicity, awareness, and funds for the Kevin Bowser Memorial scholarship, a fund established at his alma mater, John Bartram High School, to benefit needy college-bound students.

Unofficially, though, but just as important, I was trying step out of my kid-brother role with this ride.

I felt like a kid brother because I'd hung around both Kevin and his identical twin brother, Kelvin, my whole life. They were the sons of my parents' good friends, and even though there was a ten-year age difference, I was allowed to be around them whenever I wanted. My parents trusted them that much. There was such a strong, influential, and very necessary bond forged between the three of us that they didn't even look alike to me anymore.

Kevin was Kevin.

Kelvin was Kelvin.

And I was a different man because of their influence.

But, all of what we had was now in jeopardy after September 11. Each hour with no word of Kevin's possible whereabouts- and only the many replays of the towers crumbling onto themselves to mark time -made each possible scenario a bit darker than the one prior.

A week or so had passed when I let go of the possibility of Kevin being one of the unidentified injured people or one of those wandering around with amnesia or some other scenario. It was a tough decision, but I had to admit it to myself: Kevin was dead.

I decided to go to the Bowser home to essentially pay my respects, so imagine my shock when I saw him walking over to greet me. No, it wasn't really Kevin, but when I looked at Kelvin, all I saw was his brother. Like I said before, the twins didn't look alike at all to me anymore, but seeing Kelvin's eyes light up, the way he walked and hearing the way he said my name—it was all Kevin. It stopped me in my tracks. I tried to be strong and hold back my tears, but I couldn't.

As close as Kevin and I were, I had the great luxury of being able to be able to forget him if I wanted to. Kelvin did not. They were twins. Imagining Kelvin looking in the mirror every morning and not only seeing his own eyes but also those of his lost twin reflecting back on him made everything hurt a little deeper. The whole time that Kelvin and I spoke, I stared and studied the contours of his face like it was my first time seeing him. Seeing this made me feel that Kelvin's grief would be even more protracted and deeper than I thought and prompted me to want to do something to have Kevin live on somehow. I felt as if I had to: Kelvin was the only brother I had left.

Kelvin offered to help me plan out my North American ride when I announced that I would do it in order to bring some attention to the scholarship. But I wouldn't let him; he had enough going on. When he would ask me how things were shaping up, I'd tell him, "Relax brother," and that this was my idea, my task, and my deal, and I had things covered.

Truth be told, I didn't.

Because planning a nationwide bike trip was bigger than anything I'd ever chewed on, I quickly concluded if I wanted to attain all of my goals-official and unofficial-that it would be simplest and best if I registered with America by Bicycle, an established touring company. The plan was to cross North America while on their 50-day tour from Astoria, Oregon to Wallace Sands Beach, New Hampshire and then take a few extra days and ride solo to Kevin's father's home in Philadelphia. And since Kevin's dad lived one block from me, I was essentially flying all the way to the Pacific Northwest with my bicycle and then riding home.

Riding with a tour was a good call, but there was no room for deviation. If Mike Vitez was going to meet me, he had to conform to my route. Nothing was firmed up between Mike and me by the time that I took off for Oregon, so I got on the plane with my fingers crossed. At the end of each day, I wouldn't relax or even shower until I called or sent him an email, and it wasn't until we confirmed a meet in Casper, Wyoming that I finally allowed myself to calm down. But not too much; now everything hinged on me doing a great job on this interview.

Leading up to Mike's interview, I spent my solitary hours on the bike, imagining different questions and responses. I had to get this right. By the time we met in the hotel lobby, I was so tightly wound that I stood there, hot and sweaty, blurting out prepared answers to questions he hadn't yet asked.

"Just relax," he said, ushering me to sit down.

When Mike and I did sit down, he initially seemed more interested in what made me tick than anything. As I gave my answers, he scanned me up and down, probably because I was so sweaty and, again, told me to relax and maybe grab a shower. He was right, I was intense… and I did stink.

After showering, I was more relaxed and we soon started talking about Kevin, our friendship, and what his presence meant to me as a man. When we started talking about the timeline of September 11, I told Mike that I didn't think of Kevin, because, as a daily commuter, I didn't really associate him with NYC. I thought of him being in Philly, safe. I told him that I clung to that belief, because Kevin had been in San Francisco during the '89 earthquake, and while we were worrying whether he was safe, he was helping a wheelchair-bound lady down a hotel stairwell. But the reality of everything was that Kevin went into work early, logged on to his computer, and that was it.

I never totally confessed to Mike about my urge to step back from my kid-brother role but I vented enough to relax and forget that I was in an interview. It wasn't until I said that bicycling across North America was the least that I could do for all that Kevin and Kelvin had done for me and heard him say, "No shit," that reminded me that this was an interview.

"Why bike across America?" Mike asked.

I told him that the period after my father died, years earlier, had been difficult for me and left me looking anywhere and everywhere for peace. A slice of serenity came with the chance discovery of an account of a man bicycling across the US. I wanted to experience this crossing/journey for myself. But when I told my friends this, they either laughed or asked when it was ever going to be the "right" time.

It seemed destined to remain an unrealized dream, until September 11 revealed that the line between life and death could be as thin and tenuous as oversleeping one day. At that point, no one was laughing anymore. Everyone told me that the time was right.

Next, Mike wanted to know what bicycling a continent came down to, and I told him that it wasn't that complicated at all. It came down to only a few things:

Meet and get along with my roommates Scott and Steve.

Wake up before the crack of dawn and wolf down some food.

Get on the bike and pedal ninety miles per day.

Ponder life.

Meet people along the way.

Wolf down some more food with Scott and Steve.

Sleep in a hotel room with Scott and Steve.

Repeat for 50+ days.

Mike then asked if I'd met anyone special thus far and I told him of an encounter I had had while poking around in a Dubois, Wyoming gift shop. While there, I couldn't help but listen to the cashier and her friend gossip, talk about life and their inability to pay rent, cable, and make ends meet. After finding a few things and growing tired of their conversation, I went to the counter to pay for my stuff.

"Are you one of those crazy cyclists I passed on my way to work?" the cashier asked. I told her that I was.

She asked, "What would possess you to do this, anyway?"

Sharing my reasons prompted an exchange that encompassed everything from her never leaving Wyoming to life before and after September 11, and, of course, Kevin. She seemed genuinely surprised to discover that I wasn't pro war, and that it was my wish for everyone else in the world to die only from old age, but seemed to understand when I said that I just wanted people to respect life and appreciate living a whole lot more. When we spoke about Kevin and his family and I showed her a picture of him, her manner softened even more. "You both were lucky to have your friendship," she said.

Our exchange felt great and had us both sniffling and wiping away tears, but I was late in meeting the other cyclists for dinner and had to go. She grabbed her purse from underneath the counter, pulled out a few dollars and said, "This is for the scholarship fund."

I told her that I appreciated the gesture but had to refuse, because I'd eavesdropped and knew that she didn't have enough money to pay her monthly bills. I told her that when things got better for her, she could contact the foundation handling the fund and give whatever she wanted, but to get herself together first. She told me that she couldn't let me leave empty-handed and asked, "Can I give you a hug, at least?"

"Hugs are always welcome. *Always* welcome," I said. By the time we embraced, both of us were crying again.

"No shit," Mike said with a blank stare. He asked for more stories, and I told him that they were not always so poignant, like when I stopped in a roadside convenience store, guzzled a big bottle of sports drink, and then took a nap while bicycling to Blackfoot, Idaho. He looked unimpressed by this statement, until I added the timing of it all.

The road to Blackfoot was brutal because of an unrelenting sun and lack of any sort of breeze. It was so brutal that I took this nap… in the convenience store… on the floor… in front of the store refrigerator…that I had propped open with my backpack.

Mike looked at me and said, "You're something else."

"Dude, I am just me, and I was just hot and tired."

To get a true feel of what I was going through, Mike opted to ride with me the next day, but with a scorcher forecasted, he could not have picked a worse day. The road to Lusk, Wyoming was going to be 105 miles of pure oppressive heat. I am certainly not the most experienced cyclist, but by this point, I had biked through enough heat to know what it took to make it through: get up, get out, ride fast, and do it all as early as possible. Mike had other plans, though.

While I was up, fed, and ready, Mike casually sipped his coffee, tried to get notes and quotes from other riders, and checked over the route details with his driver/photographer. He did not understand the importance of getting an early start. His dawdling made me nervous about not finishing that day, but I couldn't just leave. I felt that I needed this day to sum up a lot of things in order to get a good story written. Even if it meant that it was going to be a much harder day, I had to hang around—this interview was that important to me.

As Mike pushed the questions, I pushed the pace, and we made good time in the morning. But as the mercury rose, Mike's stamina and patience eroded, and every few pedal strokes he started to ask how far we'd gone.

"Not far enough. Keep pedaling," I kept answering.

We got to one semi-flat stretch where you could look ahead and see the road undulate for miles. The longer you stared into the distance, the more the heat from the asphalt created waves in the air and made the road come alive and undulate even more. I looked back at Mike, who now had an elongated expression as if his face were made of melting rubber, and decided that I'd done everything I could to get a good story from Mike, and besides, if I did tell him something good at this point, he wouldn't remember it. I also decided that there was no way that I was going to be able to finish if we kept his pace, and I knew that Mike was never going to quit and get into his photographer's van while I was around.

So, I had to come up with a way to separate us. I asked if he really wanted to know what it felt like on these trips.

"Yeah," he said.

"Really?" I said.

"Yeah," he said.

"You're sure?"

"Yeah."

"All right," I said and stood up on my pedals and sprinted away.

Yes, it was a bit self-serving, but I wasn't being a total jerk—that had been my cycling experience. I would be riding along with someone and all of a sudden, a slice of road, a hill, or a view would call to one of us. The call was different every time, but each time, you had to answer it. No goodbyes. Nothing personal. Both people—the one who took off and the one who didn't—dealt with their demons. Later on, you would slow, breathe, and catch up with each other down the road.

When I looked back, Mike was nothing more than a red shirt getting smaller in the distance. My only reminder that I was an interview subject was a photographer who popped up every few miles to take pictures. Because of the heat, the road to Lusk, Wyoming pushed each of the riders to their personal limit, and there seemed to be pooped cyclists waiting for the tour support vehicle everywhere.

When I saw Mike later in the day, he was slumped in the passenger seat of his photographer's SUV, wearing an exhausted smirk and giving me a weak thumbs-up. As the vehicle slowed to my pace, I could see the air conditioning was visibly blasting on him and thought that Mike was going to roll down the window to say something to me. I looked forward to feeling some of that cool air but just as I slowed down some more, the SUV lurched forward and sped off. When it did, Mike gave me a wink as if to say, "Payback is a bitch, Big Man."

After dinner that evening, I went to see Mike one last time in his hotel room, which was downright frigid because the air conditioner was blasting so hard. He was fully relaxed in a recliner and chuckled as he blew out a puff of smoke from a cigar as I walked in. Mike called me "a character," and asked me a few more fact-checking questions, but when I asked him what day and where in the paper his article would run, he had nothing.

"Anywhere from Thursday to Sunday — from the Metro to Lifestyle. It depends on the editors," is all he said.

It wasn't the most definitive answer, but it was the answer I got. All I could do was walk away believing that I did my best.

Thursday came and went with no story.

Friday did, too.

So did Saturday.

My heart sank. I know that only big stories are in the Sunday editions and felt that I'd failed at my goal to achieve notoriety for Kevin's scholarship. I felt like I'd failed to help Kevin's name live on. I felt like I failed Kelvin, too.

My cell phone rang early Sunday morning, and I ignored it. It rang again, and I ignored it again. It rang again. Now, there was no ignoring it.

Before I could even get out a full "Hello," I heard my sister yell, "Above the fold. You are above the fold!"

I sat up because I knew exactly what she was talking about, but found it unbelievable. "Above the fold" meant that my story was the leading story for the paper's biggest circulation day. It meant that every Philadelphian was waking up and having coffee and breakfast with Kevin.

"Holy shit," was all I could say.

Because I had to bike 86 miles, there wasn't time to go online and read the article, but I knew that if the article made the cover, it had to be good. With my official goal of bringing notoriety to the scholarship fund and my unofficial goal of getting Kevin to live on for a little while longer achieved, I breathed a lot easier. I spent the day beaming and a bit more open to the whole experience that cycling North America offered.

As the tour continued on out of Wyoming and into South Dakota, Minnesota, Wisconsin, Michigan, Canada, New York, Vermont and into New Hampshire, every hug, smile, interaction with my roommates, and everything else felt better than it did before. I even found myself looking forward to the mountain passes we had to cycle over.

The night before we officially ended our tour by riding onto the shores of Wallace Sands Beach, the riders gathered for dinner in the banquet room of our hotel. There the tour leader gave an impassioned speech, informing us that we were about to enter an "elite fraternity" of people that had ridden a bicycle across the continent. "But," he paused "this is the last time that all of the members of this chapter of this fraternity will be in the same room, so savor tonight and really savor the ride tomorrow."

Afterward, riders stood up, one by one, to address the group about what the tour meant to them. I listened intently to their heartfelt words and did what I could to savor those final moments with my friends. I did what I could to extend the day's ride, too. I stopped for a few minutes to help a woman garden, helped a secretary hang a flag outside a dentist office, and stopped to hug as many random people as I could. When we reached the beach and I officially crossed the continent, I became so elated with my achievement that I changed tradition a bit.

The tradition is for bicyclists to "baptize" their bikes by dipping their rear bicycle wheel in the Pacific Ocean, bicycle North America, and then dip their front wheel in the Atlantic Ocean. This was the plan, but when I saw the ocean stretched out across the horizon like a living blue blanket, plans changed.

With thoughts of Kevin in my head and pride in my heart, I grabbed my bike, held it over my head and ran into the ocean. My roommates, Scott and Steve, who were once total strangers to me, did the same. Fifty days of crossing state borders, touching two oceans, and laughing every night will change a relationship. We crossed the continent into a brotherhood and were so close to the Maine state border that we decided to bike into a state, together, one more time.

Very soon thereafter, Scott had to grab a flight back home to San Diego, Steve had to grab a ride back home to upstate Maine, and I had to grab my bike and start pedaling to Philadelphia. Anne Burke, my good friend, came up to New Hampshire with her bicycle and rode with me into Massachusetts, Connecticut, and then onto New York and the World Trade Center site.

By the time I stood at a huge memorial that been set up near the World Trade Center site, 330 days had passed since *that* Tuesday in September. It was a relatively short amount of time, but much had changed in the world and within my world. I was now left with only pictures and memories where a friend once stood, but, while bicycling across the country, I managed to find something indefinably special that began to soothe my pain. Even though I wasn't too clear about what made everything so special, I stood at the memorial thinking of how I could do even more.

I probably would have stayed there a lot longer than I did, but I couldn't because the noise of vendors selling pictures of the World Trade Centers, people stopping to take pictures, and people asking me to take their picture as they stood in front of the site jarred me from whatever meditative state I was hoping to get in.

Besides, that wasn't the time or the place to think about such things: I still had things to do. I placed Kevin's picture on the memorial and got on my bike. I biked through New Jersey and into Philadelphia, and when I rounded the corner to Kevin's father's house, a drum corps from a marching band, news vans, a block party, and mayoral proclamation were waiting for me. I felt humbled by it all, and as if I'd achieved my goals, officially and unofficially. Kevin was living on.

Mike Vitez was on assignment and couldn't attend my homecoming, but his article was well received and started an avalanche of calls, emails, and letters from people contacting me about how they were inspired to do something, no matter how small, to make the world a better place. Everything that was happening around me made me feel as if I were a part of some bigger ball of good energy that I really didn't want to stop.

There was a problem, though: how do you continue the momentum of something that you were a part of without a clue as to what you just did in the first place?

Trying to solve this problem made my first weeks back home feel weird. Everyone, including me, assumed that I was going to stick to my plan of riding across North America, honor my friendship, and go back to work as usual. But I changed. My eyes were open more than ever to the possibilities of everything, and everywhere I went, there was something that I took as a sign that I should not stop.

After I had been home for a month or so, I stopped by the newspaper offices to see Mike. He wasn't there, but while leaving, an African-American reporter pulled me aside and congratulated me. He said that what I did doesn't happen everyday. I thanked him for his words, but told him that many before me had ridden their bikes across the country.

"Who's talking about riding across the country?" he said with a wry look. "I'm talking about the cover!"

"The cover?"

"Yeah, the cover," he said. "You really don't get it, do you? You are nobody," he said, explaining that black males don't make cover stories. "You are not rich, famous, an athlete, or a politician. You didn't kill someone or get killed. You are not an artist, a drug dealer, or anything like that. You aren't using, abusing, or exposing the system. You lost a friend violently and aren't even bitching or showing rage. You are a black man who just did something good and got the cover of the paper. When have you ever seen some shit like that? I work for the paper, and your shit just does not happen."

There was a sense of urgency in his voice that begged me to really try to hear what he was saying. I walked away from him believing that I had accomplished more than I set out to achieve and thinking that I'd like to do more. But, again, I really didn't know what the hell I had just done.

After this exchange, I was even more open to possible signs as to more that I could do, and soon another sign came from a highly unlikely source: a crack-head.

One evening, around midnight, I was biking home through a park and heard, "Bike man. Bike man," from the shadows.

I don't know what made me stop, but I did. "Yeah..?"

"Bike man, you the guy that rode all that way and raised that money"

Oh Lord, I thought. "Look dude, I don't have any money—it all goes to a fund that I can't touch."

"Nah man, I just want to know: is it real? Or is it a scam? Don't lie to me, because I know scams."

Before I could really answer, he said that that he hoped it wasn't a scam, because he knew "the twins" since they were all kids in summer camp together. He said that he didn't know which one was dead because they looked so much alike to him. "But," he paused, "no matter where I was in life they both treated me with *respect.*"

When I told him that it wasn't a scam, and that it was all legit he said, "Keep doing good big man...but before you go, do you have any money?"

I know that his words could have been a set-up to prey on my feelings, but there was something about the exchange that rang true. I rode home thinking *"If what I did can penetrate the mind of a crack-head, then I must have done something big, and I have to do more."*

Again, the question was, "What?"

I tried to think of something but was fresh out of ideas. Nothing struck me until later, when I received a random email from a stranger that said, "Think about this for your next trip," with a link to a site about a Cairo-to-Cape Town bicycle race. I went to the link, immediately looked at the price and the time involved, and thought, *"There's no way I can afford this."*

Days later, some clients brought me a newspaper article about the same race. I thought, "*Wow, I just heard about this, but I can't afford it.*"

A few days after that, I was thumbing through a magazine and saw the same race highlighted.

This is a big sign, I thought. I went to the site again, but this time I clicked on the map of Africa to see the route. When I did this, my eyes widened, and I thought, "I can't afford to *not* do this."

I knew what I had to do next.

The State Of Dave, 2003

Cycling across North America in 2002 not only gave me a ton of stories but also a huge surge of confidence. I was riding a wave of enthusiasm about the possibilities of life and had no clue what the future held but was prepared to do whatever I could in order to fully embrace it. I was so excited that I opted out of going to a New Year's Eve party and stayed home to make a list of things that needed getting done in order to boldly step forward: decreasing my debt, getting a passport, looking at different jobs and such. I wrote a longish email that night and sent it to my friends. I didn't think that much of it at the time, but when I didn't write anything for the following year a friend asked if I was OK. "I miss the State of Dave address," he said. The "State of Dave" nickname stuck. Because this is a series of independent essays about my maturation rather than a lengthy story about anyplace that I have pedaled, I chose to include all of "The State of Dave's" in this book, unedited, to give you a better idea of who I am and the events that got me there:

It's that time again, time for all of us to look back on the last 365 and look forward to the next 365 and beyond. As you look forward to your 365+, maybe you can learn something from my last 365.

This year, as most of you know, I bicycled across the USA to honor a family friend lost on 9/11, and on this one day in particular, I learned a whole hell of a lot about life. It was a hot day (100+ degrees) in July in the middle of Wyoming, and we're biking up Teton pass. Now Teton pass, for those that do not know, is steeeep!! It was a 15% grade at least and went on and up for seemingly forever. Now, I wasn't alone through this ordeal, I had deer flies to keep me company — deer flies are just those flies that are big and tough enough to bite through a deer's ass, so my slow pedalin' ass was a big black treat (it was so steep that I could only go 3-4 mph).

Did I mention that it was fuckin' *hot?*!

So the scene is set:, a 245lbs biker on a 15% grade on a 100 degree day with enough flies around him to make the baddest Ethiopian flinch — oh yeah, did I forget to mention that altitude was so high that I had a little trouble breathing. Anyway, I barely got to the top., I had to walk the last 1/8 of a mile, and at the top, I get off my bike and let it fall over, not caring if it broke— - all I knew was that I was fuckin' tired and wanted to stop. I was too tired to curse aloud (if you know me you know that's HARD) and am doubled over and am breathing heavy — waiting for me at the top is one of the aides for the tour who says, "Dave would you shut up and turn around." I looked at him with my usual don't-mess-with-me-it's-fuckin'-hot-as-hell stare and then it happened, it all changed.

"It" was a lot of things. "It" was the spectacular view of Wyoming and beyond. "It" was the feeling of triumph of actually conquering this mountain. "It" was not feeling the heat anymore. — "It" was not feeling the deer flies anymore. — "It" was realizing that if I could get over this mountain pass, that nothing and I do mean NOTHING was going to stop me from my goal of bicycling home to Philadelphia or any other goal that I would ever make in life. "It" was awesome, "It" was empowering, and "It" happened because I did one thing: ..... I changed my focus.

By changing my view and focus, all of my prior woes eroded into oblivion, and it is the same in life as well. Change your focus. Change your focus on your problems and your adversaries and your perceived shortcomings, and the improbable becomes very tangible. Believe that you can do whatever it is that you fucking want to do and it will come to pass — now it won't be necessarily easy, but it will happen. We are all much stronger physically, mentally, and spiritually than we think we are, and once you push through those perceived barriers and limits, you empower yourself for the next challenge that life serves you. It is so simple and yet so hard at the same time, but it does work — if someone had told me that I was going to bike though rain, go through fourteen days of 100+ degrees, get sick from dehydration, hurt like hell, and get what could be best described as the world's biggest case of diaper rash (a whole 'nuther story!!) — I may not have done the trip, but all during the summer, I changed my focus towards my friendship with Kevin and honoring him and his tireless friendship toward me and my family, and the shit did not seem so bad. Give it a try and see what happens — it can't hurt!

I could go on all day about the trip and what I learned but I won't- you'll have to take me to lunch to hear the rest of the stuff — but I thought that this may help some of you verbalize and ACTUALIZE even bigger resolutions for the upcoming 365 and beyond.

You are all very, very special to me and I wish you much love, success and conquered goals in 2003 — Happy New Year!!!

--DAVID

P.S.: Don't forget to tip your personal trainer, generously.

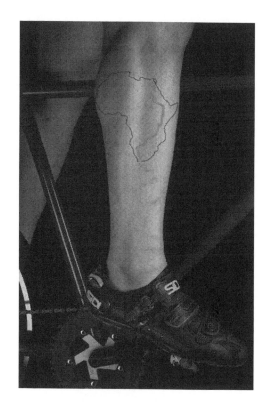

AFRICA

Every Picture Tells A Story

When I was growing up, my parents seemed to travel every-where. Whenever they returned home from anywhere in North America, Africa or Europe, as much as I wanted to see them safe, I wanted to hear their stories and see their pictures. At the time, I was just a kid that had a vivid imagination living in the pre-digital age. This meant that I had to hold on tightly to each and every detail and subtle nuance of their stories until the film rolls were developed. Only at the moment when the pictures were in my hands did I know if my mental images meshed and matched with the actual photographs of their stories. Many years later, when the opportunity presented itself to take part in a five-month bicycle race from Cairo, Egypt to Cape Town, South Africa, it was the possibility of taking my own pictures and telling my own stories that influenced my decision. So, with a firm foothold in today and toehold in the past, along with a digital camera in one hand and a bike in the other, I held my breath and took a huge leap of faith.

I arrived in Cairo a few days before the race without a clue as to what I was going to experience. But I arrived ready to capture every experience on film and started snapping pictures with an unbridled zeal.

I decided to take pictures of each sunrise and sunset that I experienced on the continent- here's my first picture. *Click!*

Two nights later, the cyclists were wined and dined at pre-race ceremonial dinner. *Click!*

The next morning, the riders were up before the sunrise, loaded their gear into support vehicles, and biked from our hotel to the pyramids and the Sphinx for a picture. *Click!*

This trip was an experience of personal firsts for me. Besides being my first extended bike race and my first time off my home continent, this was the first time that I'd ever set up a tent. I was so proud of this momentous occasion that I took a picture. **Click!**

There are at least a thousand more words about what is seen and unseen in this picture, and they all deal with my inexperience as a camper. I realized that I forgot to bring a pillow on my flight to Cairo and improvised by taking the airline blanket- which you can see is balled up in my tent. But what you cannot see in this picture are the other riders' tents.

In stepping back to take this picture, I tripped over some rocks that were surrounding some tents. While on the ground, I noticed that rocks were surrounding all of the tents around me. Being extremely naïve about the camping experience—also known as really dumb—I assumed that maybe this was some sort of camp ritual that I was not privy to. Since I was open to the experience,

I grabbed my headlamp and traipsed into the darkening desert and, after gathering what I believed to be a good amount of rocks, placed them around my tent. The *camping gods are happy*, I thought.

This rock routine kept up for about four days until, still in the desert, I clumsily tripped again over a rock. But this time, I noticed a lot more than the rock.

This time, I noticed the line of rope along with it that was tethering the tent to keep the tent from collapsing; this never occurred to me because I had a freestanding tent. I told you I was dumb.

After I quit collecting rocks, the normal tour routine was set:

- Wake to the predawn wake-up horn.

- Eat a breakfast - consisting of porridge, coffee, flat bread, and maybe some peanut butter. *Click!*

- Break down the tent and gear

- Ride an average of 130-140 kilometers

- Meet one of the two tour vehicles that would drive to the exact middle mileage point and set up a lunch stop consisting of local breads, vegetables, salt, local meats, minimal condiments, and an electrolyte drink. *Click!*

- The other truck would go all the way to the end point and establish camp and get started on dinner. *Click!*

- Eat a prepared soup when you biked in for the day, usually noodle soup and whatever leftover meat there was from the previous night's dinner.

- Set up your tent and then talk about everything and nothing.

- Get somewhat detailed directions, ten kilometers east and eighty kilometers west and so on, for the next day's ride.

- Eat dinner around a campfire. *Click!*

- Repeat over the course of 100+ days.

Once the routine was established, things were smooth, but if there ever was an issue, we were to take it to Mike. Mike was our tour leader and, to be honest, didn't add much value to the group. He really was a bit of an arrogant ass, and most days his sole concern was getting to camp, setting his tent up under a shady tree, mocking the slower riders, and drinking beer. *Click!*

Accepting Mike and his less-than-empathetic nature was easy in a place like Egypt where flat, well-paved roads and tailwinds were everywhere. But in Sudan, things were totally different; just getting there was an ordeal. Our day started in Abu Simbal, Egypt where we cycled down to the port and loaded our gear onto a floating platform. Once the platform was secured to a tugboat (that had the filthiest bathroom I have ever seen), we slowly drifted down Lake Nasser for hours. *Click!*

By the time that we docked in Wadi Hafa, Sudan, offloaded our gear from the barge, cleared Sudanese customs and loaded our gear onto the new support trucks that had been waiting for us, dusk had fallen. *Click!*

Then, cloaked in darkness, we somehow biked on a dusty street behind the new trucks to a soccer stadium. Once at the field, we officially met the staff of African Routes, the new tour company that would be supporting us for the rest of our journey, and were introduced to the "red box" system.

The red box system simply meant that you squeezed whatever you needed inside a red box that was given to you and then stored everything else into your luggage, which was then lashed down atop the huge support vehicles. The official dimensions of the red box were: Not that big x Not that deep x Not that tall. This meant that you only had enough room for your tent, sleeping bag, a change of clothes, toiletries, and a few other miscellaneous items. I got acclimated to the effectiveness and efficiency of the red box-bicycling-camping lifestyle rather quickly but have to say that the best part of the box was that it made a great place to sit at the end of the day.

Our route through Sudan was simple: follow the Nile. That was all we had to do, but things got messed up when we discussed the route to our next city, Kerma.

After looking at the map, Mike noted that the Nile curved, and brought up the mileage-saving idea of stopping at the outskirts of Town A, riding into the desert along the hypotenuse, and then ending in Kerma. If there were a picture of me at the time that this was presented to us, you would have seen an expression of total uneasiness. I saw how this plan worked, but only in theory. I felt that the real-life application of having 30+ individual riders turning into the desert sounded really, well, stupid. I didn't speak up, though, because no one else did, and because I figured that my feeling was due to my inexperience as an outdoorsman.

The day was like any other, each rider going at their own pace until they arrived at the tour company's big metal arrow pointing into the desert. I arrived at the arrow sometime in the afternoon along with riders Bart, Stephanie, Joe, and Edwina. The arrow, which pointed straight into nothingness, was easy to spot because there were five Sudanese men standing around it, staring into nothingness. Upon getting there, I confidently sipped most of my remaining water while posing for pictures with the men, and even though I didn't speak Arabic, figured they were saying, "You're a fool if you follow that arrow." *Click!*

After taking pictures with the Sudanese men, I started off into the desert with the much smaller Bart and Stephanie. Our size difference was an issue, because while my big behind kept sinking my bike into the sand, they maintained a much smoother cadence and seemingly glided along the desert floor. I lost ground with each pedal stroke and, as Bart and Stephanie pulled further and further away, learned more than I wanted to know about time, distance, space, and acoustics.

I barked, "Hold up!" while pedaling, but because Bart and Stephanie were biking along with the sound of the blowing wind in their ears, they could not hear me.

I tried to yell louder, but found that with nothing but sky for the sound to bounce off, my normally loud voice dissipated into the wind. I rode a little more and figured that I would stop in order to yell my loudest, but my efforts were fruitless because their forward movement coupled with my motionlessness only made me lose even more precious ground.

For reasons that I still don't know, I grabbed my camera and took a picture of Stephanie and Bart as they became only two dots on the horizon line. *Click!*

Initially, I was upset that Bart and Stephanie had left me, but I concluded, when I started pedaling again, that they must have just lost sight of me while focusing on going toward Kerma. I also concluded that, as I looked at every type of vehicle track crisscross the sand and thus erase any reference points I was hoping to gain, following them wasn't going to be an easy task. But I was confident that I was going on the right vector to Kerma, especially when I saw Bart and Stephanie in the distance.

It didn't bother me that they were now traveling on a different vector than when I last saw them.

It only bothered me when I got close and saw that they were neither Bart nor Stephanie. Then, my confidence turned to worry. **Click!**

After recognizing Joe and Edwina, a Canadian couple also on the tour, I was distressed, because they'd opted to rest a bit when I last saw them and started out into the desert behind me. But now, they were in front of me, and coming from the right. This meant that I was moving a lot more haphazardly than I thought.

Joe and Edwina were a bit unnerved by everything but our newly formed trio brought a bit of calm to us all. It even brought laughter, especially when we joked about which body part we were going to hang Mike from when we got out of this. We rode slowly and it wasn't too long before we saw two other figures in the distance.

Upon seeing the two figures, I fought my natural instinct to stop and yell. I just kept moving forward, screaming Bart and

Stephanie's names into the desert air. But because neither figure was Bart or Stephanie, the only sound that could be heard was our hearts and hopes dropping.

John and Traci Lynne were another tour couple from Alabama, and they started into the desert behind the three of us but were now in front of us. Seeing them confirmed that we were officially lost, big time. Seeing them also evaporated any levity that existed between Joe, Edwina, and myself and only left nuggets of exasperation and anger behind.

There were no rules for our newly formed group, but they started framing up quickly. After each venting about the brainless plan to wander in the desert, we agreed to speak our minds, pro and con, about any decision made, especially since we'd all felt opposed to the "orienteering through hypotenuse" plan, but had said nothing.

We also agreed not to waste energy by fighting the sand, and that if one person could not ride in the sand, we would all walk.

As I listened to everyone speak, I became aware of two things: 1) I was the only single person in this group and felt that I should really assert myself in some way, at the beginning of this whole mess, or run the risk of getting out-voted later on; and 2) We each had very little faith that Mike would even notice or care that we were missing.

After everyone spoke, we agreed to head toward a structure amid the tree line on the distant horizon.

As we started walking, Edwina quietly muttered, "I'm worried."

"Me too," I said.

Looking into the glow of the slow-setting sun, I remembered that I needed to get a picture. ***Click!***

As my camera clicked, there was also a huge click of a revelation in my brain: this situation was real, and we may be stuck in the desert all night.

Immediately, the uncomfortable silence that we were walking in became even more constricting. "First things first," I blurted. "We will not panic because panic equals death. Let's do a check. Who has what? I am out of water, have a long-sleeved jersey, and a few Power Bars." My idea to quantify exactly what each of us had may have been a good one but hearing me say, "*…panic equals death,*" startled even me. I made it even worse when I then asked the group if anyone had ever seen any helpful movies about people stranded someplace. No one said a word.

We continued, in silence, until the quiet was broken by the words "Fuck Mike."

I really don't know who said it, because we were all thinking it, but I know that it wasn't Edwina. Edwina was raised in Great Britain, was very proper and never cursed. She rarely even acknowledged foul language. So after "Fuck Mike" was uttered and we clearly heard Edwina say, "Yeah," we laughed. But we quickly fell back into silent steps until Joe's words, "Truck. Truck! It's the truck!" sliced through the cool, desert serenity like a buzz saw.

Before the words were even out of his mouth, Joe dropped his bike and ran, backtracking, into the desert. In the next instant, everyone else ran too, except for me. I had quickly scanned the dusky expanse that we had just trudged through, and saw a lot going on.

I saw Joe running.

I saw Edwina waving her jacket in the air.

I saw Traci Lynne waving her hands.

I saw John sprinting ahead of Joe.

I saw a lot of movement but I didn't see any truck.

I yelled, "Wait," but with the wind and emotion, no one was heeding or even hearing my words. I thought fast and pulled my camera from my jersey pocket, raised my arm and started taking pictures. *Click!*

I panned my camera toward the left... *Click!*

...then toward the right... *Click!* *(you can see Traci Lynne running in the corner of the shot)*

And even to the heavens... *Click!* *(You can clearly see the moon in this shot)*

I did all of this thinking that I didn't see anything but continued to take pictures because if there *were* a truck, it would see the flash from my camera. ***Click!***

Soon, the enthusiasm, waving, screaming, and movement leached from everyone's bodies like air from a deflating balloon. Everything stopped. Edwina, Joe, John, and Traci Lynne stood motionless where their hope and momentum had left them. I, too, stood immobile, even when Joe trudged past me, barely lifting his feet off the sand, and sneered, "Why didn't you run?"

"Because I didn't see shit," I replied, with equal din and disappointment.

With nothing to be said and nothing that anyone wanted to hear, we became five silent individuals who just happened to be walking in the same direction. Even I, a constant talker, welcomed the stillness.

Being totally honest with this account, I have to say that Mike wasn't *totally* useless, not totally. That's because on our first day, he advised us to go to a mosque if ever lost because it would always be open and there would always be someone there that could help. That was extremely helpful, because the structure on the horizon that we had been walking toward, atop a well-packed mixture of rocks and sand, and finally tillable soil, turned out to be a mosque.

By the time we reached the outskirts of the nameless town, we were dirty, dejected and still silent. We had been walking our bicycles and wearing all of our extra clothing to stave off the dipping desert temperatures. With no streetlights or even that much electricity to speak of, the town was dark and any wattage of illumination stood out like a beacon, including the camping headlamps that Joe and John wore. Our eyes scoured the sparse streets and alleys, looking for anyone who could put us on the right track.

When we did see some people walking down the street, we stood in stark contrast to their traditional Muslim garb. We were strangers here. But that didn't stop us from running toward them loudly saying, "Kerma? Kerma?" and pointing toward the ground as if to ask, "Is this Kerma?" The people just looked at us, and hurriedly, almost fearfully, walked away while muttering something in Arabic. Yeah, we were definitely strangers here.

Needing assistance and having the few people that we encountered briskly walk away from us increased our inner tension to boiling. I know this because without warning, one of us would say, "Fuck Mike" or "I can't believe they aren't looking for us," like pressure cookers letting off the occasional wisp of steam. It was only a few minutes later when a cab sped up the dusty street, but it was a long few minutes.

Cold, hungry, tired, and very impatient, we still hadn't learned our lesson about running up to people like escapees from an asylum, but we couldn't stop ourselves, either. We stood in the middle of the street frantically waving our arms to get the cab driver's attention. When he stopped, I noticed two things right away: his cab was empty, and he looked scared as hell with the five of us rushing his vehicle.

We yelled the town name of Kerma again and again, but this time, the person did not leave. The cab driver wrinkled his brow, and, without too thick of an accent, coolly said, "This is not Kerma." Relief mixed with a bit of anguish came over us, because now we definitely knew where we weren't.

Now a taxicab in Sudan is not like those that you may be used to—it is only a covered pickup truck with two rows of seats in the back cab. I asked if the driver could take us to Kerma, and eager to put an end to this day's adventure, I put my bike in the back of his taxi before he could answer. I assumed the others were with me and was surprised when I turned around and saw them standing there, conferring.

One of the reasons for their conference was that there was no way that five bikes and five people were going to fit in his vehicle, which meant we would have to separate. Another reason was that John was concerned about his EFI (Every Fucking Inch) status. And to get that award you have to ride *Every. Fucking. Inch.*

John said, "Let him go," referring to the cab and driver.

It was at this point that I had to interject my opinion and explain my single, non-married status. I said, "Look, I can take the women, find Kerma, and can come back."

"What about the rule: if one of us can't ride, then none of us ride?" John said.

"Fuck that! That was in the desert," I said. "If you think that I am going to let an empty cab with the only guy that I have met in this country that speaks decent English and knows where Kerma is leave, then you are out of your mind. So, who is riding with me?"

As the pickup lurched into gear and Joe, Edwina, Traci Lynne, and John started to fade away into the darkness, I leaned out the window and yelled, "Fuck Mike!" as a sort of rallying cry. I quickly lost all my bearings as the cabbie sped around darkened corners and only realized just how much tension had built up in my body when I exhaled and reclined in the passenger seat. My only thought was, "Boy, *were we lost.*" I became even more aware of how bad things were when I took my camera out of my rear cycling jersey pocket because it was jabbing into my back and started scrolling through my pictures of the day. Feeling that the end of the day was near though, I started chatting up the cabbie, and took his picture. *Click!*

Along the 10-15 kilometers to Kerma, we hit another town, and it occurred to me that other riders might be stranded as well. The cabbie picked up on my anxiety and stopped outside what looked like a small eatery, and, in what sounded like a frenetic pace, spoke to some people standing outside. As they spoke, the cabbie made a pedaling motion with his hands, and all of a sudden, they all started to heartily laugh. When the cabbie got back in, I asked him what he said.

"I asked them if they had seen any more white people," he said.

"Any more?"

Laughing, he said, "Tonight, *you are white,* my friend"

"Gee, it doesn't feel like I thought it would," I said laughing. I decided to take a picture to document my new "whiteness." **Click!**

The camera flash lit up the darkened street and momentarily froze the movement of everyone walking about in its lens. I turned the camera around to show some of the people their picture in the 1"x1" digital viewfinder, and when I did, it triggered a bit of posing and jostling. I decided to take another picture. *Click!*

The group started out a few feet from me, but quickly more people started to join. The posing progressed to pushing. I thought that if I took a picture, maybe it would quell things a bit. *Click!*

It didn't. Getting a glimpse of themselves escalated everyone's behavior. **Click!**

Soon, everyone near was crushing and clamoring to get in the lens. *Click!*

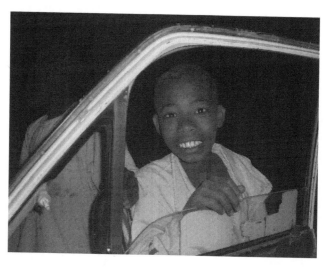

At the point that people started crawling through the driver's side door, their innocent desire to get their photo taken now bordered on aggression. *Click!*

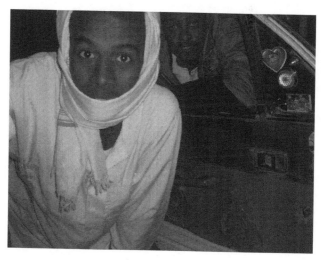

I knew that there wasn't going to be any polite way that we were going to be able to leave and yelled, "We gotta get out of here." As I snapped some more pictures and retreated to the car, the cabbie just laughed and shooed people away. He continued laughing all the way to Kerma.

We first arrived at an extremely dim café that seemed to be abuzz with people. I could barely make out the people sitting outside, but they clearly saw me. I was barely out of the cab when I was greeted with a hug and questions as to whether I knew where the others were. After exchanging stories, it came out that more than half the group had gotten lost, and the five of us were the last of the lost ones. The cabbie enjoyed our happiness, and after riding back to get the other three riders (John opting to ride in through the darkness to maintain his EFI status, which he maintained throughout the whole trip), he would not accept any money for his effort. But he did say, "You are happy. I am happy," and posed for a picture. **Click!**

As it turned out, our hapless leader, Mike, had not looked for us until nightfall.

No wait: our hapless leader, Mike, had not even noticed that we were missing until nightfall.

The two support vehicles had gone out to look for us, but one got stuck in the desert sand and the other was stuck trying to free it. Since the trucks carried the food and gear for the tour, and the hungry cyclists had eaten everything that was in the town's only café, we were left to stew in our own angst. We ended up taking over a one-floor rooming house and rooting around for blankets and even old dresses to keep warm. The only thing that got me through the night was taking pictures and laughing at the absurdity of it all. *Clickclickclick!*

Sometime around three in the morning the trucks came back, and we each sleepwalked to our red boxes to retrieve our sleeping bags to try and get a few hours of warm sleep. *Click!*

I couldn't get too much sleep, though, because the series of near misses, coincidences, and "what ifs" kept my mind and body on edge. But what made me most livid was that I already knew Mike well enough to know that his ego and arrogance would never allow him to even offer the simple apology that really would have gone a long way toward smoothing things over. Every time I pictured myself speaking with him, I heard him flippantly saying what he disdainfully said anytime anything went afoul: "Hey, what do you want? *It's Africa.*"

I knew I wouldn't be able to contain myself if I heard that again.

With everyone feeling edgy the next morning, the only thing preventing a full-scale mutiny was our next destination: a rest day in Dongala. Our Dongalan campsite was a small, enclosed quad of one-floor schoolhouses with very limited electricity and running water. By the time we arrived, offloaded our gear, and ate, it had started getting dark, which severely decreased the visibility inside the buildings. This was a problem, because we had been camping in the bush for over a week, and I was a bit ripe.

Getting lost was one thing, but taking my funky ass to my tent one more night was just too much for me to take. I needed a bath. I grabbed my soap and headlamp and marched into the dark building where the showers were but found no showers, only faucets of tepid water. There was also Edwina washing her and Joe's laundry. I asked, "Do you mind if I wash here?"

"Sure," she said not even looking up.

"Thanks." I filled up a bucket with water, stripped naked, and started washing my body.

"Quite a day yesterday," Edwina said while washing laundry and still not looking up.

"Sure was," I said, not looking up either.

The conversation about our desert saga carried on for about two or three minutes, with her oblivious to me and me obtuse to her. When she was done, she said "All done," with a tone of accomplishment and then, finally looking up, said, "Oh my!"

Cleansed of the sweat, grime, and the events of the previous day, I stood there naked and said, "*I asked.* And if you haven't seen it by now, then take a good look," and continued washing up.

So let's recap:

- Speak up if something sounds odd; you may avoid a jam.
- If you find yourself in a jam, do not panic.
- Do not wait for trucks in the desert.
- Do not assume anyone is looking for you.

- Do not assume that because you are washing laundry, that the person asking to wash next to you wants to wash laundry, too.

I still tell my *"A funny thing happened on the hypotenuse to Kerma"* story but now gloss over the details of getting lost because I don't believe that's the real story. Anyone can get lost, anywhere. By the tour's end in South Africa, getting lost wasn't even a big deal to Joe, Edwina, John and Traci Lynne. We just laughed the experience off and remarked about how much we'd shared—especially the bit about Edwina and I sharing a bath.

Now when I tell the story I slow down when I get to the part about stopping at that small Sudanese town that was smack in the middle between where we ended up and where we wanted to go. The town where a photograph started a mini riot.

Photographs of precious and even non-precious moments have become the punctuation marks for practically every one of my cycling stories. Even before that, they meant a lot to me as my parents trip pictures were what I, literally, sat on the edge of my seat waiting for when I was a kid. Those captured images became an intrinsic part of my personal culture. Today, I always keep a picture of my father and my friend Kevin with me to serve as a constant reminder of the better men that went before me as well as make me aware of the better man that I can become. Sometimes pictures can be more than just pictures; sometimes, pictures can be pieces of us.

I never thought that deeply about photographs until I found myself in that town where they didn't have them. Since then, I have started to question what life would be like without them.

How would I act if I did not have the ability to capture the mood, melodrama, and movement of time?

Would that make me more or less passionate about ideals?

Would I dress the same?

Would I worship the same?

Would I be the same?

Would I want the same?

Would I love the same?

Who would I be?

How can I call for a certain policy in another land if I can't walk around in their shoes?

How can I call something totally wrong if I can't even see myself in their picture?

How can I make something totally right if they never even have a picture?

The state of the world is as crazy as it has ever been, leading people to stand up and make disparaging and blanketing assertions about other people, other neighborhoods, other countries, and other cultures. Many state their assertions so loudly, so long, and so consistently that their words wind up being taken as fact. Now, I am not going to sit and tell you who to believe or what to think, but I am going to ask you to not blindly trust an individual's opinion about another culture, foreign or domestic, until you have walked in that other culture's shoes…or at least had your picture taken with them. *Click!*

Shut Up And Drink Your Coffee

Cross-continental bicycle trips can be a lot like college: you pay a lot of money to leave home for an extended period of time, have some fun, and maybe learn something in the process. Under this paradigm, days off during the tour are like mini Spring Breaks: you roll into a town filthy, with loads of dirty laundry, eager to scarf down a lot of food, drink anything cold, and relax in every way imaginable.

Bahir Dar, Ethiopia's northeast regional capital, was our "Spring Break" city, and we needed it after camping in the bush as well as on hazy, hot, and humid mountainsides. Bahir Dar was a sleepy town but became wide-awake once the two huge overland vehicles, which provided storage and support for the tour, rolled through with thirty hungry, dirty, world-traveling (and now world-weary) cyclists following close behind.

Before setting one foot into the hotel's darkened mahogany lobby, we could tell from the staff's body language that they had no idea what had just descended upon them. Each bellman and maid looked completely overwhelmed as they scurried about the lobby, stepping over our sweaty bodies, bags, and bicycles while straining to differentiate among our different accents. Even the groundskeepers stopped their duties to assist as each cyclist tried to quickly get to their room to rest and, most importantly, bathe.

I was no different. I moved with abandon to get to my room so I could shower, sit on the edge of my bed, dump my dirty gear out of my even dirtier bag, and then fall back on the bed, exhale loudly and shower again. Damn, that felt good. No, that felt fantastic. But I didn't relish the moment too much, because I had to get some food.

I went to the first eatery I came upon and feasted on practically the whole menu. While eating, I decided to email home.

The Internet café I found was a hub of business activity, because it was not only an Internet café, but also served as a hair salon and phone-calling center. It was great — with the exception of the Internet connection, which was only slightly faster than two tin cans and some string. This meant that there was a lot of downtime between loading photographs and writing paragraphs. The downtime and loud humming of the antiquated computer really tried my patience and made me let out a loud groan of frustration that caught the ear of a little mimic who sat near me.

Her name was Ledet, and she was about eight years old. Almost immediately, she had all of my moves down. She yawned, as I did. She stretched her arms out wide, as I did. She imitated my voice, as I introduced myself as "Big Dave" and even mangled the pronunciation of a few Ethiopian words, as I did. Whether patrons were getting their hair done, trying to make a call, or waiting for the Internet, Ledet's near-perfect imitations of my mannerisms entertained everyone. After an hour of my time spent only being able to send two very short emails, and discovering that connection speed was actually relatively fast that day, I decided to go about the rest of my day.

With her main source of material about to leave, Ledet asked me not to go. I couldn't deny her frowning face so I stayed a short while longer to appease her. But soon I grew hungry again and stood up to go. While making a move toward the door, she asked me to follow her home so she could give me a gift, which seemed wholly inappropriate for a grown man to do. My refusal of her gesture was taken as an insult and criticized by everyone in the shop, and my attempt to explain my behavior didn't make things better. In fact, it only drew harsher criticism and more admonishing stares.

"That is acceptable where you are from, but you are *here* now," said the young shop owner. After scanning the expressions of everyone in the shop and deducing that I was not going to get out of this without offending anyone, I persuaded my friend and fellow rider, Sandra, to go with me.

With each step taken away from Bahir Dar's main avenue and the hair salon/Internet café/call center, I saw more and more deteriorated buildings. The street to Ledet's neighborhood quickly became unpaved and we soon entered a muddy warren of crude, uneven structures with no discernable way in or out.

Packed mud and dung replaced brick.

Corrugated tin and wire latches took the place of wooden doors and metal locks.

Windows and even window openings were nonexistent.

Muddy ruts replaced curbs.

My size and American accent, Sandra's skin color and Austrian accent, our gear, and the fact that we were following a smiling eight-year-old garnered us a lot of attention. Each new person who joined this band of curious onlookers stared and asked all kind of questions:

"Where you from?"

"What is your name?"

"Who are you?"

By the time Ledet stopped before what looked like a storefront, I felt like a living show-and-tell project. She turned around and with a mixture of broken English and hand gestures, told us to wait for her while she went in. Once she left us, with only ourselves to really notice, Sandra and I became even more aware of the spectacle that we had become. We both scanned the crowd that swirled around us, but they seemed harmless and content just to gawk at us. I said to Sandra, "Life's an adventure."

Ledet emerged from the store with packages underneath each arm and a bemused look on her face. Even she seemed surprised to see the number of people that now encircled us, but there was something so disarming about her smile that we were both put at ease. So we continued our adventure and followed her into an even poorer section of the neighborhood, where people living there had no energy or inclination to pay attention to us. They were solely consumed by poverty and their own circumstance.

I had been taking pictures the whole time and snapped a photograph of one beggar woman as we passed. She squatted, just a step off of the muddy path, with her hand extended, rocking back and forth, her mouth agape, but not saying a word; it was as if she knew not to waste her breath asking for money in a community where no one had it. Her frail body, poor circumstances, and will to remain silent made me want to give this woman some money and take more pictures, but I never got a chance to even focus my camera because all of a sudden Ledet let out a shriek and started running away.

Even though Ledet's running was sudden and her yell was alarming, something about her gait and tone made it clear that she was running toward something and not away from us. Only a few yards from the begging woman squatting in the street we saw the contrasting sight of Ledet leaping into a smiling woman's embrace. Ledet's uncontrolled excitement, which backed the woman into a muddy doorway, cut across all language and cultural barriers. Clearly this woman, who was now kissing Ledet's tiny forehead, was her mother.

Ledet pulled her mother's head down toward her and whispered something in her ear that I can only imagine was, "Mom, can I keep 'em? Can I keep 'em?" It was at this point that her mother's eyes widened and looked up to see Sandra and me outside her door, along with half of Bahir Dar.

With all of this thrust upon her, Ledet's mother had no choice but to let us in.

Before we crossed her home's threshold, Ledet opened one of her store packages and sprinkled its contents onto the floor. It took a few seconds for my eyes to adjust to the extremely dim light, but when they did, I saw that Ledet had spread freshly cut grass on the floor. The vivid natural green of the grass glowed incandescently on the dark dirt. This was Ledet's housewarming for Sandra and me, and the Ethiopian way of saying "Welcome" — though I am not too sure that the welcome applied to the other twelve people who were now trying to cram inside the tiny one-room home.

Ledet's home was a neat dormitory-sized room with two beds along the walls and an end table between them. Each bed had a small stool at its foot, and there were two additional end tables around the room that looked as though they served as cutting board, writing desk, and everything in between. Things were packed into every possible nook and corner to maximize storage space, but nothing much seemed out of place except for a bunch of plastic bottles of varying sizes, shapes, and colors that were everywhere a bottle or canister of its size would fit. (In Ethiopia and other arid places where water and its accessibility are an issue, plastic bottles are highly valued because they are often the only means to carry water.)

Ledet played hostess to Sandra and me and formally introduced us to her mother and little sister, who went unnoticed by me until the introduction. Obviously overwhelmed by all of the strangers in her home, Ledet's little sister spent most of her time ducking behind her mother's leg, only peeking out occasionally. Sandra and I were encouraged to sit down on the beds, which were low to the ground.

As soon as we did, the entourage swarmed all over us. This group of mostly young men stood and hovered over us wherever they could. They examined our digital heart rate monitors, cameras, and watches and moved closer with each question they asked. Soon, their encroachment made the environment so cramped and claustrophobic that I found myself wishing that I were Ledet's sister and had a mother's leg to hide behind.

Sandra and I attempted to stand up to leave, but each time we did, our move was countered by a comforting nudge from Ledet's mother that said, "Sit back down and stay a while longer."

Even though the air was very stuffy, when Ledet's mother proudly showed us a drawing on the wall, it was like a breath of fresh air entered the room. The simple doodling tacked into the mud wall was drawn by Ledet's younger sister and lovingly hung, just as my mother taped my own childhood drawings to the refrigerator.

Be it ever so humble, this place was a home.

But it was a very crowded and claustrophobic home, with a lot of uninvited people, and Ledet's mother's patience wore very thin. Speaking the international language of Matriarch, she flashed a stern look and raised a wagging index finger to say, "Enough is enough. Now please leave my house." In the next few minutes the place was cleared of everyone except for Sandra, Ledet, her sister and mother, and me.

Once everyone cleared out, Ledet and her family started rummaging through everything, pulling things out from here and taking things out of there. They were moving in fast motion. With so much going on, it was hard to know what or whom to pay attention to. When Ledet's mother dragged a big smoking metal stove into the center of the room I focused on it, uncertain of what was about to happen. Sandra and I scooted back on the bed as far as possible, watching as a thick metal plate was placed on top of the smoking stove that just seemed to make the room fill with more smoke. It felt as if a magic show were about to happen.

Through fits of coughing and watering eyes, I saw that another one of Ledet's packages had been opened and hard beans were poured onto the plate. Ledet's mother moved the small dark kernels around the plate with a wooden spatula and the smoke was replaced with the full aroma of roasting coffee beans. After several minutes, the roasted beans were placed in a mortar at Ledet's dusty bare feet. She then squatted and crushed and ground the coffee beans with a heavy and tall pestle that almost reached her forehead.

I tried to assist, but my sloppy effort to grind the coffee beans ended up putting more grounds on the floor and on Ledet's blue dress than in the mortar. Everyone laughed. Ledet's mother and sister set up a very low dining table with five cups while Sandra took pictures, and in the background of the frivolity, you could hear the pinging of popping corn kernels. Apparently a container that I thought was empty had been placed on the metal plate after the coffee beans were taken off, and was full of popcorn. Soon afterward, Ledet's remaining package, containing sugar, was stirred into the coffee, and we sat down to snack.

As I savored the coffee and the company, I couldn't help but think of my grandmother, who would sometimes make me a sandwich and tell me, as I smilingly ate it, that it tasted so good because she "put some love in it." There was definitely a lot of love brewed into that cup, and it's why that one small cup remains the best cup of coffee that I have ever had in my life.

Sandra and I didn't stay much longer after that cup, though. Nightfall was approaching, and we had to make our way back to the hotel for dinner with the other cyclists. We thanked Ledet, her mother, and her little sister for their hospitality, took some more photographs to mark the occasion, and left.

Sandra and I continued to absorb the moment in our memories and made our way to our hotel via the mud-caked path in silence. When we did start talking, both of us agreed that something special had just happened, but couldn't quite sum it up. As we heard each other tell the story over and over again to the other cyclists and friends, it was easy to conclude that the whole moment was just like a cup of coffee: the magic was all in the brewing.

Any magic found in the exchange was within the process of trusting Ledet's smile, following her to her home, sitting through the roasting, anticipating during the grinding, smelling it all, seeing the single picture on the wall, and feeling the warmth. The taste of the few ounces of hot, sweet liquid was only but seconds in that entire amazing experience.

The next day, I knocked out all of my essential duties as fast as I could. I ate, sorted, washed, and hung out my clothes and then did bike maintenance. (This consisted of my looking at my bike and thinking, *Looks good to me* and walking away.)

My warm moment at Ledet's home had made me feel quite at ease with Bahir Dar. The city's din of car horns, kids yelling, people talking, and laughing resonated inside me as I strolled toward the city's bank to exchange money. I passed the salon/café/call center where my moment began, smiling, and skipped up the bank's marble steps feeling excited about the day that lay ahead. But when exiting the bank, I felt something very different.

I hadn't changed, though Bahir Dar had.

The distinct energy that I felt about the city had been turned on its head. There was no chatter, no honking horns, no laughter, and no talking; there was nothing in the city but the deafening roar of silence.

The streets were filled with a few hundred people walking together in one direction down the street with their silence transforming them into a powerful human locomotive. No photograph could capture the intensity of the movement and the profound silence of that moment, but I raised my camera and snapped two photographs anyway.

Standing on the bank steps with a camera pressed against my eye gave me the best vantage point to take a picture, but it also put me in the best position for the whole procession to see me. I couldn't help but notice a steely admonishing stare from one of the men walking down the street. His stern gaze was so harsh that it made me lower my camera and really focus myself. I wondered what the hell I had just taken a picture of.

Then, I heard it.

A woman's distant wailing, that seemed to come from a hurt deeper than physical pain or torture, poured out above and beyond the man and beyond the crowd. It may have been audible the entire time I stood on the bank's steps, but now, this sound shattered the silence, pleading for all of my attention. Before I really knew what I was doing or where I was going, I went from being an observer of the silence to walking down the steps and onto a street, immersing myself in it.

Just walking amid the waves of silent people was powerful. I waded through the group of men and women who all walked with bowed heads, pursed lips, clasped hands, and tear-filled eyes toward the only sound I could hear. From the reverence of the people, I knew that I was walking in and essentially crashing a funeral, but I stayed with the procession until I got to the source of the only sound I could hear: a lone woman sitting in a chair next to a small casket draped with red cloth.

She was rooted to her seat, her shoulders slumped in a posture that revealed nothing but defeat. While people from the procession passed before her, a few people stood behind her, whispering things in her ear and rubbing her shoulders.

I slowed my progress, let the current of people walk past me, and watched the woman look skyward, extend her arms and try to grasp something that was now, sadly, too far away. She screamed, "Why? Why? Why?" over and over again.

A woman clutching a child's hand approached. The mother grabbed this woman's free hand in both of hers and said, "Hold onto your child as tightly as you can." The mother then hugged the child tightly and whispered, "Hold onto your life as tight as you can."

To be totally honest, I don't know exactly what was said word for word but after experiencing the universal feelings of love, loss, and grief -with my father, slowly, to cancer and my friend, suddenly, when a plane flew into his building- much of the moment was translated for me. The longer I stayed, the more I felt, and the more I felt, the more I realized that I didn't belong there. This was my fascination, but this was their private moment, and I needed to allow them to have it. I quietly left the scene.

The farther that I got from the epicenter of the funeral, the more the typical din of city life filtered back into my ears, bringing the specific detail of what happened with it. I later learned that the wailing woman was mourning her only child, who could not swim, and who had drowned trying to get his ball out of the river. That was a crying shame.

The busy work of repacking my gear for another week's cycling and camping, without facilities, gave me the mental freedom to push the events of the day to the back of my mind. But on cycling trips, where you spend six to eleven hours pedaling by yourself, stuff never stays in the back of your mind for long.

When the next day dawned, our Bahir Dar Spring Break was officially over, but unlike real Spring Breaks, where you take a rest from your learning, my hours in the city had taught me so much.

On the surface, not much had changed. The hotel lobby was again filled, though this time with refreshed and freshly shaven cyclists, eager to go. The hotel staff was again scurrying around bikes, bags, and gear, though they didn't look as overwhelmed as before. Our support trucks were packed up with the engines running. We were all ready to get on the road toward the next city.

There wasn't much difference to anything.

But as I turned left and bicycled away from the now relieved-looking hotel staff and onto the main promenade toward the outskirts of town, I reminisced about my moments. With only my own pedaling noise in my ears, I passed the hair salon/Internet café and the bank and thought of just how little I had spoken throughout all of my time there.

Now, talking may not be a big thing to you, but I talk a lot.

Some would even call me loud.

Okay, everyone, including me, would call me loud.

And that is why my relative silence throughout my Bahir Dar time was so significant to me. The hotel staff's overwhelmed facial expressions, Ledet's smile and the compliment of her imitation, her mother wagging her finger, her family's genuine hospitality, the aroma and taste of the cup of brewed "love," and seeing a city silence itself for the pain of one of its own to be heard all communicated something. All of those things crossed cultural gaps and built generational bridges and did it without saying a word.

Novelist William Dean Howells wrote, "He who sleeps in continual noise is awakened by silence." And I seemed to have been awakened to everything by just keeping my big mouth shut.

These days, I am still loud, but not quite as loud since Bahir Dar.

Now, all that it takes to keep me quiet — if only for a moment — is to sit, smell the aroma of coffee, remember, smile, and feel Bahir Dar's love all over again.

Welcome Home, Brother

By this point in my bicycle trip though Africa, I had breezed through the flat Egyptian streets, had my cycling skills sharpened by the tough Sudanese roads, passed through Ethiopia's humidity and mountainous terrain, and was barely into the more arid Kenyan air and reddish clay-caked roads. Even though I was two months into this trip, I was still making mental adjustments to bicycling on horrendously varied surfaces as well as camping in constant 90-plus degree temperatures. I woke up one morning with one thought in mind: I was getting worn out.

That waking thought led to my making a big decision: it was high time for me to take it real easy and go slowly.

The tour officials told us that the next towns we were going to come upon in the following few days would be as small, if not smaller, as Moyale, Ethiopia, the border town we'd just left. By now I was well versed in exactly what "small towns" meant.

Simply put, it meant limited water, limited food, and limited access to much of anything else.

I serpentined within the middle of the single-lane road, because loose rocks were everywhere, and both sides were lined with acacia plants. Acacia plants are indigenous to the region and have spiny, sharp thorns that can grow as long as three inches and are strong enough to go right through the rubber of your tires. Sometimes, I would be riding along, and *pssss*, just that quickly I'd have a flat tire. Riding along and dodging rim-bending rocks and places where I thought tire-piercing thorns might be lurking kept my mind on edge, but seeing some kids playing ahead dulled that edge and ushered forth a smile. I looked forward to getting off my bike and getting a break from the heat as much as I was looking forward to goofing off with the kids.

When I rolled up to a shady area near where the kids were playing, they came right over and started to stare and examine my bicycle. When finished, they turned their attention back to me, and soon were back to making a lot of noise, egged on by my equally childish antics.

As the actual kids made the discovery that I was the biggest kid on the planet, the noise grew to the point that a man, dressed in a mechanic's overalls, came out from one of the local shops to investigate. He looked totally surprised to find a grown man there, and he asked what I was doing.

"Bicycling," I replied.

"To where?" he asked, in a thick Kenyan accent.

"South Africa," I said.

Looking at me very skeptically but saying nothing, he slowly stepped from the shade of the building to get a full look and to feel the bright sunny sky. Placing his hands along his eyebrows to provide a shield, he looked at the horizon and then placed his hands on top of the children's shoulders, as if to shield them from getting any closer to me.

He said nothing for a moment, then said, "You...crazy?"

I told him that I wasn't, and tried to explain my circumstances, but that didn't help nearly as much as I thought it would. In fact, he held the kids even tighter. As we sat in the shade of the garage talking, with me giving more cogent thoughts and reasoning for riding to South Africa, he slowly allowed the kids to play around me.

The ensuing pleasant conversation went all over the place but, still slightly skeptical, he asked if I was crazy a few more times. We shared a few laughs over this, and he started to ask more pointed questions about my life in America.

"Do you know the story of how your family came to America?" he asked.

Leery of where the conversation might go, I said that I knew the story of slavery and how my forebears possibly came to America.

He looked at me askance and asked, "Is this your first time to Africa?"

At this point it was obvious that the man had something definitive to say. I paused, then said apprehensively, "Yes, this is my first time to Africa."

If I had known what he was going to say next, I wouldn't have waited at all because he said, without even a moment's hesitation, "Well, then, welcome home, brother. Welcome home."

I stood still and stunned as he moved to hug me. As much as his welcoming warmth and touch overwhelmed me, it was what he did next that made me cry and indelibly marked the moment. He told the kids—whom minutes earlier he had been shielding and shooing away from me—to hug me.

"Hug him, he is family," he said to the kids, who now seemed puzzled by my behavior: playing and laughing with them one minute, then crying with an adult the next.

The best gifts are not only free, but the ones that you never expect. Before going on this trip, I had no preconceived expectations of how I would be received as an African-American. Until this embrace, the people I had encountered on the continent had ignored my African heritage. I don't know what I could have hoped for, but this chance encounter and the genuine warmth within was so much more than I expected. Feeling the acknowledgment within a simple touch and hearing the words "Welcome home" from some random people was truly a gift of a lifetime.

I stayed a little while and shared some more time, took a picture with my new "family," and then pushed on to camp.

With no breeze to speak of, the open air of the campsite was especially hot, still, and stifling. With nothing to do and nowhere to go near the campsite, the riders just sat around being bored, which made the stillness even more noticeable. When one of the tour leaders said that she was going to drive ahead in one of the support vehicles to get supplies, I, along with a few others, leapt at the opportunity. The thought of riding in a cramped truck with at least seven sweaty riders for a momentary breeze seemed like a dream vacation at this point.

The ride in the huge overland support vehicle was only twenty minutes or so down the road, but it felt divine. As the truck rumbled down the dusty road toward the town of Sololo, I sat looking out the window with a wide-eyed stare and an even wider smile. I occasionally glanced at my cyclist friends, Brian, Randy, and others, wanting to explain the reason for my smile and the degree of comfort that my homecoming gave me, but I couldn't; the feeling was too new. I just felt the breeze over my sticky skin and opened my heart even further to the African experience.

When we reached town, the tour operator left to shop for supplies while I went to a bar with some of the other riders to get supplied with a few Kenyan Tusker beers. The riders and I sat drinking with regional healthcare workers associated with an NGO (non-governmental organization) and listened to them do the same thing that people everywhere and anywhere in the world do at bars: bitch about work. Because it sounded the same as anywhere else, I quickly grew weary of the banality and stepped out from the darkness of the bar to the bright street to discover a mass of children and adults.

Randy and Brian were playing catch with a group of kids. From the bar's steps, I couldn't see much in either direction. I couldn't see many parked cars, traffic, or an agenda. I didn't hear arguing or anyone keeping any kind of score. I only caught brief glimpses of the ball as it rose high in the air and then fell, getting lost in a sea of jostling hands, movement, and smiles. All I could see around me was good times. All that I heard around me sounded like fun.

The contagious spirit made everyone surrounding get closer, at the very least. It eventually compelled everyone, including myself, to join in. I played for a few minutes and wanted to stay longer, but thought better of it after remembering that I had to bike the next day. I opted out of the game and sat on the sidelines, absorbing the exuberance like a dry sponge.

As I sat watching this crowd, two people stood out from the rest.

One was Gator Man. I never got his real name but thanks to an ear-to-ear smile as big as his four or five year-old body, I remember him because he was just that cute. I have searched for the right words to describe him in more detail since the day I saw him, but even after all these years, I still use the same ones: three-foot smile. I call him Gator Man because he wore a little tank top with a cartoon drawing with a smiling alligator on it. His cuteness was more than enough to make him stand out, but his energy made him an even more captivating figure.

Gator Man's eyes followed every movement of the ball. When the ball went high in the air, so did his eyes. As the ball passed from hand to hand, Gator Man's body danced as if *he* were being passed from hand to hand. He did all of this while laughing with delight. When Randy told me that it was Gator Man's ball that we were playing with, Gator Man's movements made sense: too small to really join in, Gator Man was acting like he *was* the ball. But soon, Gator Man wanted off the sidelines and into the game. There was one huge problem though.

He could not catch.

He tried.

We tried.

Trust me, we did, but the boy could not catch, not even a little bit. We stood only a few feet away, presented him with a slow countdown and tossed him the gentlest of lobs, but catching and holding onto a ball was just to much too ask. He would drop the ball, even when handed to him. What did we really expect though? He was barely holding onto his own fervor, happiness, energy, smile, and cuteness. Asking him to focus on a ball was just asking for too much.

All you could do was smile with him; he was *that* cute.

As cute as Gator Man was, there was one other who also caught my eye. I call her Grace. Like Gator Man, Grace was not her real name, but that is what she embodied. Maybe 11 or 12 years of age, dressed in a dirty one-piece housedress with a wrap around her holding something on her back, she joined the game early on, only catching the ball when it was thrown in her direction.

But Grace changed as the game did. As more older boys joined in, the game escalated long past simple fun and teetered on becoming something much more fierce. The elevated degree of pushing and shoving made others run to the sidelines, but as others left, Grace remained. She grew more spirited and resolute with each throw.

Eventually, she didn't passively wait for the ball to be thrown her way. Grace demanded it. Running with bare feet on the rough, potted field of high grass, Grace outran, outfought, out-positioned, outmaneuvered, and outdid every highly competitive late-teenage boy there. She *was* grace. It wasn't only that she jockeyed for perfect position and caught everything; it was that we had been testing her.

The athleticism and beautiful grace that she flawlessly displayed begged you to test her. Brian yelled for Randy to throw the ball farther out; when he did, Grace wove through the pack of boys with an eye on the uneven earth in front of her and innate awareness of where others were to catch the ball and throw it right back. No matter how far into the rugged field the ball went, Grace got it. Even after she caught the ball, it was special to watch her use textbook form to control her body to throw a line drive or use the right amount of strength to arc her throw high for a perfect lob into our hands. Grace's command of her body commanded everyone's attention. Even when the older boys tried to hold her back, she was able to stave them off with one hand and catch the ball with the other.

I work in a gym as a personal trainer, and it is my job and passion to try and get clients to perform at just a *fraction* of Grace's level. I think that Brian summed her up best when he simply said, "Damn."

I have to admit, after being welcomed home earlier in the day, part of me beamed with pride looking at Gator Man's smile and Grace's poise, along with the rest of *my family*.

I moved to sit down on the steps of the bar and smile and was eventually joined by one of the NGO health care workers.

"Nice isn't it?" he said.

"Yeah, you have no idea," I said.

Between swigs of beer, the hospital worker said, "It is a shame that most of these kids will not grow up to be your age."

Startled and quite shaken, I said, "Damn, dude, how old do you think I am?"

He said that my age had nothing to do with it, and explained that due to the quality of healthcare, AIDS, the lack of hospitals, access to those hospitals, and the hard African lifestyle, a portion of the region's people would be dead by forty, with most passing much earlier. He went on about the conditions and different ways that life could prematurely end in this region.

As he spoke, his words took mine. I sat silent and defenseless as the statistics and other data he offered assaulted me. I was not from there, and had no choice but to take these numbers and projections as fact. Even mentally skewing his numbers downward to create a more positive spin left me feeling horrified.

I didn't say much to the hospital worker afterward; I couldn't.

Embracing *my family* earlier in the day broadened my world, but now, visualizing them passing on before their time tightened my skin to the point that it was suffocating.

I looked at Gator Man's infectious smile, which might not pass onto another Gator generation, and became nauseated at being so powerless to do anything.

Only moments before, Grace's grace had left me smiling, but thinking that she might peak at 13 years old and pass on by 30 left me paling.

I wanted to say disapprovingly, "This can't be," but his words seeped too deeply into my imagination and left me drowning in my own insignificance.

With too much to explain, I never said anything to Brian or Randy, who stood only a few feet away from me and didn't hear the hospital worker's words. Too surrounded by smiles, laughter and joy, I stood up because I couldn't take it. Too weak to stay and face them, I left without hugging Gator Man or taking a picture of Grace. It was all too much.

With no fanfare or even waiting for the support vehicle, I just started walking down the dusky road back to camp. By the time the truck rode past and stopped to pick me up, the tracks of my tears and dust had made funny markings on my face. As one of the riders reached his hand out to help pull me up on the truck, he looked down at my face and asked if I was all right. All I could say was, "I will be, I think."

Contributing 2 The Experience

Thursday, September 1, 2005.

While volunteering as a camp counselor for troubled teens in upstate New York, I read an article about a guy who won a few thousand dollars for a short documentary at an independent film festival.

I could use a few grand, I thought.

I must have been thinking aloud, because one of the teens said, "Why don't you make one of those? You are always telling us to do something and your story is just as good as his. So... *do something.*"

My ever-revving mind started going, and I thought, "Yeah. Why not?"

Now, if you know me at all, you know that being unprepared, uninformed, uninvited, unaware, un-liked, underfunded, and un-anything never stopped me from attempting something before. So why let it stop me now?

The only film festival I knew of at that time was Sundance, and after doing some research, I discovered that I qualified.

After reading further, I saw that I was past the deadline.

Reading further still, I saw my new favorite words: *Late Submissions Click Here.*

After clicking on the link, I found that everything was good as long as my film was in Los Angeles by September 30. So here was the deal: in order to win a few grand to fund future bike trips and maybe to get a potential sponsor to see the motivational value of what I was doing, I needed to have a short (under 45 minutes) documentary in a DVD format filmed and mailed across the country in 20-plus days.

"Okay, this is doable," I thought.

Undaunted and unfazed, I started.

I went through the checklist of what I had:

- A good story
- A strong vision of how I wanted the documentary to look
- A strong belief in myself
- A chance

I then went through a list of what I did not have:

- Knowledge about how to make a DVD
- A sound editor
- A written script
- Any experience making a movie

Okay, I thought, *looks good*. I have done more with less. The worst thing that can happen is that I fail miserably. And if I'd learned anything from my all of my years of underachieving in school, it was that there are no real final grades out in the world—there are just harder tests to take. All you have to do is to be willing to step up and attempt them.

The next few days at camp blurred together, because my sole focus was on mentally storyboarding my vision of the documentary.

But everything I was thinking of hinged on my ability to quickly learn a computer program that made creating everything, from the simple to the complex, fun, exciting, and easy.

At least, that was how the commercial made it look.

Sunday, September 4, 2005.

After a five-hour trip back home to Philadelphia, I was tired but couldn't wait to get started. I opened the computer program for the first time to try to learn it. After tinkering around a bit, I saw that making this film was going to be tough, but entirely possible.

The next few days were spent immersing myself in this project and trying to balance it with life. I guzzled espresso doing one task, and before it was completed, I was thinking through the next task in the process. My own determination and drive shocked me, because I never, ever worked *this* hard in college, or even while being paid. It felt like something else was driving me.

Within two weeks, the visual was basically finished. The next thing I needed to do was to record a voiceover track — but I couldn't, because I dropped my computer once, and it had been malfunctioning ever since (surprise, surprise). My friend, James, a sound engineer, told me I could record it at his friend Mike's recording studio.

Sunday, September 18, 2005.

I met Mike for the first time at his place and saw that his recording studio was his bedroom and bathroom. In his bedroom was a wall of equipment and speakers, and in his bathroom were soundproofed walls and a mic stand. Right before we began, he told me that he didn't have too much time to give me, because he wanted to watch the Philadelphia Eagles game that was coming on soon. *Great, just what I need,* I thought, *another deadline.*

I stood in his bathroom and started reading my script. Cotton-mouthed and stammering, the first takes were awful, and all of a sudden Mike barged in and snatched the script from my hand.

"You do all of this on a bike?" he said.

"Yup."

"Shit, we gotta talk," he said.

For the next few minutes, Mike and I talked about my story, my friendship with Kevin, and what I wanted to accomplish with this documentary.

He said, "Man, I thought that you were some busted-ass MC trying to cut a demo tape. You are really doing something. Let's start this all over again."

I left Mike's studio a few hours later, gulped an espresso, and was off to sync up the sound with the picture. But that was not so easy, because my speech was too fast at some points, too slow at others, and I said "Uhh" and "Umm" way too much. I called James and Mike in a panic and explained the situation. They told me to relax, that they could make it work.

Mike masterfully edited in pauses where none previously existed and edited out my stutters and stammers to make me sound smarter and wittier.

Soon, I emerged from his apartment with a better audio track. I ran to the gym to train a client and then back home to sync things up.

Thursday September 22, 2005.

I was making great progress and thought that if I kept my current pace, I could finish by four — a.m., not p.m. Even though I was spending a lot of time on this project, nothing I did felt arduous. The process of creating a visually stimulating story and making my ideas come to life infused me with energy and just felt natural.

This was as focused as I'd ever been, and by not clowning around, I pretty much finished everything—except for the last 20 seconds, which I was going to film and splice in later—by 11:00 p.m.

Saturday, September 24, 2005.

Because my computer kept malfunctioning, my very last steps were the hardest and most frustrating. With time ticking down, I felt like everything that I wanted was just one-too-many fingertips away; I had to figure out another way.

One thing that has helped me throughout life has been to mentally plan for everything to go wrong and after recalling that, I remember I'd created a backup file. I breathed easy. But then, after finding that I'd deleted my back-up plan file from my computer, I saw that I was screwed. So, I tried to think of something new.

Monday, September 26 and Tuesday September 27, 2005.

I thought of a plan, but James and Mike were busy and couldn't help me out of my own mistake. I had come too far, though, and refused to stand for accepting failure.

It took a day but I got an idea - sometimes pressure is a great thing, because it squeezes every sensible idea out of you.

My idea had me literally running through downtown in order to purchase a microphone that plugged directly into my computer to record the last audio bit. The idea worked, but only in theory. My computer was so sketchy that it randomly cut on and off. But that wasn't my biggest problem. Without a sound studio, the ambient noise was overwhelming and made the last twenty seconds dreadful compared to the first twenty minutes.

Wednesday, September 28, 2005.

With the festival deadline less than 48 hours away, I quickly attempted to create as soundproof an environment as I possibly could by sitting hunched over my laptop with blankets draped over my head to dampen the outside noise. Take after take, I tried to get the right "air of professionalism" in my voice and finally got something adequate down around midnight.

I had finished everything — but wait, another hurdle presented itself. When I dropped my laptop previously, my CD/DVD drive had stopped functioning, so I could not burn the DVD copy I needed to send to Sundance.

Thursday, September 29, 2005.

Tick-tock. The deadline was now less than 24 hours away, and I was too worn and too strapped for time to attempt anything that might take too long and might not work. So I thought of something that *always* works.

Tick-tock. I got a fifty-dollar bill, put it in my shirt pocket, arrived at a computer store two hours before it opened and planned to nicely ask (i.e. bribe) them to burn a copy for me.

Tick-tock. I fell asleep on a bench outside the store and awoke as a manager was going in. I blurted out my dilemma and, in an effort to cut through any red tape, started to reach into my pocket.

But before I could pull out the fifty-dollar bill, he said, "Hey, you look familiar. Were you in the papers? Aren't you a guy that did something?"

Tick-tock. I put the money back in my pocket and said, "Yeah, I guess."

Tick-tock. I explained to him what he might know me for and he said, "Dude, you aren't going to believe this, but I was just at your site the other day. What you did was cool as hell." As he hooked my laptop up to their fastest computer, he told me that I would be out of there "in no time."

Tick-tock. In no time later, I left with one DVD in my pocket after forcing the guy to take the fifty bucks.

Tick-tock. I drove like a bat out of hell to next-day-air my film off to Sundance.

The end.

Well, not quite.

Prize money drove me to make a documentary, but it was all of the wonderful emotions unleashed while bicycling past Sioux Falls, Niagara Falls, Victoria Falls and every other place in between that drove me to make *Contribute2 the Experience* in the way that I did.

I didn't know who was ever going to see my short film, so I touched on as many of my experiences as I could in order to try and motivate any viewer to do something to make the world a better place. If people were only going to meet me through a movie screen, I wanted them to not only think of my friendship with Kevin but also think about their own special friendships, too. I also wanted anyone who knew me to understand that all of the sweat, strain, money, and time that I spent on these journeys was so worth it and that I wasn't stopping. Basically, there was a new Dave in town and the old one wasn't coming back.

Initially, I was just happy to have made a film and have it up for consideration, but in no time my pride gave way to my competitive juices. I wanted to get into the film festival, badly. Soon, I was obsessively checking the festival site a few times a day to see if the film had been accepted. It hadn't been.

I normally take rejection in stride, but after all of the physical, creative, and emotional effort put forth, I was left very vulnerable and took this "no" personally. I felt like *I* hadn't been accepted.

I had immersed myself so deeply into the movie-making process that I hadn't told my friends what I was doing, and, after getting the rejection, didn't see a need ever to tell them. But I soon got a call from out of the blue. A woman with a thick British accent phoned and suggested that my film be submitted to other film festivals. Immediately thinking that one of my friends was playing a practical joke, I said, "Yo, I don't know who put you up to this shit, but it's not funny. Not today," and hung up.

A few minutes later, my phone rang again. The same British voice said, "I assure you that I am not joking." To prove her sincerity, the woman described my film—and then I remembered that my friends didn't know anything about it.

Because of our conversation, I submitted, and got accepted, to another festival. In fact, I submitted to 32 festivals, was accepted to 27, and received special honors at three—in Philadelphia, Germany, and the United Kingdom.

When it was all said and done, I never got the few grand that I was looking for, but it all worked out because it reaffirmed the one lesson that I have learned from almost everything I experience: whether making a movie, getting a job, getting a phone number, getting a chance, or anything else in life, you have to believe in yourself. It reminded me that sometimes all it takes is one "yes" to make all the difference.

The end.

That is, until the next film.

Branded

"Stop right there."

When my friend Tom stopped me in the middle of a story I was telling, I shut my mouth, and waited for him to say something, assuming that when he did, it would be important. He did, and it was. What he said triggered the beginning of my understanding the true depth and power of something that I had previously ignored: marketing and branding.

Nine months before Tom dramatically told me to "stop right there," he and his wife, Michelle, owners of Price Communications, a brand development firm, had just hired me as their personal trainer. Because we had only recently met, they were unaware of my past. So, on one predawn morning in their apartment, when I casually mentioned to them, between sets of pushups, that I was going to be cycling in Africa for a few months, they looked perplexed and started asking questions. I made them do more pushups while telling them my African ride would be just a further extension of my previous North America ride honoring my friend Kevin Bowser. Neither of them interrupted me as I spoke; maybe it was the pushups. But when I finished speaking, they said they felt my passion and had only one question, "What do you plan on doing, marketing-wise, for this next trip?"

I didn't actually have an answer, but tried to BS my way through one anyway. I told them that my initial plan had been to ride across North America and then return to life as usual, but that I didn't account for how planning a nationwide bicycle trip would stimulate a desire to do even more. I explained that, even though it sounds crazy, the urge to ride a bicycle across Africa had sort of snuck up on me, and left me with little time to prepare a marketing strategy other than sending out a press release.

"And?" they asked.

I had nothing else and just smiled and said, "Life provides."

With that said, they both gave me a "poor foolish David" sideways glance, which effectively ended the exercise session. I'm not sure if it was pity or something else that drove them, but they vigorously began dismantling my "life will provide" marketing plan. The trainees became the trainers.

My business lesson: Hope is not a strategy.

After a while, they gave me three things:

1. A textbook on strategic marketing.

2. Four days to read it.

3. A dinner invitation for the upcoming weekend to discuss what I read in the book.

Tom and Michelle's textbook was helpful at explaining that branding was so much more nuanced than a ten-second jingle with a cute tagline, or anything else I thought, and no matter how subtle or overt, was involved in everything from jeans to Jesus, and from candy to candidates. But there was a line in the book about a company's brand being their essential promise to their clients about what it stands for, and that made me feel some pressure.

I know the high regard with which promises are held, so the thought of promising anything made me anxious. I understand, now, that while what I am doing is altruistic and life affirming, it is also a business, my life's business.

But back then, I just looked at myself as a man that was following his passion after losing a friend and didn't have enough vision to see what my actions would blossom into. The only thing that I knew was that my honoring ride made me feel more alive than ever. And the only thing I felt comfortable promising was that I was interested, willing and prepared to move forward and spread that feeling around. The practicality of applying high business concepts to *myself*, a lone man, seemed implausible at best.

I showed up for dinner four days later with an empty stomach, a head full of marketing theory and thinking, "This is going to be one hell of a meal."

Before my last morsel was chewed, Tom started interrogating me. One question that he kept asking over and over again was, "What do you want people to do after they hear about you?"

None of my answers seemed to be correct, and after a few more times, I finally said, "Something."

"You're a competitive guy and you want to challenge people, right?" he said.

"Uh, yeah."

"To do what?"

"Er, anything?"

"Are you sure? So, you don't care? You are saying that, now, all of this is more than a simple scholarship. This is beyond Kevin now. You don't care if people are trying to make the world better for cancer, or kids, or kids with cancer, or 9/11, or the environment, or whatever—just do *something*, right?"

"Yes."

I sat still at the dining room table as Tom played bad cop, walking around me, drilling me with question after question. Just as my eyes would focus on his movements, good cop Michelle, staring at me from across the table, would say something about a company having to define itself in order to not disappoint its support base. This ambush was difficult, but they emphasized that I had to have a clear and concise vision so that my brand, my promise, could be developed, delivered, and upheld. I blurted out that I didn't care to tell people exactly what to do, because, at the end of the day, all I really am is just a dude on a bike.

"So, you only want to say that 'I am not sitting around,' and that 'This is what I am doing from the seat of a bike: giving hugs, making people smile, and being Big Dave?' You want to engage people just enough to challenge them, and then ask 'What are you doing to contribute?' You want to create an atmosphere where people can read about what you're doing to contribute to the world, and then talk about what they are doing to contribute, right?"

He said the word "contribute" a few more times, and it hit both of us. "Contribute" was it. "Contribute" was all of what I wanted to say, but had not been able to express. "Contribute" was the defining action of what I was doing and wanted to do. "Contribute" was what I wanted people to feel that they could do after hearing about my experiences. "Contribute to society" was the promise that I knew I would always deliver upon, and the promise that I would never break.

"Contribute" was my brand.

Soon after that meeting, I set up the Contribute2.org website. Even though it was an .org website, there was no official organization, no board of directors, no money collected and no money offered. The site was essentially just a platform that I used to post pictures and chronicle some of my Cairo to Cape Town stories, in an effort to inspire people to always contribute.

My five-month, ten-country African cycling experience had left me physically tired, but beautifully on edge, both emotionally and spiritually. I wasn't even able to nap on my flight home from South Africa. I just sat in my seat, infused with confidence, the in-flight magazine opened to a map of the world and dreaming of the world of possibilities.

By the time I deplaned in Philadelphia, all I wanted to do was bike the rest of the world, hug as many people as I encountered, and share as many smiles as I humanly could. Within a month of landing, I gathered a group of friends together to discuss how to achieve this.

The meeting was held at Tom and Michelle's office and everyone was clearly as excited as I was. Actually, my friends were more excited, because before I could say anything, they started talking about their vision of what Contribute2 could be—magazine articles and books that I could write, and globetrotting cycling treks that I could run. I sat in the meeting, not saying much of anything, because even though what they thought David Sylvester, the man, and Contribute2, the brand, could accomplish was flattering, it dwarfed my thinking and was intimidating.

What they proposed sounded complicated, difficult to navigate, and like it would have a huge time and planning requirement. All I wanted to do was ride my bike around the world, and the thought of operating in anything but my one-man gang, attacking things in the order that I could handle them in my comfort zone, scared me. They weren't asking me to part with my creative freedom, but I was so intimidated by things that that was the message I heard. I was so intimidated that I left the meeting slow to act on my friends' suggestions.

My business lesson: Often, the most awesome thing that people can envision is the potential being who lives inside their own skin. Don't be afraid, for that being is you.

One reason I wasn't ready to take the enterprising steps necessary to go the next level was because I had already fallen into a trap of listening to the wrong voices.

People from around the world visited my Contribute2 site, and even though my brand was underdeveloped, they loved my passion. These people sent me kind, good-intentioned and ego-feeding messages, that said all I had to do was "just wait," because Oprah was going to call me. Their enthusiasm was easy to listen to, and the more I fell under the sway of their assurances, the lazier I became at my own brand development and strategy. I became more intent on getting in contact with Oprah, instead of examining what Oprah and others had done to become successful.

Looking back, I can honestly say that it's fortunate that Oprah never responded to my calls. Oprah Winfrey is not Superman, or even Superwoman—she is just a very successful woman. Even if I did get on her stage, it would have only been a personal achievement. I hadn't yet put the work in to defining a brand or developing a business strategy, and would have been ill-prepared to professionally benefit from such an appearance. I wasn't even prepared to acquire any knowledge. I would have just been a big guy on television, telling stories.

After I was published in the April 2006 issue of *Essence* magazine for an article I wrote about a store I came upon in Malawi, I started to get a glimpse of what I hadn't been seeing. The store's name was "Niggers" and my story generated a lot of attention, but because I got caught up in the honor of becoming published for the first time, and had been lazy at brand development, I was inept at capitalizing on the interest I was capturing.

Right about the time that the realization of my own laziness and ineptitude was hitting me, Wheeler del Toro, a former Temple University classmate and successful businessman, called to see how I was doing. Within only a few moments of talking, he saw through everything and launched into me for letting my two seconds of fame derail any business strategizing momentum I may have had built up. He knew that his words were stinging, but said that he was coming at me so hard because he, too, had made this same mistake of focusing on the limelight rather than business when he made the cover of *The Wall Street Journal*. Wheeler said that he wasn't adequately prepared, and he got more out of business and life from hustling than he ever did from notoriety. He also said that in order for me to get to the next level, I was going to have to hustle harder than everyone else, because I didn't have a tangible product line. "You and your story of hustling for your own dream is your product," he said, adding, "you better figure out how to turn this into a business, and not just a good story. Otherwise, you ain't got nothing."

My business lesson: Abraham Lincoln once said, "Things may come to those who wait, but only the things left by those who hustle." I don't think I can improve upon a former President.

My foot-in-the-ass talk with Wheeler was much needed, but just as I started to focus on the business side of things, "Contribute2 the Experience," my documentary that I'd made about cycling North America and Africa, started to gain popularity on the film festival circuit. Now if becoming published for the first time in *Essence* felt complimentary, then there were no words for how having my first film screened around the world felt. I again lost focus.

Everything about film promotion was all very new to me, so it caught me off guard when a woman, full of excitement and exuberance, called me early one morning to speak with me about a film festival in Los Angeles. Her telling me that I needed to come to the West Coast for a week or two prior to the screening to promote my film sounded extreme, especially for the early hour in which she'd called. When she detected a less-than-urgent attitude on my part, she asked, "What do you want to do with this film?"

She wasn't the first person to ask me, and I really didn't know what she was asking or how to answer her, so I blurted out, "I just want to ride my bike."

"What?"

"I just want to ride my bike and make the world a better place."

"He just wants to ride his bike. *He just wants to ride his bike. He just wants to ride his bike?*" she repeated my words, in a rising pitch and rising incredulity. With her exasperation bordering on anger, I sat holding the phone in silence. When I didn't respond, she lowered her voice and quietly said, "Love, if that is all that you wanted to do, then why the hell did you make the film?"

This was a damn good question, but I couldn't understand why this woman was making such a big deal about things.

Anyway, I didn't listen to her.

I didn't go California early to promote my film.

Instead, I arrived at the film festival theater on the day of my screening and realized, almost immediately, that I had made a mistake.

I say almost immediately because I was oblivious to everything as I scoured the lobby that was abuzz with filmmakers and theatergoers until I finally found a film festival program. After thumbing through the pages, seeing my name and the name of my film, I put on a self-satisfied grin and obtusely bounded up the steps to the filmmaker registration area. There, they assigned me a filmmaker badge, a table, and two chairs.

"What are the table and chairs for?" I smilingly asked.

"For your promotional materials."

"I don't have any," I responded.

The registrar said nothing, but just like Tom and Michelle several months earlier, his "poor dumb David" look spoke volumes. Quickly realizing that I had once again let my bad habits take over and had not listened to the experts, I stopped smiling and walked, deflated and embarrassed, back down the steps and through the busy lobby.

My promotion space was next to a filmmaker who had a table filled with posters, DVDs, a scrapbook, his resume, and even a few copies of a script. There was so much stuff on his table and so many people milling about that he barely had time to speak when

I introduced myself as a fellow filmmaker. But he did have the time to flash me a patronizing smirk when I sat at my bare table with just a backpack.

Sitting alone, at a bare table, with no one coming up to talk to me wasn't some theory that I was reading about in a textbook. This was all too real. I sat there letting what everyone had been trying to tell me about planning, preparing, and promoting my business take hold in my thick head. I sat there, doing nothing and prepared to take this life lesson sitting down, until the filmmaker next to me did something to tick me off and wake me up.

He took my chair.

It wasn't that he took my chair and flashed me a dismissive look or said something condescending to me. It was worse. He took the chair without even acknowledging me. He took my chair as if I didn't exist and gave it to one of the people standing around his table. By being unprepared, too hung up on the limelight and lazy, I had made myself invisible—even less than invisible. This one act drove home the point that every person who walked by my table to surround his could have been a potential sponsor for my next ride, or a potential rider, or a potential contact, or a potential *something*. I sat there, angry at myself and thinking of Wheeler telling me that I had to find a way to get the story of my hustle out there, and that if I didn't, I "ain't got nothing."

I quickly assessed what I had: a table, a backpack with my laptop, a good story, an audience of potentials, a loud voice, and one chair. It wasn't much, but it was more than enough to change the tide. I pulled out my laptop and quickly made a file of my most compelling photographs. I set them up so that they randomly displayed across the computer screen, stood on my one chair and loudly asked, "Who wants to know what it's like to bicycle across North America and Africa?"

A few people turned my way, and when they did, I told them my entire story in a short entertaining burst, so that even the casual passerby would get the gist and maybe a laugh. People started chatting me up. Soon I had more people listening to my story and milling around my bare table, giving me their business cards. It wasn't much, but I promoted my film, learned a good lesson, and even got a chance to even the score with the dismissive chair thief of a filmmaker. As I stood sorting business cards, I offered my remaining chair to him, suggesting that, unlike him, I wouldn't be needing it.

I flew home from the film festival thinking of how much my life had changed since September 11, 2001: in less than five years, I had gone from being a small-time personal trainer who had lost a friend to a cross-continental cyclist who used his experiences to create various forms of media that were being read and screened around the world. It was now 2006, and without much planning but plenty of passion, a lot had changed.

I knew that I had an inspiring message and a unique story, but also knew that, with only a vague sense of purpose and continued laziness, it wasn't going to go far. I stayed awake for the whole flight just as I did when returning from Africa, but this time was different. Instead of thinking about new opportunities, I thought of *lost* opportunities and was focused and ready when I landed. Once this happened, things started moving quickly.

Shortly afterward, I met with Tom and Michelle and an associate of theirs who was inspired by my film to design a logo for Contribute2. She handed me a drawing with the letter "C" in the form of a bicycle wheel, combined with the number "2" to form a heart and said, "Dave, you're all heart." The logo was a great start on the road to moving my brand forward, and long overdue, but I needed more.

There's a saying: "The smartest man in the room is the man who knows what he doesn't know." Now, I didn't feel like the smartest guy in the room, but I knew that I needed help, so I decided to go to the University of Pennsylvania's Wharton School of Business Management.

I contacted one of their professors, Nelson Gayton, who agreed to meet with me at a coffee shop. Before he took one sip of his coffee, he pointed at me and said, "Dave, you are a business." The whole time we spoke, he kept hammering that point home and reminded me that as soon as I bicycled outside of Philadelphia and the United Sates with the purpose of engaging people to inspire them, I had actually become a "global business."

Our discussion was more of a casual conversation about me, rather than a specific strategy session for Contribute2, but he did point out that I shared a common, yet faulty, thought process that prevented many businesses from being successful: I thought too small. He said that looking at things with too narrow of a lens hindered, and was possibly fatal, to a business' success. "Businesses can always scale things back," he said, "but they can rarely ever ramp things up enough to catch the wave. You have to think big in order to get it all right."

As he was leaving the coffee shop an hour later, he pointed at me and said, "Dave, you are a business, so please don't waste one iota of brainpower dreaming small."

My business lesson: Do not waste your time dreaming small.

One of Professor Gayton's suggestions was that I start patterning myself after philanthropic organizations that I admired and the individuals who ran them. Doing this made the connective lines between companies' brands, their mission statements, the way they approach funding, and how they summon and control action readily visible. I took a long hard look at myself with a "bigger" lens. I saw that my actions generated a lot of enthusiasm, like big organizations. But I also saw that, unlike a lot of big organizations, because I was not listening to Tom, Michelle, and others, the intent of my actions was open to interpretation, and thus misinterpretation. To many, my brand was a series of random and unrelated events.

My business lesson: Your brand should be a dynamic and connective thread that purposefully weaves through everything you do.

His words made it obvious that, if I wanted bigger, I had to be bigger. I had to grow up, acknowledge my faults, and focus on them in order to get out of my own way and not have my business hampered by the stupid things that I do.

My business lesson: Don't let your business take on the bad habits of your personality.

My business lesson: If you surround yourself with people who are strong in areas where you are weak and you don't listen to them, then you are a fool.

Next, I looked back over a grant proposal that had been rejected earlier that year. At the time that I received the news, I just groused about not getting the money, but I was different now. I wasn't dreaming small any more and was instead thinking big. I was through bitching and was doing things differently. I approached a person who had been on the grant review panel and asked what I could have done differently to gain approval.

I took notes during the assessment of my proposal, and found that the reviewer remembered it being "all heart, all passion and, consequently, all over the place." I addressed each of these concerns when I wrote another grant proposal about bicycling

South America to a different organization. In that grant proposal, I dreamt bigger and asked for more money, clearly defined myself and my mission, presented a budget along with proposed outcomes, and then let people critique my work, telling them to be harsh. It must have worked, because I received the money.

My business lesson: People respect and admire heart and passion, but will only fund them if they are grounded by a defined plan and a clear vision.

A serious car accident stopped my proposed South American trip from happening, but because of marketing, in part, everything worked out. In order to rehabilitate my body, I needed to spend a lot of time at the gym, in the pool, and on the bike, and needed something to think about while doing it. The fact that my brand was getting derailed just as it was starting to form really gnawed at me, and drove me to push just a bit harder in and out of the gym.

Overall, my knowledge of branding and marketing remains very limited, and during the last decade, since September 11, I have done more things wrong than right. I have wasted other people's time by not heeding their advice about working on the details that would take me from an idea to a tangible product. But I have grown. I haven't wasted time by dreaming small, and I continue to apply many of the lessons in this chapter to myself and continue to grow. I even got my act together enough to author and self-publish this book. But more important than all of that, by acknowledging my past failings and expressing a willingness to trust and listen more, I have built a sturdier personal brand.

My name is David Hale Sylvester, and my personal brand and promise to you is to passionately contribute to society in any way that I can. In order to keep that promise, I am committed to humbly listening, learning from my mistakes and always evolving. That is the price that I gladly pay to promote my brand.

Oh, wait. One more thing…

When I returned from Africa, I went to see Tom at his office. I was telling him a story about a day I'd spent riding in Tanzania. With extreme heat, no breeze but that which I created, no shade anywhere in the country and nothing but warm and awful-tasting water in my bottles, it was a hellishly rough day.

"But," I said, "I saw something ahead in the distance that made me pedal hard as shit. I knew that Coca Cola red from kilometers away and pedaled my ass off to get a cool drink. Shit, I didn't even care if it was cold. I just knew that there was soda there and that I was going to sit right down and—"

"Stop right there," Tom said. "*That's* branding."

This chapter is dedicated to my good friend, Tom Tag, who passed away from cancer on March 26, 2010, and without whom I would not have been able to Contribute2.

God Bless You, Tom.

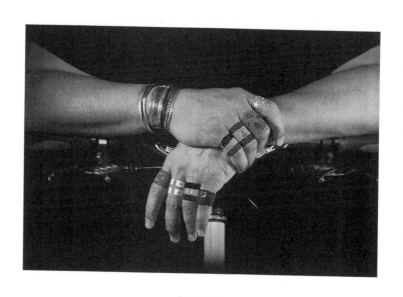

ASIA

Out Of The Blue

See only fluorescent lights. Hear beeps. Try to focus. Want to move your body but feel it restrained. Feel very scared. Feel pain like you've never felt before. Feel violated as your clothing is cut down your sleeve to your waistline and up your pant leg to your belt line. Feel the sensation of fabric, damp with your own blood, being pulled off of your skin. Feel naked in every way imaginable. Feel chilled. Know that you are in trouble. Grope for answers. Feel your tears drip down the corner of your eyes and slowly roll down into your ear. Feel it itch. Listen to voices talk about you, but not to you. Hear a voice urge you to "hang in there," but also hear a lack of empathy in its tone that would actually convince you to do so. Be unable to scratch that itch. Even though your whole body hurts, feel your leg hurt even more. Question why you are on your back, unable to move and hearing someone ask, "Can you feel this?" Want to speak but not know where to start or what to say. Want to scream "Why?" but have a puddle of your own saliva sit in your throat and force you to swallow down any of your utterances. Taste an acrid taste in your mouth and nose that you can't identify. Feel more confused. Feel a warm, soft hand touching yours. Want to feel it more. Hear the voice attached to that hand introduce herself as the chaplain. Focus enough to know that chaplains only come around for a major boo-hoo situation and not a minor boo-boo situation. Grapple with your mortality. Feel a chill within that warm and soft hand. Weep a deeper tear that blurs the fluorescent lights even more. Be annoyed with yourself for creating even more tears that you can't wipe away. Don't focus, because when you do, there seem to be more people working on you than you thought. Don't blink because each flutter feels like razors on the underside of your eyelids. Want to yell, "Help," but feel that, all things considered, you are being helped. Remember, driving on a sunny day and then spinning round and round. Remember the world going black. Try to piece together the events of the day. Have each of your senses assaulted. Feel it all.

Life can change in a heartbeat, and a car hitting my truck only two hours after I woke up one sunny September morning in 2006, was my *bump-bump*. That crash left me with a mind, body, and spirit that I no longer knew.

Right before that car came out of the blue to hit my truck, I was a happy man with a well-balanced mind/body/spirit formula existing within me. That existing equation had effortlessly buoyed me with a great sense of confidence while I became a personal trainer, fitness instructor, body builder, motivational speaker, world-traveling bicyclist, and everything else I ever attempted in life. I was happy living with my belief that my mind, body, and spirit could and always would work as a unit. I was so happy about things that I was days away from leaving to go bicycle another continent, South America, and sharing that happiness.

A nutritional bar company responded positively to a grant proposal I'd written and awarded me $9,000. With the generosity of the grant, I purchased a new bike, a laptop, camping gear, prescription sunglasses, and an airline ticket.

The plan was to fly from Philadelphia to Cali, Colombia and then take five months to bicycle down the Pan-American Highway to the southern-most city in the world: Ushuaia, Argentina. The proposed purpose of my trip was simple, yet true to my mind/body/spirit equation: I was going to encounter, interact with, and hug as many people as I possibly could, then communicate my cross-cultural experiences to inspire others.

It was Labor Day Monday, and with my flight leaving that Thursday, I assumed that packing my bike and all of my gear into the cab of a pickup truck and driving to a barbeque to show my friends would be a cool thing to do.

But you know what happens when you assume?

In the blink of an eye, a drunk, stoned and unlicensed teenage driver bulleted through a red light and shattered my assumptions about what I wanted to do that day and hoped to achieve in South America. His car rammed into the right side of my truck, tossing it and everything inside to the left. Immediately unconscious, my limp body slammed into the driver's side door with the steering column slamming into my leg. As the truck spun around like a top and spilled the truck contents along with the mind/body/spirit equation that I held so dear around the streets and sidewalks of the sleeping West Philadelphia neighborhood, the tilt steering handle pierced my leg at the knee.

Semiconscious and unable to focus any of my senses, the initial aftermath of the accident felt like a sick dream. I had no idea whether I was imagining a haze of smoke, or if it was coming from the collision. I was shocked into clarity, though, when I heard someone ask, "Is he dead?" I couldn't see anyone, but I knew the voices were speaking of me. Even in memory, that question chills me. *"Is he dead?"*

My initial reaction was to scream, "Of course not!" but nothing audible ever made it from my mouth.

I grew even more frightened and contracted every muscle fiber I could control to give some sign of life and say, "Please help me." But again, nothing much happened. It was only moments before I was able to move, but even one moment shackled from what you want is too much.

It was no more than a fraction of an inch when finally I moved, but that was more than enough to send a nauseating wave of pain through my body. I wanted to scream even more than before, but again, my body betrayed me. My agonized yell, mixed with wreckage smoke and my own saliva, worked to choke back every one of my words.

A Good Samaritan, thinking my truck might explode, wrenched the driver's side door open and placed his hands on me. "Please help me. Please," was all I could think, but could not say. I felt nothing but gratitude as my body was freed from the wreckage. But as my leg was un-impaled from the steering column, a second shockwave of tortuous pain surged through my body and forced me in and out of consciousness. Still unable to scream, I kept swallowing my own frightened shrieks. This was no dream.

Here I was, a man who had lived everyday embracing freedom. Now I was entangled in a wreckage, left with a body that didn't seem to work and a mouth that couldn't speak. Left helpless, I was in hell.

Being thrust into my worst personal nightmare induced a panic within me that made me try to push the Samaritans off when they took me from the wreck. But my pain, shock, disorientation and adrenaline surge left me unable to command my body parts and I collapsed like a puppet cut from its strings. My head just wobbled and dropped, and when it did, I caught a glimpse of my bloodied body and my exposed left knee joint that was now at an awkward, inhuman angle.

That was when everything that I had just experienced really set in.

That was when I regained my voice.

That was when I started screaming.

The intensity overwhelmed me and reduced my life's next remembrances into a jumble of fuzzy, yet painfully sharp images: being lifted into the ambulance, seeing a piece of my truck half a block away from the accident scene, getting a passing glance of the guy who hit me and hearing the scream of his passenger. It wasn't until I lay in an emergency room, immobilized on a backboard and with eyes that stung with debris and tears, that my memories became cohesive again.

At that point, I remember hearing the chaplain introduce herself to me and really needing to feel and touch her warmth. But a cacophony of expletive-laden screams from the other men in the accident kept drowning her soft voice out. Their shouts of "Chill, bitch, chill," "Get off me, motherfucker," and "That shit hurts" sounded like insanity to me, but jarred me enough to focus and visualize the scene: I was now one of three black males involved in a car accident.

From their screams, I concluded that they were as injured as I was, if not worse, and had gone through all that I had. Now ripped from our clothing and identification, we were naked and had nothing to distinguish us as victim or assailant, friend or foe, smart or smart-ass. Still unable to see clearly, I focused on the voices of the emergency room staff and perceived a tone of indifference, at best, and a certain dismissive tone, at worst.

Maybe it was real.

Maybe it was imagined.

In any case, I was petrified of doing anything to adversely influence the quality of my care. So, as the driver and passenger of the car that hit me yelled and cursed at the doctors, I decided to distinguish myself by staying mute. The chore of having to take the perception of my blackness into account angered the hell out of me, and added to the anguish I felt, but I couldn't take a chance. I was left with my whimpering tears as my only emotive recourse.

The pain, pain-numbing drugs, and screams of the others made it a struggle to focus on the conversation between the doctors and nurses working on me. I wanted to know just how banged up I was. When I blurted out details of my past and proposed bicycle trips to try and start some sort of dialogue to get some information, I heard some talking, but not to me. When I asked directly whether I would bike again, I heard nothing but petrifying silence.

Finally, after what seemed like forever, a voice said, "That's impossible."

I wanted to respond, but the painkillers slurred my words as well as my sense of time and my orientation within the building. I was only vaguely aware of being wheeled from the main emergency room to the X-ray area and to other rooms, but when a person came in to read the results, I woke up.

The words "There is something in your leg" cut across everything I was feeling.

Apparently, the almost two-inch knob on the tip of the tilt steering handle had broken off in my knee when I was pulled from the truck. The knob was buried so deep that it could not be seen during the physical exam. The drugs I'd been given continued to warp time, so I don't know if it was 30 minutes or three hours before the nurse gave me the extraction plan, but I was completely sober when it was delivered. While the doctor and nurses cleaned and numbed my knee, I restarted the conversation that they had previously ended with the statement "That's impossible." I told them that nothing was impossible. Even though the drugs reduced my active pain, nothing could ease the anxiety I was feeling about my predicament.

I was in an emergency room, seriously injured, feeling like my life was in doubt and all alone. I was more than scared; I was desperate. I needed someone, so I tightly clutched the only direct human contact that was near, the chaplain's hand. Weeping the whole time, I held her hand tightly during the extraction. The drugs dulled the pain, but the sensation of the knob inching out of my immobilized left knee millimeter by millimeter was surreal. I writhed toward the right, toward the chaplain's supportive touch. I felt like my body was being contorted beyond all capacity. I repeated the words "Nothing's impossible" over and over again, mentally and verbally, because I needed to hear and feel it, even if it was from my own mouth.

"Nothing's impossible. Nothing's impossible."

Once the knob was extracted, the pain was still tortuous but endurable. Even so, the trauma of the accident made me believe that "my time" might still be at hand. My life didn't flash before my eyes, but I did quickly reflect, and realized that I had never *really* exhaled since the crash.

After taking a deep breath, I thought that if this was going to be the end of my life, the only real regret that I had was that I might not be able to see or thank my mother and a few other friends and family members. Otherwise, I felt that I had a good run. I then finally exhaled, stopped fighting to stay awake, closed my eyes, and drifted off. When my family and friends came to see me at the hospital, I couldn't see because of eye patches, but I felt them, and they felt great.

As I was being discharged from the hospital, the nurse wheeling me out said, "Any accident that you can walk away from ..." All I could mumble as I pressed on the wheelchair to stand then leaned on the nurse and then rested on the car before finally collapsing in the back seat was, *"This is walking?"*

My first few days at home were an anxiety-fueled mess. My home provided shelter, but failed to shield me from my friends' stares of pity at my slow movement and scarred face. My bed brought sleep but since my slumber was plagued with nightmares that had me waking up with tears in my eyes, it brought no rest. I was constantly tired and wondered if I would ever feel refreshed again. My formerly confident mind was now so doubtful of everything that it told my body to do nothing—including quench its thirst, because it was too exhausting to walk to the bathroom. My spirit that had greeted each day with a smile was now stunted. My mind/body/spirit formula no longer computed, and I didn't know who I was anymore. All I knew was that this was not *me*.

My time out of the house was strange, too. Listening to a bicyclist's eyewitness account of an accident that I barely remembered felt bizarre. I felt freakish and wanted to vomit as he eyed me up and down and described how he could not ride his bike for two weeks afterward, and that he never thought he would see me walk again. It was just as bad when others saw pictures of the accident scene. Their descriptive words like "miracle," "godsend," "marvel," and "blessing" made me excruciatingly uncomfortable.

Unable to bend my knees, even my attempt to properly humble myself and find solace in prayer was frustrating. I was left with just rolling on my side and crying.

Crazy things can happen when you are trapped inside your house, and even crazier things can happen when you are trapped inside your head. My idle days waiting for the swelling to go down sufficiently enough to get an MRI were spent surfing medical websites, and making the most obscure connections. Within a few mouse clicks, my depressed mind went from having obvious knee issues to having cancer. Once I calmed down, though, the scenarios set in.

The best-case scenario was that my knee ligaments and tendons were ripped or torn and would require surgery to repair.

The worst-case scenario was that I would have to have a total knee replacement.

In either case, the situation was maddening, because I could not go on like this. I had to get "me" back.

Days after the MRI, I sat gripping the phone, prepared to hear the worst. My friend and orthopedist, Dr. Richard Scarlett, did me a personal favor by calling me to give his opinion. He had no idea that I was a tightly wound ball of tension, but managed to say the exact four words that slackened my every muscle: "Man, are you lucky."

I sighed with great relief as he explained his assessment of my knee, making it a point to say the word "lucky" a few more times.

We spoke about nothing special for a few more minutes, but he said four more meaningful words before hanging up: "Shit, you are blessed."

Thanks, Rich.

The next day, I went to Dr. Israelite, my assigned orthopedist, to get the official opinion. He could tell from my smile that I knew the good news of not needing any surgery, because the two-inch tilt steering knob went into my knee exactly where it could to do the least amount of damage to the joint. Essentially, the knob only dented my knee cartilage.

Dr. Israelite twirled the knob—which I now always keep with me as a good luck charm—between his fingers as he cleared me for aquatic therapy three times a week and said, "Man, are you lucky." Each sentence felt fantastic, and when he gave me an indication that I might recover a good portion of my mobility, I didn't even try to hold back my tears of joy. I just hobbled to the bathroom to humble myself and cried even more.

At my first aquatic therapy session, I stood in warm, chest-deep water with six senior citizens, two of whom were ladies sharing the name Myrtle. Though we each had different injuries, the seven of us were going to get started together. The instructions we were given were simple: walk the length of the pool forward, backward, and sideways.

I was in trouble from the word "go." The seniors walked by me with ease as my resolve and strength eroded with each step. Fighting the water was a struggle, and by the time I stopped on the side of the pool to catch my breath, I was a lot closer to being wiped out than warmed up. As I stood there huffing and puffing, my ego was bruised, but it became even more battered, when one of the Myrtles, waiting for me to finish the drill, said, *"Damn, what's wrong with you?"* Now that hurt.

Myrtle's simple question really did hurt, but when a dear friend called me late the next night to remind me how pitiful I was being, I stopped hurting and woke up. She knew what motivated me, so she told me that if I really wanted "me" back, I was going to have to fight to get it.

Thanks, Susanne.

I have long believed that a man's thought process is what ultimately defines him and right up to the point of impact "being better than I was yesterday" was my normal defining thought pattern. The accident forced me into a surreal and very far from normal place of self-pity though. "Being better than I was yesterday" was no longer enough for me. I needed my body to move because it would make my mind move on a forward path and thus give my spirit its ebullience. I needed all of this because I didn't know, or like, who I had been forced to become. In short, now I had to be better than *who* I was yesterday, and I had to do it by tomorrow.

With this new thought process in mind, the three sessions per week of aquatic therapy that I was cleared for were not nearly enough. I needed to be more aggressive. Still unable to train others, but more than able to train myself, I got up before sunrise each morning and was in the pool and fighting by 5:00 a.m. I fought the water forward, backward, sideways and every which way possible, up to three times a day. Because I had an intimate knowledge of my body, an in-depth understanding of body mechanics, and an awareness of the distinction between muscular soreness and joint pain, I went well beyond what I would professionally recommend as a personal trainer, or even as a friend. But I felt that a new David Hale Sylvester had to be developed. This was what I had to do, and how I had to do it.

To put my mind and spirit at ease, I composed—but never mailed—letters to the young man who hit me. The notes were painful to conceive, and even type out, but I had to put all of my feelings out on a page, from my anger to the irony that I, a mentor, should "meet" a troubled young man in this worst of ways. I knew from the trial what his injuries were and that he, like me, was due for a lifetime of discomfort and pain. I wished us both strength, and hoped that we each got whatever message we were supposed to get from our chance meeting. Doing this may seem odd, but my spiritual being needed to be done with all of this so I could move on.

The plan to get my mind and body in sync was simple: jump into the deep end of the pool and sink or swim. The accident reduced my body and its movements into a mass of unsynchronized parts, and I needed something to force them all into a rhythm. The only thing that I could think of was to tread water. I could have waded from the shallow end toward the deep, but I needed the jolt and the pressure.

I took a calculated risk, and though it was a lot more of a fall than a true leap, I jumped in. With a very angry lifeguard standing at the pool's edge, I fought the pain and stiffness. While taking in mouthfuls of chlorinated water, I fought Myrtle's comments, my thwarted plans to bike South America, and everything surrounding the accident.

My personal "Brawl Against It All" was totally exhausting and lasted less than two minutes. But as I clung to the side of the pool with the lifeguard yelling at me, I smiled and laughed because I'd gotten the prize I was looking for and needed: a reference point.

I now knew that my body could work in sync for two minutes. If it could do that then when pushed—and I was going to push it—my body could perform at that level and beyond. I was looking forward to every day after that.

I trained and pushed my body for months. During that time, by chance, an opportunity came my way to speak to a group of drivers who had been caught driving under the influence.

I rarely prepare for speaking engagements, usually preferring just to go with the flow, but this time was different. I was unaware of how much pain and anguish I still felt until I sat by the door, watching people from every demographic file past me into the classroom. I couldn't have prepared for this even if I wanted to. Each of the forty or fifty people who walked in brought forth a new memory of the accident that trampled all my ideas of what to say.

By the time I stood before the packed classroom, I was more than just cotton-mouthed and nervous: I was petrified. With so many feelings grating me raw, I really wanted to channel everything into one very long and very loud primal scream and walk away. That was what I wanted to do, but I knew that screaming at this group wouldn't accomplish anything, so I stood there quietly thinking of how to communicate my point.

After a few moments of thinking, I clapped my hands together, one time, and barked, "Look up!" I ordered everyone to look up toward the ceiling and keep their eyes there. I then spouted off as many stark and vivid details of my remembrances of being trapped in the truck and my time in the ER to try to make each of them feel the suddenness, sadness, fear, and helplessness I felt. While I gave these details, I walked around the room touching people's legs and arms and jostling their chairs, but constantly telling them to look up, because they were immobilized, like I was, and had to deal with it.

Recounting and revealing everything I felt during the accident was extremely difficult, and left me barely able to hold onto my own emotions. Before I became too overwhelmed, I told them that it was not my mission to tell them not to drink or not to do drugs. I didn't want to bullshit them by telling them that I was perfect. I told them that my mission, as I saw it, was to tell them who I was, what I had been doing in the past, and what I wanted to do with my future, and point out that each of us, driver and victim, was living proof that life gave us a second act and another chance.

"As crazy as it sounds," I said, "we are in the same fucked-up boat, and I can tell you that I am not going to waste my second chance—and I hope you don't waste yours." With that, I left the room.

Because I was pushing myself harder than ever and looking for things to push me, I decided that the Ultra-marathon man's impending visit was a sign. Dean Karnazes was an Ultra-marathoner who was coming through Philly in November as a part of a personal campaign to run fifty marathons in fifty states in fifty consecutive days. Philadelphia was going to be his 48th consecutive 26.2-mile run. As soon as I heard about it, I knew I had to be at the race to watch him run. I wasn't going to run myself, but ride alongside him and glean some of his energy. I emailed Dean, who had corresponded with me in the past. He got back to me within 24 hours with a simple note that said, "It would be an honor to have you ride with me."

On the morning of Dean's run, the sunny sky and crisp air reflected the beaming smiles and energy from the other runners. Bicycling the first few miles around Philadelphia was tough but invigorating, and made me feel like myself again.

As the day wore on, though, my energy eroded to the point where my body groaned with each pedal stroke. As the fall sun set, sweat ran down my body. I slowed to an aching crawl, as if I were a rusting version of the Tin Man. The only thought that got me to the finish was the knowledge that every pedal stroke took me closer to where I wanted to go, and further from where I was. In the end, the marathon distance turned out to be more intense than I thought, and made me too tired to bike for weeks afterward. Still, it was a hell of a ride.

Thank you, Dean. I so needed that.

The accident put me through a lot of physical, emotional, and spiritual changes during the latter part of 2006. I was left saddled with a notable limp, one less bicycle, a smashed laptop, reoccurring nightmares, no plans for another cross-continental trip, a lot of debt, and a thinly veiled threat of legal action from the nutritional bar company that had awarded me the grant money, because I hadn't biked a continent as planned. From the moment the car collided into me, each day was a struggle to regain "me." Each day that I regained "me," there was a struggle to then retain "me."

But this struggle made time fly by and before I knew it, 2007 was fast approaching. I knew that I was progressing on the right track, but there was much about me that was still out of sync. I didn't want to start off the New Year this way, and wanted to push my own agenda a bit. I figured that I could use a cold focusing slap in the face, and that nothing could be colder, harder, and more focusing, than the Polar Bear swim in the Atlantic Ocean.

The Polar Bear swim is just what you think it is: a person jumps into ice-cold water. I was nervous about doing the swim, so I convinced some friends to go down with me. But, I was open to the whole experience. As I waded into the cold waves, I looked at the cloudy horizon and prayed a simple prayer to every divine being I could think of. *Give me strength, please.*

I closed my eyes and immersed myself, staying until I could not take it anymore, and then came out. I then stood on the shore looking out to where the waves met the horizon, had another spiritual talk, and went right back in.

I don't recommend this for everybody, but this oceanic baptism of sorts was the absolute refocusing slap I needed to start 2007.

Thank you, Ilana, Leigh, and Monique, for joining me.

Late in January, my friend Brian Rodgers, who I met on my Africa ride, called to see how I was doing. I was in a less-than upbeat and optimistic mood, and didn't withhold any of my feelings about what I had been experiencing. Brian must have been shocked to hear this, because shortly after our conversation, he sent me an email that changed my life's direction. In the email, he wrote: "If *you* can get depressed, then God help us all. Now get your shit together and ride Asia." Brian was referring to an Istanbul-to-Beijing bicycle trip he was taking part in that August.

I thought about it for a minute and then contacted the nutritional bar company and asked if they would get off my back if I did a "continent swap" of sorts and biked Asia instead of South America. When they agreed, biking Asia became my supreme focus.

Thank you, Brian.

I honestly don't think I can tell the story of how I pulled off taking this expensive cross-continental bicycle trip across Turkey, Georgia, Azerbaijan, Turkmenistan, Uzbekistan, Tajikistan, Kyrgyzstan, and China. All I can say is that even though this accident seriously tested my will, it didn't strip me of it. In fact, it emboldened it. I worked at such a high level to recover fully and regain my ability to walk right, bike right, and train right, that as soon as I achieved one goal, I replaced it with another task. Fundraising for the trip replaced physical rehab. Giving presentations replaced cycling. Trip planning replaced swimming. Things changed, but my overall focus was resolute.

But let me be very clear: I would not have been able to do any of this without my friends or family. Each day, they ushered me through to another day and through to another goal. They saw me though the achievement of all of my goals, including seeing me through to ride another continent, Asia. I felt so much gratitude for their place in my life, so I decided to take them with me in the form of 122 passport-sized photos taped all over my bicycle.

Months later, I found myself looking up at a dark football flying through a dusky sky. Acting purely on instinct, I jumped into a game of catch that some other riders had started in the middle of the Turkmenistan desert. My stride, on the uneven sand and dirt clearing that we camped in, was a bit choppy, but as I dodged a tent while trying to catch the ball, I made a discovery. I was running.

I was running.

I was actually running in spite of what the emergency room doctor said would be impossible.

I was running in spite of what I had allowed myself to believe.

I was running in Turkmenistan after biking all day, and I was well on my way to biking to Beijing.

There are many more things that could be said about that encounter, but I can sum it all up by saying: I saw. I played. I smiled.

Later that night, I lay in my tent looking up into a brilliant starry sky and rubbing the small scar on my knee that will always remind me of September 4, 2006. I did not rub it in pain, though. I just massaged it and thought about my life and all that I had been through. It was then that it occurred to me that it had been just over a year from the date of my accident. I continued massaging my knee along with memories, and before I closed my eyes for the evening, one thought stood out among all the others and made me smile: I finally had *me* back.

The chance occurrence of this accident touched every aspect of my life. Because this experience touched me so, what began as a part of my life that I was not ever going to write about has turned into one the most emotionally wrenching essays for me. Reliving each movement and every emotion in order to try to properly convey it to you resurrected my anxiety-fueled nightmares of being trapped in the truck.

But it did something else as well. This accident reinforced the fact that I am very, very, very, *very* fortunate, and I attribute much of that good fortune to the overall conditioning of my mind, body, and spirit. I encourage others to follow suit.

Enhance your body. Every medical professional who looked at my injuries told me that the conditioning of my body, state of health, and muscle tone before the accident helped me absorb the impact better, and recover after the accident faster.

Enhance your mind. The combination of the intensity of the pain from the accident, the uncertainty surrounding my future, the uneasiness of my being perceived as weak, my pride, my ego and my own stubbornness led me to make the gross mistake of suppressing my true feelings. Feeling fully but not speaking freely delayed my recovery, and it was only after I started opening up to my friends, family members, a therapist and even a blank journal page that I felt emotionally cleansed and free to move forward. In other words, free your mind and your ass will follow.

Enhance your spirit. I will never forget those moments of being alone, strapped on a gurney. Lying there and grappling with my mortality was agonizing and left me thinking of the things that I said without feeling, and left my mind dwelling on the things that I'd left unsaid. Since that day, I exercise my spirituality by doing my best to communicate exactly what is on my mind, express what is in my heart, and live in the moment.

As much as I search, there is just not enough depth within the English language to convey the love and gratitude I feel for all those who helped me through this. Somehow, every word I come across falls short. But until the day comes that I find the proper words to communicate all that I feel, let me just end this essay by saying:

Thank you all—you saved me.

This Sure Ain't South America: A Letter

My automobile accident cast a pall over my being that made me doubtful about my ability to recover from it, especially since everything I wanted to do was hampered by the crash. I wanted to contact my friends, most of whom assumed that I was already in South America, but couldn't because my phone—with all my personal contact information—had been smashed. I wanted to notify the company that gave me the grant money to do the trip but couldn't because my computer—with all of my professional contact information—had been smashed. I wanted to see a way out of this but couldn't—neither figuratively or literally—because my eyeglasses had been smashed. When I did borrow a laptop two weeks after the accident, I just wanted to write something that would ease my anxiety a bit.

The first draft of this letter was much darker that the one below, but while typing this email, a show about Olympian Wilma Rudolph aired on television. For those that don't know, Wilma Rudolph is an American who sprinted to an Olympic gold medal in 1960 after being born prematurely and with infantile paralysis. Her stirring story was exactly what I needed to hear and prompted me to scrap the first draft and tearfully write this one, this time ending with a quote that Wilma Rudolph had used which reminded me of something my mother had said to me earlier that day: "If you want to hear God laugh, tell Him that you have a plan."

Here it is:

The plan was to enjoy my Labor Day holiday by casually running some errands through my hometown, because I was going away for a few months. The plan was to drive through West Philly, pick up one more piece of camping gear in University City, go to Center City, return my friend's truck in Bala Cynwyd, and then go read more about Cali, my landing city in Colombia. A great plan in a great city... but I never got more than two miles from my house.

Two youths, going west on Walnut Street in a speeding car, ran a light and hit me as I was driving through the intersection. No screeching tires, no horns, no warning – just impact, or as the police officer pointed out, multiple impacts. My car twisted around and was hit at least twice by that car and then was knocked into another one.

From the point where our cars collided to the point where my car stopped was over 150 feet. Where I am physically and emotionally from that moment is a lot farther. My car, my plans, and my life were pointed in a vastly different direction than where they landed.

Laptop, cell phone, glasses, sunglasses, data, phone numbers, and information—all were smashed and gone. I had corneal abrasions from debris flying through the air—which have since healed, although my doctor thought my eyes were still damaged until I pointed out that I could only ever see the big E on the eye chart *before* the accident. My neck and back are stiff, but doing well right now. My knee, my knee: even writing about it two weeks later is hard. When I was pulled from the wreckage, I saw my knee, literally—I could see bone. As it turns out, there was a knob from the car lodged in my leg that could only been seen though an X-ray. The extraction of that hurt like hell, even with the major drugs I was on. I'll get an MRI tomorrow to see what other damage there is – wish me luck. Emotionally, I vacillate from my normal confident self to someone I don't even know. I will be doing nothing in particular, and the sight of my knee will flash through my head and I'll freeze up. Damn, this is hard.

I am lucky.

So, so very lucky. I am lucky to be here. I am lucky to have no broken bones. I am lucky to have my sight – the doctor said that my thick glasses probably protected my right eye (shout out to Prada eyewear). I am just plain old lucky. For those who found out and have said prayers and called, thank you. For those who are just hearing this for the first time and might pray for me, thank you, too. For all of those that I will be calling on to hug me, cheer me up, and keep me going though whatever rehab process I will have to do, thank you in advance.

God may be laughing, the timetable may be shifted, but it will take a lot more than this to stop me from cycling my third continent, and I hope that whatever your plans are, you too will pursue them through thick and thin.

DAVID

My doctors told me I would never walk again. My mother told me I would. I believed my mother. —Wilma Rudolph, Gold Medal-winning Olympian

State Of Dave 2007

Never has the feeling of love been more tangible, comforting, and real to me than when I was in the ER of the hospital in September. There I was, less than 96 hours from leaving for yet another ride of a lifetime, and little did I know that just by driving around and running an errand, I was already taking my biggest ride yet.

In the emergency room, I was scared and my body was tired, but I didn't want to fall asleep for fear that I wouldn't wake up. Having seen enough episodes of "ER," "Emergency," "Grey's Anatomy," "General Hospital" and even "Scrubs," I knew that complications could crop up at the damndest times. I cannot begin to tell you how scared I was.

I held on, though, and stayed awake. Now don't get me wrong, I am no hero or Superman. I was frightened and crying like a big Chunky-soup-eatin' mama's boy.

I told the attendees as many names and phone numbers as I could remember.

I closed my eyes and thought of all the people I had met and all the places I had been. I had no idea what was going on or what exactly happened. Very confused and still disoriented, all I knew was that my leg hurt like hell, and I was freaking out. One minute, I was driving down the street, and the next, my body was being dragged from a truck with my eyes barely able to focus but able to focus enough to see my exposed knee joint. I babbled about my family, my travels, and about Africa, because I wanted a connection with someone, so that he or she might care for and about me. I was in need.

With my body immobilized by the backboard and neck brace, I had no eye contact, no connection, and no command of the room full of people who were there to help me. Sure, there were plenty of people surrounding me, working on me, talking about me, but no one was talking *to* me. It was just a mixture of pain, lights in my eyes, beeps, and conversations going on all around me.

They checked all orifices of my body for bleeding, and as they were sticking a finger in my ass, I said, "Buy me a drink first" though it came out inaudibly as "Bymmeehadrnkyfirst." When the attendee translated what I said to the doctor he said, "Hey, you have a sense of humor. That's good. Hang in there."

With painkillers taking fast effect, I could barely stay engaged as the doctors and attendees discussed my status, but my heart sank even deeper when the chaplain introduced herself. Only a voice and hand with soft skin, she introduced herself, and knowing that a chaplain is only called in to relay bad news, I fought the sedatives to stay awake. The voice asked me about my trips, and as

I babbled the details of what I had done, another voice said "that's impossible."

Tearfully, I repeated the words "Nothing's impossible." as the knob was extracted from my knee and don't know whether I was saying that as possible final prayer, a final call for help, a final pep talk for others, a beginning pep talk for myself, or as a way to try and establish a connection with the people working on me so that they would work harder, but I repeated the words.

I hung in there and was never so happy to see my sister's and mother's faces and hear their voices. The feeling of love was very much needed at that time. My friends and family did so much for me in the time that followed:

- They called me from the West Coast to let me know that they could be on the next flight, if needed.

- They brought enough guacamole, chips, and cookies to feed an army.

- One who is an orthopedic surgeon read my MRI results and consulted me before my doctor did.

- They took me to get a pedicure – hey, my feet got messed up in the crash.

- They brought me a plate of fried chicken and mashed potatoes (although a better friend might have brought me something strong to drink and some dessert...)

- They looked me in the eye and told me, "I rushed right over, as soon as I felt like it": isn't sarcasm great?

- One urged for me to stay awake for a few more seconds, so she could pray for me over the phone.

- One who is an attorney drove down from Long Island with her physician husband and beautiful two-year-old daughter from —on a weekday—to sit with me for a few hours.

- One sat with me and watched episode after episode of "Flavor of Love" Season Two with me.

- One dropped a laptop off that he was about to give to his wife and said to return it whenever. (By the way, you'll get it back whenever.)

- And my mother looked at me in my teary eyes and said, "Don't worry, you have people all over the world praying for you."

Whether they came bringing jokes, food, company, or even more food – I felt it. Whether they called, emailed, or texted – I needed it. Whatever it was that they did or whenever they did it, they all conveyed that powerful thing called love.

This whole ordeal hurt, but it would have hurt a lot worse if there were not people there physically and in sprit who loved me. Love is a powerful thing. At no point during all of this did I want or wish for a plasma TV, a Benz, or any other kind of tangible thing; what I wanted were the simple things: a reassuring smile, a familiar voice, my mother's hand, another second, a second chance. And I really and truly wanted and needed a hug.

Every year, I seem to learn something new or reappraise things and start to value something that I should have been centered around all along, and this year it is pure and simple: love.

We don't often get second chances, and as I age, I see that I've been lucky enough to get two, three, and umpteen more chances, and I am trying to take advantage of every one of them. I wish you and yours many second chances that you can take advantage of, and a deeper appreciation of the awesome gift called love.

We may not talk daily. We may not know the subtle nuances of each others lives. We may not even see each other yearly. We may be just two people who pass each other in the day, but if you are receiving this, then I cherish you and your involvement in my life.

Consider yourself hugged, thanked, cherished, and loved by me.

Happy Holidays

PS: I am going to try and get to South America sometime in the spring.

DAVID

It is okay to be hurt because we will survive it and grow from it.

If we insist on avoiding pain, we stagnate.

— Dr. Anne Burke

What Are You Gonna Do When You Are Big, Black, And Scary?

"You may leave Africa, but Africa never leaves you," is a great line that I once heard, and I wholeheartedly agree.

I traveled to Africa at the right time of my life to let its marvelous beauty fully captivate and intensify my every sensation. My African bicycling experience hit me like a drug that compelled me to fall in love. The unique, warm, and magnificent moments left my being afire and very reluctant to loosen the grip on any of the bonds formed there. Indeed, I left Africa, but Africa has never left me.

I imagine that other bike riders of Africa felt the same way, because when the same tour company offered a tour of Asia, many of them leapt at the opportunity. The inaugural Silk Road bicycle tour started in Istanbul, Turkey and traveled on to The Republic of Georgia, Azerbaijan, Turkmenistan, Uzbekistan, Tajikistan, Kyrgyzstan, and ended in Beijing, China.

Entering any cross-continental bicycling tour is not a casual decision. In addition to the costs that easily eclipse ten thousand dollars per rider, each individual must be strong-minded, tenacious, determined, and adventurous. Each of those from around the globe who partake must be prepared to cycle an average of eighty miles a day over varied terrain for at least six days a week, and camp out in all types of weather and altitude.

The tour company operated this Asian venture in the same efficient manner as it did the Africa tour. A typical day started with a wake-up horn before sunrise. We would pack up our tent and gear, seventy pounds per rider, and then pack it onto one of the two huge overland vehicles that provided storage and transport. Both trucks rolled out after the cyclists broke camp, with one vehicle traveling to the day's mileage endpoint to establish a campsite and the other vehicle going to the day's mileage midpoint to set up a lunch table. This is an oversimplification of the minimalist system that kept this four-to-five-month tour rolling along, but not by much. You can probably see how under the wrong circumstances, the characteristics needed to endure a tour like this could easily transform into inflexibility and obstinacy, and rip apart a group.

As I have said, the experience of cycling Africa was just like a drug, and we were hooked. But the problem with drugs is that the first experience becomes greatly idealized in the mind. We were now like strung-out addicts, blind to how hooked we really were, hoping to catch the elusive intensity of that African high somewhere in Asia. We looked past any cost and beyond any potential hurdle and paid the price. We entered into the Asia experience, never taking it on its own terms and unfairly comparing its magic to Africa's. At least, that's what I did.

It didn't take long for Asia to disappoint. Our first border crossing (Turkey to Georgia) was the first time I heard someone openly express disappointment and a desire to leave the tour. After camping in a cold, rainy field, one rider stood in deep mud and declared, "I want to go home. I am not having fun." With dirty cheeks that glistened with tears and raindrops, she had clearly had enough. "This ain't Africa," she said.

Her outburst prompted a small group of riders to surround her with a warm, reassuring hug that made her stay, but the "I am disappointed that Asia is not Africa" door was now wide open.

A few weeks later in Azerbaijan, it was my turn to want to leave. I started to realize just how much I was hooked on the African experience, and explored the option of leaving the tour and finishing the following year.

I would have left if not for two special people. First, Phillip. The tour mechanic made me reconsider when he told me, "If you are here to inspire people, then think of all those that won't be inspired if you quit." Next, my fellow prankster and longtime friend, Scott Miller. He asked, "If you leave, then who the hell am I going to laugh with?"

From day one, cliques naturally formed. Initially, they were based on hanging out with those cyclists we knew from other tours but, as time wore on, natural and national selection took place, and new alliances took shape.

Normally cliques aren't too much of an issue, but on this tour, the elements (15 – 122 degrees F), topography (zero – two miles above sea level), and the terrain (endless miles of desert) limited our interaction with people other than ourselves. Days would go by without seeing or speaking with the local populace. Like regimented soldiers, marching day after day through unknown territory, we were becoming leaner and meaner, and never even realized it.

My clique was mostly American. We enjoyed a sarcastic, smart-ass sense of humor. We saw the other groups as a bunch that took life (and our practical jokes) personally and way too seriously. They saw us as being boorish, unrestrained, immature, and obnoxious. Relatively early on, I found out what people thought of me when a fellow rider told me, "Dave, some people will never get past your size and the volume."

Without many outsiders to dilute our ever-increasing fractiousness, tensions continued to build throughout Turkmenistan, Uzbekistan, Kyrgyzstan, and Tajikistan. By the time we got to China, something was bound to happen.

Now, there are fireworks in China.

Let me clear that up. Fireworks are made in China.

No, let me clarify even more. Fireworks were invented in China.

They are sold everywhere in China and are a constant source of amusement for almost everyone. With nothing else really to do while camping in the middle of nowhere, those in my clique would shoot them off, just like the Chinese citizens did. Whether it was the single firecracker, a bundled brick of a few hundred firecrackers, or even a 1/8 stick of dynamite called a Thunder King, we would light it, startle each other, laugh, and that would be the end of it – for us at least.

As we smiled, though, the other riders who didn't share our humor furrowed their brows and felt assaulted. These riders took any explosion of fireworks personally, and even blamed us for the random times that any Chinese citizen blew off firecrackers around camp.

At this point, I could have and should have listened through their constant frowning. However, like the others, I was getting leaner and meaner. I reflexively matched their contemptuous glares with contemptuous acts and didn't try to understand them at all. Instead, I waited for them to approach us directly to ask us to stop, which none of them ever did.

By the time their random self-mutterings grew into angry yells at me, things had already gone too far. Their words left me amused and laughing, because by that point, I didn't have any more fireworks – but my friends did. One of my friends had never lit a firecracker before, but now, tired of the other clique's pettiness, was eager to light a few. Though hesitant at the last second, always being one who tries to follow through on intentions I took the lighter, ignited the strand, and said, "It's just this easy" and walked away. All we heard was Pop – pop – pop – pop – pop – pop – pop – pop – pop – pop – pop – pop – pop – pop – pop – POP!

How long did it take you to read that last line? That was about all it took to change everything. It was time for the real incendiaries to go off.

One rider—I will call him Jake—who always leapt up in the air as if he were avoiding a firing squad, barked, "Fuck you, David! You come back here and clean this paper up. You are littering! You come back right fucking now and clean this shit up, and you do it now."

I honestly don't know what it was about his rant about the red paper firecracker remnants that particularly got under my skin, but it did. I turned around and shouted, in the same tone, "Nah man, fuck you. I'm not cleaning up shit."

He screamed, "Fuck you!" once more and took a step toward me.

Edgier, I barked back, "Fuck you." Regrettably, I took about twenty steps toward him and tossed someone's hands off me.

As he boldly stepped toward me, I thought, *I am sick of this guy's crap.*

Both lean and mean alpha males in our own rights, we inched toward a face-off. I held my emotion, but once we stood with nothing more than a whiff of testosterone separating our noses, and he turned up his flip-top shades to reveal the contemptuous disdain in his eyes and sneered, "I wish you would," I lost it.

A small smart-ass voice inside my head quietly said, *Your wish is my command*, and in one powerful, unthinking primal vent I pushed him down and said, "Get the fuck out of my face!"

He toppled backwards to the ground and scampered back up, ready to fight.

Others had quickly stepped in. I raised my unclenched hands in the air and never took an advancing step or touched him again. I just stood my ground as others stepped in and more expletives were exchanged.

"I'm gonna kick your ass," he yelled.

"I'll give you what you want," I yelled back almost as quickly.

With at least five people around, things calmed down as quickly as they'd escalated. Jake went to his hotel room yelling that I was a "small person" and something about my likability, and everybody else looked around, dazed at what just happened.

I regretted losing my cool and immediately wanted to speak to someone to straighten this whole thing out, but Scott suggested that I go with him to get something to eat. As I sat just staring at my food, I had a feeling that this wasn't going to end well.

By the time I finished staring at my food and returned to camp, the facts had been whispered down the lane, contorted, distorted, and overdramatized. The far-ranging story that was spun about what happened caused some riders to glare at me. When one rider told me that he heard that I randomly ran over and pushed Jake down from behind and then threatened to sodomize him with a bike pump, I incredulously asked, "*Who* did that?"

"Well...*you did*," they said.

Yeah, this was not going to end well.

I met Hank, the tour owner who I have known since my 2004 African bike tour, in the lobby of our hotel, just after a small faction of cyclists had left him. They screamed for my ousting, stating that my action violated the "bike ambassador" code of conduct pledge that each of us had signed prior to the tour.

Hank remained seated and silent while I stood, admitted to, and apologized for pushing Jake down, also adding that, as far he was concerned, the matter was over. He said nothing specific but did note that my behavior was not what he was accustomed to and reminded me that there was nothing he could do because his participation in this trip was as a rider, not an owner. He said that he was leaving all major decisions to his trusted tour operators, and that they would talk with me later that evening.

It was late after dinner when I was called to Hank's hotel room. As soon as the door opened and I only saw him and his two trusted operators, Danny and Mike, in the room, I breathed easy, thinking this may be all right after all. After sitting down and retelling my side of the story and learning that they hadn't spoken with Jake directly, except to know that he was embarrassed by his behavior and was not speaking on the matter, I breathed even easier. Without Jake there to give his version, I felt that the matter was over, and that the harshest penalty doled out would be for me to take a few days off and rejoin the tour at a later point.

That was all dashed when Danny said right away, "Dave, we spoke amongst each other, and we think that you should be off the tour." He paused. "For the safety of the other riders."

At that precise moment, I felt the weight of every intangible thing in the room. Their stares, their perceptions, their decision, and their words fell on me and stunned me to the point of incredulity. All I could meekly respond was "Wow," but I was thinking, "WOW ... did you *really* say *'for the safety of the other riders?'*" The weight of everything compressed me deep in my chair.

I did not want to be seen as an enduring threat. I wanted to be reinstated to the tour. I wanted to bike the remaining two weeks of the tour into Beijing. I wanted a lot, but I didn't have a lot of time or options of ways to convey anything I desired.

I thought fast and concluded that if I remained calm and maybe even made a joke, they might be disarmed and all would be cool. Referencing the fact that each tour rider received a free commemorative cycling jersey, I smiled and blurted out, "Do I still get a jersey?"

But they had jokes too and said that I would get a jersey "*via the mail.*"

They did not waver from their point until Hank said, "Dave, we have a whole tour to worry about. Maybe you should go ahead a few days to our next rest day in Xian, and let's revisit this then."

I felt this was reasonable and nodded like a bobble-head doll in an effort to get everyone in the room to agree. I really felt that everyone was on board until Danny spoke up from his perch.

Sitting on the edge of one of the beds, Danny shook his head, and practically his whole body, and said, "No, no, no. I don't want to give him hope."

Former heavyweight boxing champion Mike Tyson once said, "Everybody has a plan until they get punched in the mouth."

How right you are, Mr. Tyson.

The sentiment behind the words "*I don't want to give him hope*" was a punch that let me know that this situation was impassable and highly personal. Minutes later, I stumbled and staggered back to my room like Tyson's proverbial boxer and warbled the words, "I'm out." My roommate, Scott, and fellow rider, Tiffany, sat stunned as I relayed the basic terse details: the riders would be out of the hotel by 9:00 a.m., at which time my bicycle and gear would be offloaded from the tour vehicles, the tour would move on, and I would be on my own.

My first thoughts and words were about going home back to Philadelphia, but both Scott and Tiffany yelled, "Hell no! We're too close." The word "we" resonated deeply within me, but the practical realities of the details of staying made my head spin.

I needed some fresh air. Still acting very much like a stunned boxer, numbly reacting and moving on pure instinct, I went outside to go to an Internet café. I remember walking with Tiffany, but recall nothing that was said. I kept talking, just enough to keep the conversation moving.

It was only when Tiffany stopped walking and kept snarling something at me that I woke up. Tiffany repeated the same sentence over and over again: "Dammit. Just make lemonade!"

Her energy shook me from my haze, but also made me take notice of the brisk and windy night air, as well as the fact that she was smoking a cigarette. Mesmerized by the dissipating nicotine frame around her face, I said, "Thanks. But you know, you really have to give up smoking."

"You really are a dick," she said, laughing, and although the exchange lightened the mood, it was not nearly light enough for me.

I entered the café feeling an array of emotions, but each was too raw and too constricting to express. I found myself staring at the keyboard, entranced by my own issues, unable to even log on. I left shortly thereafter, still in a fog, but when I got back to my room, Scott informed me of his basic plan for me to bike into Beijing. He even had a name for it: *The Shadow Tour*.

As I started scurrying around for all my stuff the next morning, the tour operators informed me that they would allow me to pick up my bike and gear in Xian. Xian was another two days' cycling away and the tour's next rest day. This was a relief, because that would give me an opportunity to plan my next steps, and I was doubly relieved when Tiffany, who is fluent in Chinese, agreed to accompany me on the bus there.

I saw Jake putting air in his tire as I was leaving and approached him. He expressed genuine shock at the news of my dismissal and only said, "I didn't ask for this."

On the bus ride to Xian, I sat staring out the window, dazed and wondering what I'd just gotten myself into. When we arrived, I met up with a few injured riders who had gone ahead to get some rest, and who also expressed shock at my dismissal. They immediately started helping me organize things for the Shadow Tour, but my efforts were half-hearted, because I really believed that I would be reinstated.

That was my belief until I received an email from Scott with the subject line: Get the Shadow Tour on the Road!!

Scott wrote that he lobbied on my behalf while riding with Hank for a day, without him saying much of anything. But Scott believed that he got all the answers he was looking for when Danny stood up by the dinner campfire and announced that I had been "kicked off" and that he "did not want to hear any more about it."

The email touched on a lot of raw emotions, but the last sentence made me feel that if I stayed on somehow, I wouldn't be alone. *"Fuck 'em, I'm sure they'll be happy to see you everyday riding with us, unaffiliated. The roads of China are for everyone! See you tomorrow. Scott"*

Once the tour arrived in Xian, some riders told me they felt my punishment was too harsh, which was nice to hear. But what shocked me was what they said next. Most riders expressed little to no feelings for Jake, who routinely levied vitriolic outbursts at the staff, his girlfriend, and tour riders, but vented his worst on cars that cut him off in traffic. The motorists who encountered Jake would be yelled at, have their cars kicked or dented, and even almost get punched. The riders felt that the firecrackers blown during the tour were the more egregious and actionable offense, and told me that they would lobby for my return if I apologized for setting them off.

I sat down with Hank one last time in an effort to be reinstated. After I said that he, the tour company, and I had a history, and that my outburst was an anomaly, he calmly looked at me and said, "Dave, come on. What do you want? You are this big black guy and you beat up another rider. I can't have you terrorizing the others."

I was so focused on getting back on the tour, that I didn't fully react to that statement and just went on to explain the huge difference between beating someone and pushing someone down.

He said that he had others to think of, and again, that I was "a big, black, loud guy who curses a lot."

To prove his point, he told me that on the day before the Silk Road tour started, Scott saw me in the hotel meeting room that had become a makeshift bike shop and yelled, "What's up, motherfucker?"

I apparently "bellowed" back, "What's up, motherfucker?" and ran over to embrace him with an affectionate bear hug.

This scene happened in full view of other riders who didn't know either of us, our history of bicycling Africa together, or our longstanding friendship, but who did know that we were with the tour. One of these riders ran over to Hank and asked who I was, because they felt that I was "scary."

"You scared them," he said.

I sat listening to all of this while slumped in my chair. I felt that his argument and tactic of using my own genuine warmth against me was inane, absurd, and highly insulting. Even though I could have said it better, I blurted out, "You're fucking kidding, right? That was almost four months ago. So because someone may be a bitch, I have to carry that burden? Shit, I didn't even say the first 'motherfucker'... *and I get in trouble???*"

Let me say this now. I was truly sorry for my thoughtless act of pushing another man down, and had no problem apologizing for that act. But because I wanted back on the tour, my previous thoughtless action shackled me with a heavy perception that left me harnessed in a very deep hole.

As a person with a normally loud voice, I could not raise my voice one decibel, because that would make me too threatening.

As a big person, I felt I couldn't even sit up straight—because I would then be too big, which would then be taken as too assertive or aggressive.

As a black male, I couldn't do anything, because it apparently only amplified my size and volume.

Expressively castrated, I had no recourse but to slump deep in my chair, slump deeper into my hole and take my characterization as a big, black, and scary terror.

To try to put things in perspective, I listed other incidents that had happened without penalty or uproar on the tour, ranging from one rider jabbing another with a fork, to a rider pouring vodka on another rider's head and attempting to light a match, to a staffer transporting marijuana in our tour vehicles. These were met with a disdainful look that said, "Don't whine, big man."

Hank knew that he had me over a barrel at this point, because he then took the liberty to analyze my character. He stated his belief that perception was always reality; because of that, I really was a *big, black, and scary* guy. He also said that I wasn't really a nice guy, and that I could do more with my size and personality if I weren't as loud and so "typically American."

His words jarred me, and the more he spoke, the more it hurt, because it sounded as if he had felt this way long before any altercation.

I wanted to say so much about his choice of words and his thought process, but knew that it wouldn't come out calmly, so I just sat and listened. As I paid attention to his words, I found myself almost chuckling, because I thought, *How scary could I really be?* I mean, if I were in a room alone with someone half as threatening as he was describing, I sure as hell would not feel too comfortable dismantling his character. I would think that this scary person would beat my ass.

Hank got a lot off his chest, but I spoke up when I felt that he went too far. I told Hank that he had the right to kick me off the tour, but that was all. He didn't have the right to even suggest how I should be big or black—or American, for that matter.

Though I didn't need to, I informed Hank that I was not bicycling Asia because of him and therefore, would not be quitting because of him. I told him that I would be shadowing the tour for the remaining two weeks to Beijing.

My decision and my choice of words made Hank's demeanor grow even more contentious. After reiterating his "big, black, and scary" points, he flatly said, "Well, I just hope that you don't attack any of my other riders."

With getting back on the tour being out of the question, the only other matter on the table was my reputation. I felt compelled to ask when, exactly, I had crossed the line. I asked if I was too scary when I offered my services as a personal trainer to people, or too black when I offered hugs to a few homesick riders. Just when did it happen?

He looked at me as if I were a bother, and shrugging his shoulders, said, "Dave, what do you want? You're a scary guy."

And with that, the Shadow Tour began.

When I got kicked off the tour, I really did feel like a boxer who'd been punched in the mouth. I had no plan, but with the initial support of Scott, Tiffany, Catriona, and Brian, I made it through to the bell. Now, I had a fighting chance to make it through one last round.

I vividly remember walking down the hallway from Hank's room and down two flights of steps to my own, but I don't remember much of what I was thinking, because my mind was awash with details. Getting kicked off the tour changed everything. By the time I entered my room, I was almost overwhelmed by all of these thoughts, but I quieted my mind by narrowing my thoughts and actions to just a few things.

First, I centered myself by being honest. I pointed the finger at myself because pointing a finger anywhere else at this time would make me lose my focus. There was no one else to blame; I'd lost my cool, gotten myself in a jam, and now, regardless of anyone's decision or thoughts of me, I must deal with it in order to get myself out.

The next thing I did was to recall my goal: Beijing. Much more than a destination, bicycling to Beijing and experiencing Asia was a promise that I had made to my family, friends, and supporters, not to mention myself. And now, with my world being turned upside down and reduced to just a few things, breaking a promise was the last thing that I wanted to do.

After that, I thought of time. By the time I finished speaking with Hank, I had less than twelve hours to figure out what I was going to do, and to get my mind around the fact that the remaining two weeks of the tour were not going to even remotely resemble the first four months of the tour. The only thing that got me over that mental hurdle was that I believed that I could make it through anything for two weeks.

The next variable I had to take into account was everything else. Getting kicked off the tour meant that I could no longer mindlessly cycle along, or mindlessly do anything anymore. I had to think now. When I did this, I saw the connections and how everything came down to me.

Being detached from the group meant no tour support vehicle, which meant I now had to physically carry all of my gear. I now had to sift through every item I'd purchased and brought on this trip, differentiating between a "want" and a "need," until I trimmed the weight of my gear down to nothing. Nothing was spared. I went through everything until it was a (still heavy) 30-pound backpack. This was hard to do, but hardest on my mother, because in my zeal to lessen my load, I inadvertently tossed some souvenirs I'd purchased for her. Sorry, Mom.

Developing rhythms gets you through most things, and cycling a continent is no different. My rhythm was to get up and get off to a fast start, then slow down as the day went on. Pedaling along with extra weight, though, meant that my rhythm, cadence, and instincts about cycling were going to have to change. I was going to have to pedal slower, consume more calories, and have a sorer body as well as a longer day.

All of this affected my wallet, which was going to be a bit of an issue, because being kicked off the tour meant that I would have to pay for hotel rooms and meals that had been covered with my tour fees. I was essentially paying for things twice.

I sat on my bed, taking all of this into account. With everything stacking up, it looked like the next two weeks were going to be extremely difficult, but if my life experience taught me anything, it was that a strong body, strong mind, strong will and good friends could get you through anything.

What made me believe that I could endure was that I knew there really was only one person who could possibly stop me from getting to my goal: me. I also knew that I wasn't going to let myself down, so I believed that I could get through this.

I was now prepared for the Shadow Tour to begin.

The one matter I refused to deal with at that time, though, was Hank's calling me big, black, and scary at least six different times during a twenty-minute conversation. Dealing with that was not going to get me to Beijing, but it did stick in my mind.

Once I had my attitude where it needed to be, I had to get my bike in order. It was locked outside the hotel but wasn't there when I went to find it. I panicked until I learned that Chuck, one of the riders, had decided to surprise me by taking it and having it cleaned and oiled for me. This was a great relief, because I never clean my bike.

As he handed it to me, Chuck said, "Dave, shadowing a tour with a dirty bike is just plain old wrong." Thanks, Chuck.

On day one of the Shadow Tour, I woke up especially early. After copying the day's directions from the tour map in the hotel lobby, I really felt the additional weight—both emotional and physical— I was cycling with right away.

By the time I reached Xian's quiet countryside and felt the gentle breeze, though, I was calm. When one of the support vehicles came roaring by, tooting its horn while I coasted down a mountainside, I instinctively smiled.

Today is gonna be a good day, I thought while watching the truck disappear around a bend. But my smile disappeared when I saw the support vehicle stopped at the mountain's base and the driver outside looking at a map.

It turned out that the directions the tour left in the hotel lobby were incorrect. Both of us had taken a wrong turn down the mountainside and now had to go back up. The driver started to offer me a ride back up the mountain, but stopped in mid-sentence when he looked over and saw that Danny's girlfriend was riding in his truck that day. He shook his head, extended his hand to shake, and said, "This shit sucks. Good luck."

I was only a few hours into the Shadow Tour, when I was presented with my first figurative and literal mountain to handle. My Shadow Tour plan to get to Beijing would only work if I was able to hang with the actual tour. So I had to get up that mountain. As the support vehicle slowly ground its gears going up the mountain, I ground my own mental gears. I immediately started to make all of the critical physical and emotional calculations I'd need to get up the mountain, but I'll never know what solution I would have come to on my own because people kept interrupting me.

Five elderly Chinese men surrounded me and began talking to me, even though it was painfully obvious that I didn't speak Chinese. The heavily smoking men had watched the exchange between the driver and me and deduced what was going on. They surrounded me, looking over my shoulder at the map in my hands, and would not shut up to let me think. The more I turned my body away and tried to ignore them, the more animated they became. At the point when they started touching me in order to get my attention, I decided to shut up and try to listen.

Bicycling across lands puts you at ground level and immerses you in the culture. Almost immediately, you start honing a communicative instinct. The key is figuring out when to trust those instincts.

At first, I was only acting like I was listening, but as I began to pay attention through their yelling, touching, cigarette smoke, and my own resistance, the language barrier between us lowered. Whether through each man slowing the cadence of his Chinese words or a simple touch, I started to learn a lot. Whether it was the crude drawing on a dusty parked car, or the gesture of pointing toward the mountain with one hand at a steep angle and the other hand at a much more slight angle to the side of the mountain, I realized that the men were trying to communicate something important to me.

I trusted my instincts and listened to the information, which was amazingly audible. The five smoking Chinese men indicated that I didn't need to go back up the steep mountain and could circumvent the steep incline via a shortcut they were pointing to.

It was a huge gamble on my honed communication skills, but I heeded their advice, which worked. Thanks, five guys. Now please quit smoking.

Their road was less steep and did get me to my destination city, but it got me there on a totally different vector than the tour. I biked through the streets of a small Chinese town with a lost look on my face, consciously looking for other cyclists or a tour vehicle, as well as subconsciously looking for another set of helpful smoking old Chinese men. I found neither. I was left on my own.

I could have cycled longer, but with nightfall getting closer with each pedal stroke and the task of finding a place to stay for the evening ahead of me, I chose to stop. The task of getting a hotel room made me anxious for two reasons: I do not speak Chinese and I do not like to haggle.

Before I go on, let me explain that haggling for the price of everything is a part of the Chinese culture, and that a common language is essential to haggling. I pedaled up to the first hotel I saw, and while walking through the marble-laden lobby to the front desk, thought, *Gee, having a hotel room or an established campsite waiting for you at the end of a 70-mile-or-so ride sure is sweet.* But

I couldn't allow myself to think about such things and wiped the pleasant expression off of my face by the time I reached the front desk.

I stood at the front desk with a focused look on my face and held up the exact amount of money I was prepared to spend for a room clearly fanned out, like a hand of cards. I pointed to the wall of room keys behind the desk and then, holding my breath and hoping for the best, slowly backed away toward the door.

Admittedly, it wasn't much of a plan, but it was all I had, and it proved effective. Midway between my third or fourth retreating step, the clerk motioned for me to come back toward the desk. As I filled out the registration slip and tried to chat with the clerk, I noticed something interesting. Each slot behind the desk was filled with a key, making me the lone patron in a five-floor hotel.

My own footsteps sounded creepy echoing up the staircase and down the unlit hotel corridor. Everything was so dark that I was surprised when my electronic key card worked and opened to a spacious room. Tired, alone, and muddling through the events of my first day, and planning what was needed to even approach my second, I collapsed backwards on the bed and closed my eyes. I lay there wondering what I had gotten myself into and whether I really had what it would take to get out.

My spirits lifted later, though, after I showered and found some food along with some other things I was looking for. It turned out that the tour hotel was less than 100 yards down the same street I was on but I never saw it because I approached the street from a different direction.

More important than the pool tables or bowling alley or any other amenity the official tour hotel had, it had my friends and their encouraging energy. Scott and I met to grab some dinner. Afterward, when I pointed to my darkened Hotel d'Desolate at the end of the street, he patted me on the back and said, "Hang in there, bro. It's only one night."

With my head hanging low, I went back to my room to, again, fall backward on my bed. I lay there thinking until I had to go to the bathroom.

Bathrooms in some foreign countries don't have bathtubs, only a showerhead and a drain in the floor. This leaves you with a soaked toilet paper roll, but it also gives you your own personal steam room. I unfurled my yoga mat, which I had classified as a "need" when prioritizing my gear, and turned the floor of my bathroom into my personal steamy yoga studio.

Now naked and very much alone with my thoughts, I went through a series of yoga postures in an effort to stretch my body and to clear, calm, and clarify my mind. I closed my eyes and relived the tour—both the good and bad—and thought how hard the next days were going to be.

I pictured Tiffany yelling at me to "Make lemonade, dammit," and thought of her words with each posture repetition. The more I repeated the postures and words, the more I felt the new soreness of riding with additional weight. "Make lemonade."

The deeper I pushed into the postures, the more I thought of being branded "big, black, and scary," and the more I felt horrible for contributing to that brand.

"Make lemonade." I repeated these words again and again, further thinking of the constriction of the perception, and as I did, the shower water mixed with my tears. "Make lemonade."

My mind drifted everywhere as I repeated the words until I focused on something that made me laugh aloud: I hate lemonade. Regardless of what any advertisement may say to the contrary, I feel that lemonade is always too tart, too sweet, too something, but never just right. I never order it. But now, alone in a hotel in the middle of rural China, I was mentally making it.

I laughingly yelled as loud as I could, "I fucking hate lemonade, but I am gonna make some anyway and drink all that shit all up!"

My shower/yoga/mantra/battle cry reinvigorated me, but I deflated a little when I turned on the TV only to find that the only thing broadcast in English was a three-hour retrospective on Celine Dion. That was just too much for this man to take.

Refreshed from a fresh pitcher of "lemonade," I woke up well before sunrise and was out and on my bike within thirty minutes.

It was some time around noon when I came across Jake's bicycle on the side of the road. Assuming that he was relieving himself in some nearby tall grass, I waited for him.

"Hey, I don't want any trouble," he yelled with a blend of agitation and surprise as he exited the bush.

I yelled that I came in peace and just wanted to apologize, because I never had the opportunity to do so. Not advancing at all and letting him come to me, I continued, telling him that everything was over and that my standing there was not about the trip. When face-to-face, I said, "I fucked up and I'm off. This is about doing the right thing."

Because it was the fire in Jake's eyes that had set me off, I wanted him to see the sincerity in mine when I apologized, so I asked him to remove his sunglasses. He hesitantly complied, but only seemed to breathe easy when I apologized for putting my hands on him (making it clear that I was not apologizing for lighting the firecrackers). He graciously accepted my apology and said that my expulsion was not what he had asked for.

"Relax, dude, it doesn't matter anymore. That shit's over, " I said, shaking his hand.

Doing the right thing only cost me a few minutes of my day. As we got on our bikes, I said, "See you when you pass me, brotha," and that was it.

As the Shadow Tour continued over the next few days, Scott became convinced that I was actually riding better with the additional weight, but he did warn me. He said that that riding with my gear in a backpack would kill my back and that I should use the bike rack another rider had given me to carry my gear.

With the feeling of being abandoned in the middle of China still chafing me emotionally, I snapped that I wasn't "giving these motherfuckers the satisfaction." I also said, "I may be big, black, and scary, but they better add the word 'strong,' too. Besides, if I can't ride with a little extra weight on my back, then all my years of lifting weights for a living were a lie."

What Are You Gonna Do When You Are Big, Black, And Scary?

A few nights later, the tour stayed in a hotel that provided a guard for the tour's bicycles and support vehicles in their enclosed parking lot. After again haggling for a room, I locked my bike up next to some local citizens' bikes at the opposite end of the lot. I went up to my room, showered and took a nap, but was roused from my deep sleep by a knock on my door. I groggily opened the door, but before I could say anything or focus on the face of the person standing there, he started talking.

His first words were, "Big Dave, things are getting very petty."

The person was someone who worked with the tour and who told me that I had to remove my bicycle from the parking lot because I was not on the tour anymore, and the lot was "for tour bikes only."

Thinking that this was a prank by one of my friends on the tour, I peered out into the hallway, but focused on the situation at hand when I saw no one.

"It's a big-ass lot," I said.

The staffer agreed and apologized for the petty nature of the visit, adding that I couldn't enlist the help of the tour's interpreter, which I hadn't.

I gave the worker a hug, went downstairs, unlocked my bicycle and carried it up to my fourth floor hotel room.

Yeah, things had gotten petty.

It hadn't been my purpose, but my not leaving when banished and still managing to have a good time in exile was incensing some to very trivial levels.

Two days before reaching Beijing, I was sitting in a coffee lounge and laughing with my friends when a couple of riders walked up to the window, glared at us all, and then stormed off down the street. Another rider sitting by herself at another table saw this and told me not to worry, because many within the group were "just not nice people."

"Really?" I replied. "Tell me about it."

What Are You Gonna Do When You Are Big, Black, And Scary?

I sat down and had a brief conversation with her about everything that had gone on during the tour. When I stood up to leave, the rider said she was very happy that I had stayed with the tour. I smilingly agreed and started to walk away, but just then, she grabbed my forearm, pulled me toward her and whispered, "You know what? *They can't kill the Big Man.*"

Damn, did I need to hear that! It's the little things like that comment that made a big difference to me.

The Shadow Tour never could have happened without my friends Brian and Scott letting me crash on their hotel room floor to help me save money, or Tiffany swiping a sandwich for me one day, or Catriona spending part of her day riding with me, or if Isabelle hadn't made me laugh by saying, "You should have beat up Hank, he's the real asshole." There were others, too, but I would not have been able to deliver on my promise or reach my goal if it were not for them.

The last night before you pedal to the final destination of a cross-continental bicycle tour is a special one. It is the last night that everyone is guaranteed to be in the same room before scattering home to their corners of the globe, to meet again only in picture, memory, and colorful story. This night was special for the Shadow Tour as well, because after 1000 kilometers and thirteen days of exile, it was the night I got my commemorative cycling jersey, the one that was included in our tour fees, the one promised to me when I got kicked off the tour. Our size information for the colorful shirt, which had the names of the eight countries we bicycled through on the sleeves, had been taken in Turkey, and the shirts were shipped to the tour hotel in China. Brian told me that he would pick mine up at the dinner, but I told him that I had been "riding and hiding" for two weeks and would do it myself.

"You have a big pair of balls on you, man," he said.

"Yup."

The group dinner was in the hotel's large banquet room. I walked straight to Hank's table, shook his hand and said that I didn't want trouble but just wanted to pick up my jersey and then go to Kentucky Fried Chicken (which is hugely popular in China) for dinner.

Hank smilingly grabbed my hand and laughed and said, "Damn, I didn't know that the big man could lay so low." He then invited me to stay for dinner, suggesting that this night should be a night of healing. Part of me didn't want to stay: this was *their* dinner. But a much bigger part of me is greedy and can never turn down free food, so...

I entered the room, sat down at a table with my friends, and started eating. Between bites, a few riders made me feel more than comfortable by coming over to shake my hand and stating that they were glad to see me there. Watching the others admiring their tour jerseys and anticipating getting my own felt good—until I was informed that my jersey never made it in the delivery.

Right then, I felt like an outsider again.

I quickly finished my food and went back to the hotel room I was sharing with Brian and Scott. When Scott entered the hotel room, he tossed me one of the new jerseys that had been ripped to shreds and said, "What do you make of this?"

I sat up looking perplexed at the tattered shirt, and told him I had no clue.

After playing whodunit with other riders in the hotel hallway, we learned that one rider (not Jake) had been so angered by my mere presence at the dinner that he literally ripped his jersey off his body and tossed it into a banquet room trash can.

Brian came in, and after hearing the odd details and holding the ribboned garment, said in a velvety smooth Texas drawl, "Jeez, these motherfuckers are crazy."

Later that evening, another rider stopped me in the hotel hallway and angrily inquired why I was at the dinner. He took a step forward and said I "didn't deserve dinner." He spoke for a few minutes, making a point to repeat and emphasize the word "deserve" a few more times, and end with, "You aren't one of us."

This whole ordeal left me torn; I was self-conscious of my size and not wanting to intimidate anyone, but also felt the need to assert myself in order to be respected. By trying to be all things to all people, I was being nothing to myself. It wasn't until I unconsciously, submissively, and literally backed into the wall that I woke up and spoke up.

I said that my dinner presence had been okay with Hank, but that wasn't enough to satisfy his ire.

"Well, he didn't check it with us," he snapped.

Now fully engaged and very insulted, I snapped back, "I have nothing at all to do with you." I didn't have to, but I briefly told him that the tour was no longer feeding me, supporting me, or transporting my gear, and because of all of this, I'd thrown away stuff for my mother. "*For my mother*," I said angrily. "And you know what?" I continued, purposely pausing to glance to my left and right but never taking my eyes off of his, "We are just two dudes in the middle of a darkened hallway in the middle of China and anything can happen. *Anything*."

He just looked at me, oblivious, and walked away.

I was ready for all of this to be over.

The next day marked two very special occasions. After meeting in and cycling Africa together, Brian, Scott, and I were about to finish cycling our second continent together. This was also the end of the Shadow Tour.

To celebrate everything, I taped the tattered cycling jersey ripped to my backpack with clear packing tape, and—with no other riders around to hear or complain—we lit our remaining firecrackers. It was a blast, every pun intended.

I had spent the day riding with my friends, but as the tour reached Beijing's Tiananmen Square, the official tour end point, I slowed my pace a great deal. I stood twenty yards or so away from the group, feeling a bit envious of their moment, smiling and posing for a ceremonial picture. But my envy was erased when two riders protested my presence *in the area* and opted out of the tour picture.

One of the tour's support vehicle drivers said that some part of me needed to be in the picture.

"My tour ended weeks ago," I said.

He snatched my bike from my hands and rode through the snapping of the pictures and yelled back, "This was all bigger than you — and who would have thought there was anything bigger than your ass?"

Thanks.

The tour hotel lobby was burgeoning with guests, bicyclists, bike boxes, luggage, bellmen, hotel staffers, and a lot of good cheer. Amidst all the confusion, it was impossible to get a room. The nervous concierge, who didn't speak English, just kept pointing to the tour rooming list taped on the front desk as to say, "Find your name and find your room." This continued until a staffer, fluent in Chinese, intervened on my behalf and got me a room.

Thank you.

I might not have wanted to get to Beijing more than any of the other cyclists, but, after what I had been through, I felt that I worked harder than anyone to get there. I hurt. While everyone reveled in their achievement, I made sure to hug those who had helped me but kept my emotions in check and did not linger. I had to hold in what I felt a little while longer.

Once I was alone, though, and the festive atmosphere in the hallway was nothing more than a muffled sound on the other side of my hotel door, I finally gave myself permission to fully feel all that had happened. I felt empty.

I felt even more hollow when, after four months on the road that took me through eight countries, I was able to break down my bicycle and pack up my remaining gear in less than an hour.

What the hell just happened? I thought.

At that point I just put my head in my hands and wept for a long time.

When I returned home, my friends expected me to bound through the door with interesting stories just like when I came back home from Africa.

I didn't.

After everything that went on during my last two weeks in Asia, I just couldn't.

I just came back home.

Since this is a book of independent essays, you may have been intrigued by the title enough to read this one first. As you read it, you may have arrived at the comfortable conclusion that I am whining, or that I am an overaggressive asshole.

You might be someone that thinks that I am loud, brutish, troublemaking and typically American. Or you could even be a person who thinks that I am a truly a big, black, and scary individual. Your opinion is your right. But before you close the book on me, figuratively and maybe literally, I ask you read a little further because one big issue is still on the table: *What are you going to do?*

What happened in this chapter is not something that is indigenous to China, or a trait commonly found in international bicycle tours. But what happened to me is a real possibility for adventurers and non-adventurers alike.

Don't be swayed by any of the details of what I felt or dealt with. Remain focused on the raw situation, and you will see that no one is insulated from situations like this.

Your mistake does not have to be a physical gesture such as mine. You may merely go against the grain, be the lone dissenting vote, be the one who worships, be the one who comes out of the closet, be the one who says yes, be the one who did not say no, or you may be the one who said nothing. I cannot stress enough that you can be anywhere, doing anything.

You mess up and, all of a sudden, find that you are the one who is out, excommunicated.

So what are you going to do?

This isn't about me, now. I already did what I did, to do what I needed, to get done what I had to get done.

I am not a tough guy. I am simply someone who messed up and stepped up, endured, learned something, and will handle things better next time. I didn't have to write this chapter. I could have left this story untold, but after looking deep into my own eyes, I am eager to share my lesson.

So it is all in your hands.

What are you going to do when the pendulum of fate sways against you and someone else's perception becomes your ensnaring reality?

What are you going to do when you are tested by a predicament that you created?

Are you going to be able to make lemonade that is not too tart or too sweet—and if it is, be strong enough to drink it?

What are you going to do when you're stuck in a foreign country and have to go the distance? What are you going to do when your "ugly side" is perceived to be your only side? What are you going to do when someone says they don't want to give you hope?

What are you going to do?

What are you going to do when you are the big, black and scary one?

Dedicated to Brian, Catriona, Scott and Tiffany.
It couldn't have happened without you.
Many Thanks – Much Love – Much Respect.

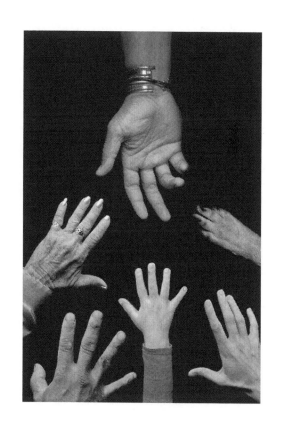

NORTH AMERICA²

State Of Dave 2008

A year ago, I became one of those idiots you see on TV jumping in the ocean. On New Year's Day 2007, I, along with a few friends, officially became "Black Bears" — we would have become Polar Bears, but those people got there at 11 a.m. and we were operating on CP Time (colored people time) and instead strolled into the Atlantic Ocean at 1 p.m.

I had been through a lot the year prior: planning a solo bike trip across South America, getting hit by a drunk driver, sustaining injuries that forced a cancellation of the trip, entertaining the thought of never walking or riding again, and a lot of other BS. I wanted to start this year off drastically different.

So, I ran to the water, and as I did, I kept muttering to myself between icy shortened breaths, "Give me strength to make me make it happen. Please let this year be different."

I never defined "it", but I knew that whatever "it" was that I was going to need much strength and mental fortitude to achieve it. I was at my wits' end, because no matter how good and positive of a front I put up after the accident, I was scared. I was scared because the doubts that I had about my own will and my body's ability were mounting, and I had lost my faith and confidence in myself.

So the year started off with me:

- Not having a bike trip to do.

- Needing a cross-continental bike trip to do to fulfill a contractual agreement or else I'd face legal action.

- Working hard as hell to get back to "normal."

- Not having any sort of plan.

But one event led to another, and things started turning around, slowly or quickly—I still don't really know which. Within the next 365 days, I accomplished much more than I could have ever imagined but the biggest feat by far was that my confidence was restored.

I once heard a line in a movie that went something like "Relax, everything you could ever want or be, you already have and are." It is kind of true, because I had the strength to dig "me" out of my doldrums the whole time and just never knew it. The whole time I was training and rehabbing myself to be "normal," I was accessing that strength. And as my leg, body, and mind got healthier, I was still accessing that strength and so I ended up working harder than ever. As weird as this may sound, in my weakened state I became more keenly aware of my own strength than ever before, and that fed my confidence.

But this letter is not about me or my enumerating any of my accomplishments. They really are no big deal, because I am the only one who wants to do what it is that I do. And I am not going to compare my trials to yours. We all have our own issues—know that right now, somewhere on this planet, even Bill Gates and Oprah are complaining to someone about something.

And I am certainly not saying jump in the nearest ocean on New Years Day, ride a bike across a continent, lift weights, be goofy, or anything like that — that is just *my* life.

All I am saying is that in '08, I wish you increased faith and confidence so that you can achieve it — whatever "it" may be.

I hope that this year you recognize, realize, and access the strength, will, fortitude, and passion that you already have to be the best possible "you" that you can be.

And furthermore, I hope that everyday that you see the sunrise, you are in a better place physically, emotionally, and spiritually than you were before.

Be well my friends.

See you in the ocean.

DAVID

Touring The Country From A To Z

March 13, 2008. On this night, I had a conversation in a crowded Manhattan restaurant that moved me. My dinner talk was with Jenna Jannovy, a veteran editor for the ESPN.com website, and we discussed the response I was receiving for an article I'd written for the website. Even though this was the first time we'd met, there was something very cool, genuine, and knowledgeable about Jenna that resonated with me and prompted me not to take any of her words for granted.

When she said that my article had revealed a huge audience of people interested in and inspired by my story, I listened. And when she later said that I was a cross between Ray Kinsella and Forrest Gump, and added, "David, if you stand on your platform and ask, they will come," I listened to and believed her. But it wasn't until she commented that I had a *duty* (as well as a distinct advantage) to do something with that platform, because I "was a real person," and not some fictional character, that I was moved.

I was so moved that I could have spoken with Jenna all night, but had to leave in order to catch my first of two trains that would take me ninety miles back home to Philadelphia. As I hugged her goodbye and rode my bike through the NY streets to the train station, thoughts about Ray Kinsella, Forrest Gump, the number of people surrounding my "platform" and possible ideas for that platform ping-ponged in my head.

Before I go on with the story, you know who Ray Kinsella and Forrest Gump are, right? Ray Kinsella is Kevin Costner's character in the movie *Field of Dreams*, whom the baseball ghosts told to "build it, and they will come." Forrest Gump is Tom Hanks' movie character, who started a league of followers just by running.

I was just in time for the first train to Trenton, New Jersey, but arrived too late for the last train to Philadelphia. Under normal circumstances, that would have left me waiting overnight in the station for the next train, but this wasn't a normal circumstance. Jenna's words would not let me sit still.

Jenna was right. I did have a platform. My email inbox still overflowed with notes from people who had read my story. She was also right when she said that I had a duty to do something with it. *But what?* I thought. I sat fidgeting in the station and then a spark of an idea hit me. It wasn't much, but I was too restless to let it go. Impulsively, I jumped on my bicycle and rode the forty-plus miles home. Along the way, the idea blossomed.

I was going to ride across North America. Again.

I had no idea what I was going to do or hoped to achieve on this ride, but it made sense as I pedaled through the crisp late night air and into the warming sunrise. Later, I thought the idea was crazy, but who else but a crazy man bikes home to Philadelphia from Trenton, New Jersey in the middle of the night?

So, I stuck with it.

Before I continue, I should say that I believe that ideas are powerful and that I instinctively give more time, consideration, and thought as to why any idea will flourish rather than why it won't. If the idea is mine, I approach it with a bit of extra zeal and a willingness to sacrifice in order for it to succeed.

When I got home, I looked back over the emails I had received from readers of my article and gave them serious thought.

One man, in recovery, said that my words about my father had helped him stay clean for one more day.

A whole fourth grade class in Kentucky wrote to me.

A man who had gone to high school with my father ended his note with, "Your father would be so proud."

An elderly African-American woman said that I made her proud.

A mother detailed her morning of lying in bed with her two young sons, a globe, a map of the country, and my article. She thanked me because she said that my words helped give her a "simple moment" that she'd dreamt about since giving birth.

Each note contained raw emotions that touched, honored, and energized me to work harder.

Next, I looked at *Field of Dreams* and *Forrest Gump* again.

After doing all of this, a series of rapid-fire conclusions set the basic parameters for what I was going to do.

Since people were viewing me as some sort of All-American guy, I decided I should do something on America's birthday. So the starting date for my trip would be Independence Day, July 4.

From my previous rides, I knew the prevailing winds blew west to east. So the West Coast was set as my starting point.

Although I am an independent personal trainer and my clients had generously supported my previous endeavors, two months was the absolute longest time I could afford to do this — and that was pushing it. With a July 4 start, ending in September was set.

Since it was my friend's death that had prompted my initial journey and current life path, I decided to end on September 11. That date made ending in New York City pretty much a done deal.

Any "platform stand" I took had to be sooner, rather than later, to capitalize on any name recognition I might have. So doing all of this in 2008 was set.

Now, all I needed was a hook - something to let the people know how touched I had been by the responses I had received.

A lot of ideas bounced around my head until my friend David Mandell said, "Well, Dave, if you are going to ride all the way across North America again just to thank people and show some appreciation, then you might as well help 'em do something."

Dave's comment made everything click.

He was right. This wasn't about me riding through the country; I'd already done that. This trip was about me *doing something* while riding throughout the country.

It was settled. I was going to bicycle solo across North America for the second time, starting from somewhere on the West Coast on July 4 and ending on September 11, 2008 in New York City. And I was going to help people along the way.

I still didn't have a starting point or any idea of who I was going to help or how, but I had more than enough information to start planning. Trust me, I have done more with less.

Once I concluded that I wanted to bike through New Orleans to help the people in that area, a southern route was set. After consulting the people at the Adventure Cycling Association, I set a starting point of San Diego.

I wanted to help everyone, but my time was limited. I narrowed my list down to the groups of people who had recently emailed me: women, children, veterans, and substance abusers.

Next, I took the biggest cities and started matching up various charities. I called the charities and said, "Hi, I am David Sylvester, and I am coming through your city while bicycling across the USA this summer, and I want to volunteer for a day. Yes, I know it's hot…No, I'm not crazy…Yes, I'm sure…No, no, don't hang up, just listen to my story."

It took a lot of calls and explaining, but eventually my solo service tour of the nation fell into place. At the last second, I also decided to try and stop at as many Obama headquarters as possible, but that was secondary to the service work I wanted to do.

I tried to get a sponsor, but no one showed any interest, so I gave a few fundraisers to be able to afford the trip. I raised enough to have an operating budget—not much, about $100 or so per day, but enough. As I said, I am willing to sacrifice for my ideas.

The trip turned out to be amazing, because, in order for it to go smoothly, I needed to rely on the kindness of random people across the nation, and once again, people didn't fail me. This trip also gave me a lot of time to self-reflect and conclude that there was enough of an arc within my story for a book on my travels. In fact, after all that I experienced on this hastily planned and underfunded tour, I believed I was the one to write that book — this book.

But there was a big catch.

I had never written a book before. So, I decided to test myself by writing this chapter. I believed that if I could sum up what I went through on this tour in one chapter, I'd be good enough to write a whole book.

It took many attempts and a few months, but I did it and mailed copies to everyone I met along the tour. Then, I got started right away at writing this book, leaving this chapter as the last one to edit. This version is slightly different (and I hope better) than the one I mailed out, but both versions convey what I wanted to say to everyone.

Which is, in large part: Thank you.

I never saw or spoke to Jenna again, but would like to think that my tour, this chapter, and maybe even this book was the "platform" she spoke of.

With that, I give you: Touring the Country, from A to Z.

A is for Apex.

I have taken part in three cross-continental tours where the route and mostly everything I did was planned out by a touring company. So, I felt a lot of pride when I was able to plan a solo cycling/service tour in less than four months' time. At the time, I felt that this was my personal apex.

My proposed stops were:

San Diego, California: Father Joe's Mission and homeless shelter.

Phoenix, Arizona: The Foundation for Blind Children.

Las Cruces, New Mexico: Mesilla Valley Hospice.

El Paso, Texas: Dismas Charities, a halfway house.

Austin, Texas: Planet Cancer, an organization that helps people in their 20s diagnosed with cancer.

Austin, Texas: Bark for Peace, an organic dog treat manufacturer.

Austin, Texas: The Lance Armstrong Foundation.

Galveston, Texas: YMCA.

Galveston, Texas: Wright Cuny Recreation Center.

New Orleans, Louisiana: New Orleans SPCA.

Mobile, Alabama: Penelope House, a domestic violence shelter.

Nashville, Tennessee: Campus for Human Development, a comprehensive homeless shelter.

Nashville, Tennessee: Magdalene House, a drug addiction center for women.

Washington, DC: Walter Reed Medical Center, US Army hospital.

And lastly, arrive in New York City on September 11, 2008 in time to attend the name-reading ceremony and hear my friend Kevin Leah Bowser's name read.

B is for Breadth.

Sitting in front of my TV, I thought the newscasters gave me a good sense of the destructive swath of Hurricane Katrina. The media's concentration on the city of New Orleans made it seem as if it were the only place really affected. But after biking through the region, I can tell you that TV did nothing to prepare me for the breadth of what really happened to this area.

Riding on the causeway into New Orleans, it was easy to see how a hurricane could devastate a city that sits below sea level. But I didn't get too far into my thoughts, or the causeway, because bicycles weren't allowed. It was only after the police pulled me off the causeway and I hitched a ride into the city that I could continue with my tour or my thoughts.

When I made it into New Orleans and volunteered at the SPCA, I met a diverse cross-section of residents who were more than eager to tell me what they went through and what they felt could have been done differently during the hurricane. I left the city full of these various perspectives, and feeling that I had a good sense of what happened, so I was surprised when I heard another side of the Katrina experience, seventy miles away.

I had just spent the day riding along US 90, a beautifully scenic coastline road that connects the cities of Biloxi Bay, St. Louis, and Gulfport, Mississippi. The day of riding on wide, freshly-paved roads, with the buzz of construction everywhere on my left and white sandy beaches on my right, made all of my thoughts carefree. I walked into a store and innocently asked why this bustling area seemed devoid of people.

The clerk looked at me in disbelief, with eyes that asked "Don't you know?" What he said was, "It's only this way because it all was erased. Katrina took it all." I felt dumb. All I could think was, *This never came through on my TV.*

That night, I didn't find too many people to speak with about their experiences. But, when I got four flats and a shredded tire all before 9:30 the next morning, serendipity brought me the person I needed to talk to. Arthur, of Gulfport, Mississippi, was the only passing motorist who bothered to stop and help me as I sat by the side of the road. He offered to drive me around in his pickup truck to find a bike shop, but didn't quite know where one was. "Things have been shifted around quite a bit," he said.

As we drove along from vacant storefront to vacant storefront, Arthur and I chatted, and two words punctuated almost every one of his sentences: "since Katrina."

When I told him that the news coverage I saw made it seem that New Orleans was the only area really affected by Katrina, the search for the bicycle shop came to an abrupt stop. He said, "You seem like someone that wants to learn, and if that is the case, I'm gonna teach you." We made a U-turn.

For the next two hours, I sat mostly silent while Arthur drove around the Mississippi gulf area, pointing out annihilated shorelines, high water marks on trees that ranged from five to nine feet, open areas that had once been neighborhoods and communities, and other things that never made it to my TV.

The more he spoke, the more I saw. I couldn't help but notice Arthur's pain and frustration as he spoke of uprooted families wanting to rebuild but not even able to afford to stay together. The more we drove, the further away we got from what I thought I knew. I sat stunned and ignorant and scribbling notes about towns like Waveland, Mississippi, a town of 7,000 habitable homes before the hurricane and only 35 after. Really absorbing the fact that Katrina's footprint of devastation involved other cities, counties, and states made me feel awestruck and insignificant in the face of Mother Nature. With eyes wide open, I understood when Arthur said that Katrina's damage was "generational."

Arthur and I never found a bike shop, but I didn't really care, because I found his knowledge much more meaningful. He refused my offer of money for his trouble and "teaching fees," but he did tell me to do something with all the notes that I took.

(I'm trying, Arthur.)

The day after meeting Arthur, I heard a Mobile, Alabama woman's story. Her story was no more special than anyone else's but because I experienced it first-hand, without edits or commercial breaks, I felt the anguish a lot more.

Her home was out of the flood zone, but Katrina didn't know this. Within hours, it was over. Even after the water receded, the simple act of approaching her home was difficult. She told me that she had to disconnect herself emotionally from everything before she returned, because she knew that Katrina had "savagely" reduced her home and everything in it to some stuff that she "just happened to own."

She said that she was able to maintain her focus while doing what work needed to be done. She said that she was even able to maintain her focus while her husband sobbed and searched for ways to save family pictures and other items. She told me that she held it together, but when she found her wedding gown, that was just too much.

That was when she cried.

Even though years had passed since Katrina, seeing this woman's free-flowing tears and watching her rub her fingers as if she were still touching the moldy fabric of her dress made me feel every nuance of her story.

When my tour was over in September 2008, I sat in front of a TV and watched another hurricane reduce another city into twisted rubble. Hurricane Ike destroyed the city of Galveston, which had really rolled out the red carpet for me. Many of the businesses that I had visited or biked past were severely hit or destroyed, places like Island Cycle, Island Bicycle, the YMCA and the Olympia Grille. I spoke with a friend who lives in that area and asked her how bad it was. Despite my experiences, nothing could have prepared me for what I heard: "David, I am so glad you got a chance to see Galveston, because it's all gone now."

C is for John Cooper.

If one person I met on this tour deserves his own letter designation, it is John Cooper, a 70-something-year-old Mohawk, Tennessee resident who restored my faith in humanity and ensured that I would finish this tour —and did it all with one phone call.

John and I met one rainy afternoon at a gas station outside of Mohawk, and he was so enamored with my story that he offered to give me a tour of his airfield. Since it was on my way, I took him up on his offer and pedaled my "Obama for President"-stickered bicycle up the road until I saw a "McCain for President"-stickered truck parked outside a small hangar. Under the cover of his hangar, we sat and had a comfortable conversation about our lives and collective world travels. I use the word comfortable because John told me that he wanted me to meet his parents. I have to admit that I thought John was a little crazy — he wasn't a young guy — but went with it and said, "Yeah, sure."

John took a step out of the hangar into the rain, shielded his eyes, looked up and started speaking quietly. "Mom, Dad, I want you to meet a pretty cool fella ... "

I didn't get up to see what or whom he was talking to at first, but something genuine in his tone made me stand up and step out into the rain with him. Once I did, John pointed toward a rise of land in the distance where a two-story farmhouse stood. I strained to see exactly what John was pointing to against the rainy sky, but took his word that his folks were resting beneath the two headstones I saw.

I didn't want to go, with it still raining and especially after having such a unique parental introduction, but I still had to get some miles in before nightfall. When I got up, John said that he, too, was waiting for the rain to stop because he had another introduction he wanted to give me. "You've had a bike's-eye view of the world. I wanted take you up and be the one who gave you a bird's-eye view of things."

Three days later, little of my life had changed except for the state. I was now in the southwestern corner of Virginia, and it was obvious from the weather reports that I was going to be in unseasonably cool rainy weather for a few days. I still hated cycling in the rain but got on my bike, put my head down, got a steady pace going and just held it.

I held my pace for a few hours on the country roads until a truck pulled up directly beside me. I instinctively veered toward the right, but the road shoulder was washed out, and I had nowhere to move. I gave a side-glance to the truck that was still there, but never took my eye off of my front wheel and where I was going. With no traffic in either direction, I wondered why this guy wasn't moving to his left or even moving on.

I got my answer in the next few moments.

A single burst of gunfire went up in the air.

A haunting cackle came from the truck.

The sound of screeching tires cut through constant pitter-patter of falling raindrops.

The truck sped away up the road.

This moment left me shaking and alone, with only questions to shake me even more.

Was the truck going to turn around and come back toward me?

Was the truck going to turn and around and come back from behind me?

Was the cackling truck driver going to drive to high ground ahead of me and shoot at me?

Why?

I stood looking everywhere, through wet and fogging glasses, and grabbed my phone to make a call.

No service.

Frightened and angry, I biked a few more minutes and stopped to look at my phone. No service.

I biked even further up the road into the surrounding farmland, with my nervous feet slipping off the wet and muddy pedals. Every time I stopped to make a call, there was no signal. I pedaled a little further: still nothing. Then, I walked my bike a few steps further and saw that I had a weak signal. I dialed, but could not hear the person I had called. I barked out the details of where I was into the phone just in case someone was on the other end of the line. I got back on my bike, and kept it moving.

It was seven nerve-wracking miles to the next town, and as I gave the few details I had to the authorities, I realized just how scary this whole scene was.

By the time I got to a hotel and actually had phone service, things had gotten out of hand. The friend I had called earlier apparently could hear me clear as a bell, and when I didn't respond to anything they said, got distressed and called my mother. By the time I spoke with my mother, she was extremely worried, and I was pretty despondent.

"No one cares," I told her. I said I had been kidding myself all of these years to think that I actually was doing anything of value to change the world, and all of my time and energy was a waste. "I am officially out of the human philanthropy business," I declared.

My mother let me rant about no one caring, but when I said that I was going to abandon my planned mission and grab a bus back to Philadelphia, she told me to "relax" and rethink it in the morning.

When I hung up, I was adamant and made plans to ride to the bus station. But all of my plans changed when I checked my voice mail later that night.

An unfamiliar but friendly voice said, "Hey buddy, this is John Cooper, the guy with the airfield. I know that you are a man on a mission, doin' good things and with a schedule, but I also know that it's raining and gonna keep raining, so if you need me to pick you up and take you wherever so you can stay on schedule … well, I'll do it. Like I said, this is John Cooper and I just wanna know that you're safe. Take care, buddy."

That was all it took. This one simple phone call helped me digest the events of the day and strengthened my resolve and faith in life. I called my mother the next day, before I started pedaling, and said, "I'm back in business."

Thank you, John Cooper. You are my angel.

D is for Do.

Someone once asked if I had a personal credo. I didn't, but thought the idea sounded cool. I thought quickly and said, "Do what you can, when you can, as you can, but always do something." In Hoover, Alabama I met a woman who embodied every word of that credo.

I bicycled up to Jack's Family Restaurant for breakfast, leaned my bike on the side of the building, strolled in, and got the unsought attention of every patron in the place. Being 6'3" and 250 pounds in bike tights and a Captain America bike jersey will do that.

While I waited in line, the customers asked me questions about why I was biking that morning and where. By the time I ordered my food, every customer had heard my whole cycling story and purpose. I sat down to eat and map out the rest of my day, but before I could take a bite, the cashier came to my table.

"This is all I have, all I got in tips, and all I can spare, but take it and do some good with it at one of those charities you're working at."

In her hand were 45 cents.

She mistook my surprise and honor as something else. She looked down and said, "I'm sorry. I wish could do more."

It took me a few moments to gather myself, but when I did I said, "Miss, you have already done more than enough."

E is for Emergency.

When I announced that I was going to ride solo across the continent, most of my friends' thoughts turned to the possible dangers I might face. I guess that's normal, but other than the John Cooper story, I came across only two minor emergencies. One was in Arizona.

Because I had biked through the extreme heat of Sudan, Turkmenistan, Uzbekistan, and other places on my previous travels, I believed that I was prepared to handle the heat of the Arizona desert. But maybe because I was older, or alone, or both, there was something about this heat that felt especially wilting. By the time that I pedaled into the small town of Gila Bend at 11 a.m. it was 110+ degrees and I stood, drained, at the motel registration desk, thinking, *I gotta leave a lot earlier in order to beat this.* Looking at a map that showed no road turns and just a straight shot into Phoenix, I decided to start biking at night, when it was cooler.

It was about 2:30 in the morning when I biked from the motel parking lot and still about 88 degrees.

I got on the road, established a nice pace, and kept it. I just cruised along, with my eyes trained at the point on the ground where my battery-operated handlebar light stopped illuminating. Powered by my thoughts and the music in my headphones, I rode for about an hour or so and found myself becoming more and more comfortable in the darkness, using it as a meditative tool.

Just as one of favorite songs came on, a live version of The Allman Brothers' "In Memory of Elizabeth Reed," I came upon a car. It came up so fast — or rather, I came up on the car so fast — that I almost hit it. The car wasn't moving; it was just a car on the side of the road.

The fact of a car wasn't alarming by itself, but the fact that the car was on the side of the road, engine off, all the windows down, no one inside, in the middle of nowhere and in the middle of a starless night – that was alarming as hell. All of a sudden, the darkness I hadn't been paying attention to, had even been taking comfort in, became twisted. I felt immersed, as if potential dangers were just waiting a few inches beyond my light's capability. My mind raced to horrible places.

Maybe the car's occupants had passed me earlier in the night and pulled over to the side of the road to scare and attack me.

That's not my normal thought pattern, but darkness, surprises and fear can really change how you think quickly. My flight instinct said, *Turn off your light so you can't be seen.* I didn't listen to that instinct, because then I wouldn't be able to see. My fight instinct said, *If someone is plotting to attack you, you better give them a whole lot of big Dave.* Now, that made more sense.

I stood up on my pedals, yelled as loud as I could, and sprinted straight ahead. After sprinting and war crying until I was almost breathless, my practical instinct said, *Well, that certainly was a waste of time and energy*.

At that point I stopped, fumbled for my phone and earpiece, and called my friend Maurice back in Philadelphia. Maurice is a long-time friend. He was just stumbling in from a night on the town, and he becomes a real smart-ass when he's been drinking. When I told him what had happened he said, "Hey, this is the part of the movie where the black guy gets killed."

Jerk.

I can be a smart-ass too; I told him he was going to talk to me until the sun came up. Maurice came up with the theory that people had been sleeping in the car, with the seats reclined, and that my screaming had probably scared them more than their car scared me. I doubt it. But I never did find out what was going on in the dead of night.

My other emergency was in Balmorhea, a West Texas town that has springs, spas, and a peaceful feel to it that just naturally s-l-o-w-s you down. It wasn't as hot as Arizona had been, so I reverted back to my normal pattern of being on the road by 6:30 in the morning. Even though I was in the town for only a few hours, I fell under its peaceful charms and wasn't on the road until around 8:30. Okay, it was closer to 9, but I was tired from riding 112 miles the day before and was taking it easy.

Just out of town was a fenced-in ranch. The ranch was nothing special, but the horse on the other side of the fence was. Maybe the horse wasn't that special either, but the way the morning sunlight shone on its coat made the animal look special. When I slowed my pace in order to take the whole scene in, I noticed a barking dog running with the horse.

The horse and dog kept running with me.

Then I noticed a barking dog, another dog, and no horse.

Then it was a barking dog, another dog, and another dog.

Then it was a barking dog, another dog, another dog, and another dog.

Then it was a barking dog, another dog, another dog, another dog, and another dog.

This went on for a few minutes, until I noticed that the barking had stopped. But there still was a dog, another dog, another dog, another dog, another dog, and now, no fence.

The dogs had run in unison while penned up behind the fence. Now free, each was taking different speeds and vectors — but all toward me. I don't know what breeds the dogs were, I think one was a retriever, but all of them were fast.

Within seconds they were all around me. One was angling for my legs, two were running beside me, another was behind me, and I had lost complete sight of the other one. My first instinct was to spray them with my water bottle, but I'd been so tired that morning, I'd forgotten to fill it up. I threw it at one of the dogs to slow him down.

My next instinct was to — big surprise — "give 'em a whole lot of big Dave." But that didn't work either, because just as I stood up to gather more speed and sprint away, the dog I'd lost sight of appeared in front of me. To avoid hitting him, and possibly toppling over and injuring myself, I squeezed the brakes hard. The braking force made my rear wheel jump up and my bike swerve in an unnatural way that startled me and froze the dogs for a second.

The swerve made my front wheel point toward the street, and I pedaled in that direction because there was more room to maneuver. Doing this enabled me to shake a few dogs, but not enough. I kept sprinting, slowing, and swerving on a weighed-down touring bike with a geometry that made it difficult to do any of those things.

Four out of the five dogs eventually gave up, but not the fifth. That dog was the meanest, the strongest, the fastest, and in for the long haul.

I was alone on a stretch of road with nothing left but one final push. Now it was a mad sprint to the death. Focused on just going straight and fast, I stood up and pedaled. I could feel the dog right beside me. I wanted to look but everything I'd learned from sports, skirmishes, and life said, *Don't look back. Just keep moving.*

I'm not perfect. I let my right eye stray and noticed that the dog was trying to get ahead of me, just enough to be able to lunge. I don't really think "dog," but if I were a dog, that's what I would do.

It was only a moment, but it felt longer. The dog leapt and just missed me. I mean *just* missed me. If I hadn't been standing on the pedals, he would have had me. I rode for a few yards until I could see that the dog was heading back to his pack.

Every dog has his day, but that day wasn't it, for either of us.

F is for the Faces.

Being alone gave me a lot of undistracted time to notice things that would otherwise slip by. In that time, I noticed how much I could discover in just one face.

The first face that jumped out at me was on a 100+ degree day somewhere way past El Paso, slightly past Van Horn, but not quite in Fort Stockton, Texas. I was leaning back on a bench, sipping cold water, and enjoying the shade of a truck stop, when a passing trucker walked by and said, "What the hell are you doing biking in this heat?"

Because it was so hot, the trucker didn't even stop to wait for an answer and just left me staring blankly at US 10's steady flow of traffic and asking myself the same question. I sat there pondering, and poured my remaining water over my head — and as I wiped the sweat and water from my eyes, they focused on a set of faces. Faces with the letters M-I-S-S-I-N-G above them, and other faces with the question, "Have you seen me?" below them.

Alone with my thoughts, I found myself wondering where these faces were and whether they were alive or dead. I later pedaled into the heat, thinking about how the faces of the loved ones who had put these posters up had changed since the missing ones had been gone. From that point on, I continued to focus on the faces I came across, and found it illuminating.

Over espresso and muffins in Austin, Texas a cancer survivor's face gave me strength and perspective. An addict's face in Baltimore, Maryland tugged at me emotionally when it said, "Help me," because it reminded me of a recovering addict's face in Nashville, Tennessee that said, "Dave, we all deal with our demons each and every day."

A face I encountered somewhere between Gila Bend and Phoenix, Arizona winced while telling me how it felt to get shot, while a very kind face in Nashville, Tennessee shocked me when it said it had shot someone.

I learned a lot about life and living by just sitting and listening to the residents of a New Mexico hospice, who stared death in the face daily. I wanted to look away from the face of an abuser I met Alabama, and I saw the faces of abuse victims in too many states. The struggling face of a handicapped war veteran in Washington, DC made me question the true price of any conflict. I saw the face of love everywhere — and even caught a glimpse of lust when I saw my own reflection staring at a beautiful woman in Gulfport, Mississippi.

My "face fixation" reinforced the fact that there really is no typical face and made me consider what people noticed about my own face. My smiling face started a great conversation with the wheelchair-bound victim of a drunk driving accident in Scottsdale, Arizona. One woman in Mobile, Alabama wanted a picture of my face because she felt that I was "a winner." But that opinion contrasted sharply with another in Austin, Texas, who looked at my face and called me a "broke loser," and the New Orleans face that called me a self-absorbed, cocky asshole.

I won't begin to tell you who was right or which one was wrong, but it did make me take a hard look at my own face. Here is what I see:

I see eyes that perform poorly on optometrist's exams, but through great life experience, now have an acute sense of vision and foresight. I see a mouth that once only had volume, but now speaks with more value. My skin I treasure, because everything about it reminds me of my mother, from its complexion to the way it helps me endure and keeps me safe, humble, and as beautiful as she. I see a face that beams with confidence because it reminds me of the greatest man I ever knew, my father. But overall, I look at my face and see someone who has evolved and is happy- what more could I really ask for?

It's interesting. Take a look at your own face. What do you see?

G is for Going at the speed of life.

I believe that when you ride a bicycle, you travel amongst people slowly enough to hear and feel what may bother and elate them, but fast enough to not get bogged down by them —unless you elect to.

Whenever you bike to someone, they appreciate your presence even more and admire your effort for just showing up.

On a bike, you create your own scenic overlooks and gain an appreciation of miles, kilometers, time, distance, elevation, temperature, and wind resistance that you would never get in a car.

Once you get off the bike, you have a new vision of yourself and a higher appreciation of your own power.

Essentially, when you are on a bike, you are simply going at the speed of life.

H is for Hugs.

I love hugs, and am proud to have exchanged an embrace's unique warmth in the 45 states and 30-plus countries that I have visited in my lifetime. But in Tempe, Arizona, I received a hug like no other.

The night before my special embrace, I was given a last-second opportunity to give a five-minute speech to more than 150 entrepreneurs at an event sponsored by the Club Entrepreneur Network. My impromptu motivational talk about my travels and what I hoped to encounter on my solo bicycling/service tour engendered such a passionate response that I was easily able to stretch my five minutes of stage time into fifteen. When I finished speaking, I stepped off the stage and right into a sea of hugs and high fives, which felt great. But it felt even greater to secure the promise of three tandem bicycles for my next charity, the Foundation for Blind Children, a campus for people of any age suffering vision loss.

The next day, I addressed a small gathering of the Foundation's students and told them of my gift. They were extremely thankful but puzzled as to why I would do such a thing, especially since I wasn't blind and had no connection to the Foundation or Phoenix. I told them that it was the smile of a blind Kenyan I'd met on my African trip that drove me to do this.

This smiling cyclist had joined our tour in northern Kenya, where I was having a tough time. The conditions were tough, and everyday, I seemed to be breaking something different on my bike. On this one day, it was hotter and more humid than anything we had previously faced, and while riding up a steep hill, I broke the bolt that held my seat. With no extra bolt, I had to ride standing up the rest of the day and take frequent breaks. During one of my breaks, while I sat in the shade and watched other cyclists ride by, grimacing and groaning, I watched this blind Kenyan ride by, smiling.

On the back of this tandem bicycle, this blind man was feeling every sensation that I was, but his beaming smile communicated that he was feeling it all on another level. His grin reminded me of the parts of bicycling that I sometimes take for granted and made me want to give that gift to others one day.

My answer to the Foundation's students prompted a further conversation about dreams and the sensations that make us smile. The more I spoke, the more these students seemed to get the essence of me and started making me cry. When one of the students asked to hug me, I gladly accepted but was totally unprepared for the feeling I experienced.

I know that blindness forces individuals to view inanimate objects with their hands, but never gave any thought to the sensations they felt when viewing living things. I also never gave any thought to how those living things feel being seen in this different manner.

It is electrifying.

Each touch in this large group embrace was different, and each person was in turn "seeing" me differently. One touch/view was light and deft as it went over my back and shoulders. Another contact/glimpse was firmer on my skin and firmer still at my joints. Another brush/sight almost massaged my body.

Each press and knead saw deeper into me. I found myself being viewed in a way that I had never felt or experienced before anywhere on the planet and struggling to think of a way to properly express my appreciation.

By the time I left Phoenix's Foundation for Blind Children, we were all richer. The foundation had received the promise of the three tandem bicycles, and I had received the hug of a lifetime, along with a much broader definition of the word "vision."

This truly was an uneven exchange.

I is for Ideals.

On each of my bicycle trips, I have had the honor of pedaling in established pathways of legendary trailblazers.

In 2002, I started bicycling across North America on Lewis and Clark's famed trail.

In 2004, my first months in Africa were spent following the path of those who charted the course of the mighty Nile.

In 2006, my proposed trip was to bike along South America's scenic Pan-American Highway.

In 2007, the fabled stories of the Silk Route brought me to Asia.

Each trip made my mind wander and wonder about what those before me saw, felt, and thought about while traveling. This tour was no different; I elected to follow part of the Underground Railroad bicycle path (maps provided by Adventure Cycling).

Exercising my personal freedom to travel up and down the very same Alabama and Mississippi hills that Harriet Tubman and others used to free hundreds of slaves forged a deep connection to their achievements. Being on the same landscape and imagining the exact details of the will, courage, effort, sacrifice, organization, wisdom, intellect, and intensity an individual needed in order to escape enslavement vivified each painful point. Whatever I felt grunting and groaning through one pedal stroke after another was nothing compared to the feeling of moving forward during the night while being hunted and hated.

Establishing this connection enabled me to see more. I understood that in addition to everything else, Harriet Tubman had to be a dynamic saleswoman, because she constantly sold the ideal of freedom. She had to communicate the ideal that freedom was not a city or even a destination, but an environment that provided more latitude, safer conditions, and opportunities — and she had to communicate this quickly, quietly, and constantly every time one of her charges looked into her eyes.

I sat outside my air-conditioned hotel room one night, further imagining that she must have had to remind them that their journey was not theirs alone and was going to be a source of power, inspiration, and pride for many generations beyond them. What a woman, and what an ideal.

My trip along the Underground Railroad bicycle path made me more thankful for Harriet Tubman and others for their sacrifice and endurance, and also strengthened my resolve to strive to make the world a more ideal place.

J is for Junk.

I have taken a different bike on each of my cross-continental trips and loved every one of them, except for this one. This bike was, by far, my least favorite. In fact, almost every time I looked at it I thought, *What a hunk of junk!* Who could blame me? In two months of riding I had:

28 flats.

3 different tires.

1 replaced rear wheel.

1 cracked stem.

1 replaced rack.

My cracked stem led to a serious fall in Virginia that made me hate the bike even more. It was my own fault, really. Everyone kept recommending this brand and make, but I didn't listen to that little voice inside my head that said, *Don't do it.* I should have. It probably would have saved me a lot of anguish.

As soon as I finish a tour, I retire my bike by stripping it down to the frame and hanging it on the wall as decoration. Even though it's just a bike, I feel an attachment to the machine, and it feels like dismantling a friend.

Not this time, though.

This time, I couldn't wait to get to a bike shop and take this thing apart. Even now, after some time has passed, I still look at it and think, *What a pile of junk.*

K is for Kiss.

At the Mesilla Valley Hospice in Las Cruces, New Mexico, I delivered lunches to the patients. With each tray of food, I gave a warm smile and offered a big hug. One patient found my hug offer especially delightful.

Her name was Myrtress, and she was adorable. She was so adorable that I asked this seventy-plus-year-old woman if I could give her an extra hug and a kiss. "Ooooh, I'd like that," she cooed.

As I bent down to give Myrtress a peck, her attending nurse stopped me and said that I could not kiss her on the forehead. "That's my spot," she informed me. The nurse explained that she kissed Myrtress on the forehead daily, just to remind her that she was around. Even if Myrtress was sleeping, the nurse said that she would gently give her a kiss before leaving for the day.

I complied, but as I leaned over to kiss Myrtress on her cheek, it was apparent that she had other plans. She smiled, hugged me friskily, and licked my face. Her sly wink afterward made everyone in the room laugh, and left me to carry on my duties with a face red with embarrassment.

At the end of my service day, I went back to each room to say goodbye to each patient. Everyone was sitting up and awake when I stopped by, except for Myrtress, who was lying down. I quietly entered her room with the plan to whisper, "Goodbye," but before I could utter a word, an imprint of full lips on her forehead stopped me. The red dye and wax mark on Myrtress' forehead touched me. It was the perfect signature for a gesture that said it doesn't take much to touch someone's life, and even less to make an impact.

Even though I had nothing to do with it, that kiss will probably go down as one of my favorites of all time.

L is for Life.

Sometimes the damnedest things keep you hanging in there. I met Ann, a ninety-year-old Arizona woman who had outlived her husband, her siblings, and her peer group. She was now the "last man standing." From the way her eyes lit up when I sat down to listen to her story, it seemed that she had just been waiting for someone to let her share her lifetime's worth of perspective. "I have a lot to say," she said, and then promised "to be honest" about it all.

With CNN's Headline News playing in the background, she opened up about everything, from the world affairs that were being covered to a few casual comments about sports.

But Ann saved her fire and passion for speaking about a woman's place in the world. She talked about women fighting for the right to vote, fighting for the right to choose, fighting for the right to be counted, and fighting for the right to be. She said that when she was a girl, women "could not even talk about sex, and now, now, now, women can have it ... As much as they want!" We both laughed at that one.

Ann spoke with such an unrelenting zest that I found myself forgetting her age, and it was only her constant swallowing of saliva that halted her speech and made me see her as she was. But even that worked to Ann's advantage, because it meant that she never wasted a word. It was that zest that drenched her every word, though that also made her statement of recently contemplating suicide almost unbelievable. But I believed her—she had said that she would be honest.

When I asked her about the notion of taking her own life, she said that she had lived a full life and had nothing much to live for. But she wasn't going through with it now, because someone needed her: her candidate.

The 2008 primaries were in full swing, and she was really into politics—*really* into politics. It was her unbelievable passion for voting that kept her hanging on to her life. We spoke for a little while before I had to go, and the cool thing about Ann was that she never tried to sway me to her side, or even revealed her side. She only spoke of the right to be counted. "I don't care," she said, "the black guy, the white guy, the white woman. Just vote," she said. I left shortly thereafter, but as I was leaving, I told her to not to forget to vote.

Ann just balled up her fist and said, "As long as there is a breath in my body."

M is for what can happen in a Moment.

The duties at Las Cruces' Mesilla Valley Hospice were simple, but interacting with patients was essential to all of them. One of the patients, an eighty-year-old man named Robert, was told of my story before I came to visit and visibly excited as I entered the room. When I walked in, accompanied by Scott Miller, my good friend who biked with me from Phoenix to El Paso, Robert flashed an ear-to-ear grin and said, "I am so proud to meet you."

Robert regaled us with stories of every aspect of his life, from his athletic younger days to the first day he rode a bicycle, and right up to his telling his doctors "not to bother" when they wanted to amputate his leg, because it wouldn't prolong his life. "I told 'em to leave me some dignity," he said.

When Scott and I were leaving for the day, we went to Robert's room to say goodbye and extended our hands to shake. He flatly refused, saying that he could not say goodbye while lying down and willed his cancer-wracked body to sit up and then struggled to stand on his withered right leg. Once he stood tall, Robert hugged us both and said that we "added another week to his life."

I was alone in an El Paso, Texas coffee shop when I read an email from the hospice that brought tears to my eyes. It was a note from the staff saying that Robert had passed away; it was only the fourth day of his "added week."

Even though I'd known this man only for moments, I couldn't help feeling hurt. When I called Scott to inform him, his voice cracked in disbelief. "He was so alive … we were going to add a week to his life. He said so," he said.

We were both sad that the energy of our privileged moment with Robert had failed to give him additional time but took solace that we had exchanged a lot during the time we had.

Robert's willingness to struggle in order to stand told us just how special that moment was, and our tears showed just how much had been exchanged.

N is for Names.

What's in a name?

If your last name is Einstein, does that automatically mean you are smart?

If your name is Lance Armstrong, does that mean you can ride a bike?

I don't know about those things, but I do know that there is a cross-continental bike ride in your destiny if your name is David Sylvester.

I can say this comfortably, because at the very same time I was riding my bike across the continent, taking a southern route, another man named David Sylvester was taking a northern route on the Tour De Dog.

That David Sylvester was riding across the country with his dog, Chiva, in order to enhance awareness for animal shelter issues. We discovered each other because each of our friends were doing online searches for press information and found the other.

I gave David a call while I was stuck in Galveston waiting out Tropical Storm Edouard. We had a long talk. I discovered that in addition to sharing the same name, we were finishing our tours around the same time and even lived near each other.

When we were done cycling, David and I made arrangements to meet for lunch, along with Chiva, of course. I was running late for the meeting, and David called to see where I was. The friend I was with saw the name David Sylvester on my phone and asked, "How are you calling yourself?"

"It ain't me," I said.

O is for the power of One.

In August 2008, I became the very first bicyclist to cross the Galveston causeway, legally. This crossing, which came with a police escort and news photographers, happened because I have personally replied to every email that I have received— every one. Doing this isn't easy and has taken a lot of time but I have been so touched by what people have written that I have to.

One of those emails was from a Texas grad student named Zeeyon who remained in touch with me over the years. When she heard that I was bicycling through Texas as a part of my tour, she told me that "I had to come to Galveston," and that, if I did, it would be worth it. I obliged and rode into Houston where I met her friend, Ron Contreras, and his brother. With his brother providing support, Ron and I spent the seventy-mile ride into Galveston talking about my travels and my belief that I could change the world, or at least enhance it, by giving one smile, one high five, and one hug at a time. I kept yapping to Ron but never got the sense that he took my beliefs too seriously until we got to the causeway entrance.

Once we got there and he saw the members of the press, the police, city councilman Juan Pena, UTMB Nursing School Dean Raymond Lewis and others, I believe he changed his mind a bit. After meeting Zeeyon for the first time and starting on the causeway, I was aware of the stiff headwind, aware of the people honking and cheering while hanging out of passing cars, and aware of other cyclists, but I didn't really feel it. I sensed everything while cycling, but was only aware of one thing: Ron's screaming, "One man can change the world! One man can change the world!" over and over again.

Ron's words gave me more than enough energy to sprint away, but humbled me enough to restrain myself, so I could hear him say it just one more time.

P is for Packing.

For my first trip across North America in 2002, I packed a laptop, two pairs of cycling shoes, four pairs of cycling shorts and jerseys, more clothes than I needed, toiletries, two rain jackets — yes, two — and more.

For my Africa trip, I packed everything listed above and also brought along more clothes, a tent, a sleeping bag, mosquito netting, malaria medication, and even more toiletries. I took so much that I forget until I see pictures and think, *Wow, I forgot I packed that*.

For South America, it was easy to remember what I packed, because it was all returned to me, smashed, after it was gathered from the scene of my accident.

For my Asia, trip I packed … well, it doesn't really matter, because when I got kicked off the trip, I had to throw most of it away.

Packing for anything, let alone a cycling adventure, is tough. Before you set one foot out of your door or pedal one mile, your thoughts are consumed with "What am I going to take?" and, more importantly, "What can I comfortably leave behind?", each question defining the line between "What I want" and "What I need" more and more.

I needed a clearly defined want-need line with this trip, because there was no support—it was just me. With that in mind, I packed light and tight and only took two pairs of cycling shorts, two jerseys, a pair of quick-drying convertible pants, a quick-drying shirt, a pair of sandals, a laptop, a pair of flip flops, a first aid kit, some basic toiletries, and not much else. Even though many other things would have brought me comfort, I couldn't afford the weight. Even if I could carry the weight, I didn't have the space. But as with every trip, there is one thing that weighs next to nothing and takes up no space, yet always provides enough ballast to keep me moving forward: music.

I know that I am not being a shining example of the safe cyclist by saying this, but it is the truth. I really don't think that I could get from here to there without some tunes and my headphones. Whether it is Mobb Deep, The Smiths, The Allman Brothers, Sleater-Kinney, Pete Rock, Elliott Smith, Art Blakey, Prince, Atlas Sound, Blu and Exile, J Dilla, Liz Phair, Raphael Saadiq, old school hip hop, old school R&B, or something new that I just latched onto at a cafe, music is the diverse and universal language that moves me across the planet.

Q is for the Quality of food.

People often ask me to comment on the quality of food I have eaten, assuming that it is better in the USA than in Africa or Asia.

I won't say any place is better or worse, but I will say that they are very different.

In Africa and Asia, getting food was often simple. I would walk through an open-air market, see pieces of an indigenous animal grilled or stewed with some type of herb-based sauce, point, purchase, and eat. It was real simple: What I saw is what I got.

Here in the USA, eating food is a tad more complicated. You are drawn into places by soothing color schemes and cleverly-crafted imagery and then you read a menu that describes things with the most tantalizing terms. You think that you are ordering something reasonably wholesome, but the actual food product that reaches your body has been over-prepped, blanched, nitrated, and nuked by more engineers in lab coats than any one caring person in an apron. This is all an oversimplification, but you've essentially purchased just the illusion of food: What you see is what you want.

I never thought about food that deeply, but something on this tour made me think a lot. I was on a seriously tight budget, for starters, which meant that every decision I made was based on expense. By eating what I could afford as opposed to eating what would nourish my body, I ate at many of the same establishments and ate the same things as many Americans on a daily basis. Yet, by the time I had biked from San Diego to Mobile, I hadn't lost any weight. My conditioning had improved, but the weight loss I had experienced by this point on other tours was not there.

If I didn't lose weight after bicycling 60-80 miles a day — which means that I actually gained weight — then what chance does the average sedentary American have? What chance does anyone have?

This section is not about bashing any particular restaurant, so I am not naming any. This is about how the "What you see is what you want" thought process keeps us eating low-quality food, which in turn keeps us heavier and unhealthy. I will admit it: on this tour, it was tough to eat healthy.

Maybe I should amend that last sentence.

I should say that, with the endless cycle of repetition of chain restaurants where even the wait staff looks alike and only the zip codes truly differentiate each eatery, it is easy to eat unhealthily. Too easy.

But all is not lost. The times that I did eat at locally-owned restaurants, it was fresher and tastier and was served by independent owners and mangers who spoke openly and passionately of buying local, farming local, hiring local, promoting local, and keeping the money local.

All of them gave me the biggest smiles and best hugs, and most wore buttons or had banners hanging in their storefront windows that repeated the battle cry: Keep Austin Weird! Keep Mobile Funky! Save Staunton!

These were places like:

- The Purvine winery in Tempe, Arizona
- The Drifter Pancake house in Silver City, New Mexico
- Chope's in Las Cruces, New Mexico
- Kinley's Coffee House in El Paso, Texas
- Emerald City Press in Austin, Texas
- Fair Bean Coffee in Austin, Texas
- Smooth Tony's in Galveston, Texas
- The Spot in Galveston, Texas
- Baja Bean Co. in Staunton, Virginia

If we aren't careful, we will squander the best and coolest thing about this large and diverse country: the individual spirit.

R is for Revolution.

I don't know if the Latin phrase *in vino veritas*, which means "There is truth in wine," applies to beer, but it should. Over some beers, I was talking with a friend, Harvey Cohen, about my plans to ride and volunteer my way across the nation, and he said, "Dave, you aren't just talking about simply doing a bike trip, you are talking about a revolution."

He was right. I was talking revolution, but not the violent overthrow kind. My revolution was an organic and beautifully human type of revolution that was predicated on people recognizing and sharing their power and influence. Let me explain: I know that there is a lot of power within my smile. My smile can be the difference in someone's day being great or crappy, so I go to a lot of places smiling. The acknowledgment of that power boosts my self-confidence and makes each moment of each smiling encounter of each day exciting and potentially great. So, then I go to even more places smiling.

Now here is the revolutionary part —your smile is as powerful as mine, maybe even more so because I'm sure you're better looking than me.

That means you have the power to change lives.

Harvey and I had more beers and worked out the tour tagline: "How Many Revolutions Are in You?" It fit because the word revolution could reference the turn of a bike wheel as well as the revolution that could be started by, stimulated by, emboldened by, and transferred by something as simple as a smile.

So I set out on my cycling-service, unaware of my service tasks, but prepared to do them all smiling in order to make someone's day more pleasant. Here are some other revolutionaries I met along the way:

The people who slapped my outstretched hand to give me five as I biked by were revolutionaries, because they made me pedal harder.

Melanie Andrews, a woman I'd never met before, is a revolutionary because she met me at 5:00 a.m. on the first day of my tour to feed the homeless alongside me.

Larry and Sheryl Leonard are revolutionaries because they took part of their vacation time to be with me and make sure that my tour got off to a good start.

The Phoenician female runner who winked at me as we passed each other is a revolutionary because she made me smile for the rest of the day.

The drunk guy in a Delaware bar is a revolutionary because he gave my tired body a much-needed emotional boost when he said, "Even drunk, what you are doing sounds cool."

Edu, an eleven-year-old boy in a coma whom I held hands with was the most special revolutionary I met, because without saying a word, he communicated a lot with me.

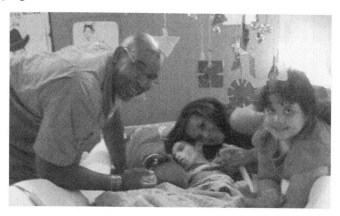

I have an infinite amount of smiles, high-fives, hugs, and revolutions within me.

How Many Revolutions Are in *You*?

S is for Safety.

The concept of safety meant different things in different places but meant something everywhere.

The word itself was printed in the various signs, pamphlets, and guidelines that I had to sign at every place I gave service. The feeling of safety was something I felt as I walked through the many security checks at Father Joe's Missions in San Diego. I felt another facet of safety as I listened to the homeless residents tell me how much it meant to have a warm meal and a comfortable place to eat it.

The concept of safety existed in the craftsmanship that went into the extra-large corridors, soft edges, railings, and other protective details for the blind individuals who went to the Foundation for Blind Children in Phoenix, Arizona.

Sometimes being kept safe meant not being seen, as for the women at domestic violence shelters where anonymity was paramount.

One elderly woman told me that more than anything else, "Everyone needs a safe place."

Safety wasn't only for humans, either. At the New Orleans SPCA, safety meant that well-maintained, climate-controlled trailers stayed parked in a nearby lot so they could whisk animals to another state in case of another hurricane.

Safety existed in many forms and even salvaged a speech I gave. During a presentation I was giving to homeless men at Nashville, Tennessee's Campus for Human Development, a man stood up and asked what could they possibly learn from my story of bicycling all over the world. "We can't even get across the city," he said.

I was about to say one thing, but a huge sign above the door that read, "Help Keep This Environment Safe," changed my thought pattern.

I told the man it was not my expectation for him, or anyone else, to get on a bicycle and ride anywhere, but only to respect my story and try to draw a parallel to his own. I pointed to the boldly lettered sign and said that that if my travels around the planet had taught me anything, it was that anything could be done from a position of safety.

I told them that when you are unsafe, you clamor like a fiend for your safety. Once you attain that safety, you exhale while planning how to get to an even safer place. I told them a story about a time on my travels when I felt unsafe and the resourcefulness I had found within myself to extract myself. I told them to look around and take stock of where they were. "This is a safe place," I said. I added that if they took advantage of the books, tools, people, and programs available to them, in this safe place, the possibilities for that man and others were endless.

My answer rambled on but it was enough for the homeless man to say, "Thanks, man."

T is for Tapestry.

I was by myself on this tour but never alone because I was constantly surrounded, protected, enhanced, empowered, and warmed by a beautiful tapestry of people. Each thread was vibrant—black or white, McCain supporter or Clinton backer or Obama follower, man or woman, wealthy or homeless—and were interwoven to create a vital garment for me. Here are just a few threads:

Alexis, we met at a picnic table in Lexington, Virginia, and you put me up in your mother's home in Staunton. The great hospitality was worth the three wasp stings I received. Thank you.

Kim, from Chicago, we met over laundry in Galveston, and you have gone on to read countless chapter drafts—Thank you.

Katrina, we first met in Lanzhou, China, when you lived in Seattle. We kept in touch and met again in Washington, DC, and you joined me a day later in Baltimore, Maryland to ride with me to Newark, Delaware. Thank you.

The Texas A&M couple who picked me up when I had a flat in desolate West Texas and happened to have read my ESPN story—what are the odds?— thank you.

Melissa of Austin, Texas - since we are talking about odds, what are the odds that we happen to meet and that your mother and my friend, Kevin, worked together at the same company and died together on the same floor? God bless them both. And thank you.

The pleasurable experiences I had in Gila Hike and Bike in Silver City, New Mexico; Landis Cyclery in Phoenix, Arizona; Mellow Johnny's in Austin, Texas; and Black Dog Bikes in Staunton, Virginia made all of my flat tires and bike issues worth it. Thank you.

The Balmorhea, Texas woman in the restaurant who struggled over to me with her walker to give me a good luck hug and pay for my meal—thank you, your touch was honoring.

The heavily tattooed motorcycle guy at the Virginia gas station who gave me a Gatorade and said, "I have no idea what you are doing or where you are going, but whatever it is, you are earning it," while I lay out flat, napping on the concrete— thank you for acknowledging my effort.

Patricia, from New Mexico, chaps and a smile never looked so good. Thanks.

Cheryl of Knoxville, Tennessee, thank you for taking the initiative and helping me continue on.

Heidi, of Austin, Texas—to be called the "real deal" from someone with your strength, beauty, and spirit meant the world to me.

Ilana, your words and feelings infused me with strength.

Nashville City Councilwoman Erica Gilmore, thank you for the proclamation.

Ruth, from Istanbul, this trip would not have happened without you.

U is for Underestimating.

On my other trips around the world, I always had someone around to speak with about any emotional encounter that I came across. There was always another person riding beside me or around the campfire that could provide me with a sounding board or another lens to look through. But on this trip, I had no other lenses or sounding boards and, for all of the mental preparation I put into this trip, I grossly underestimated what those people meant to me. I hadn't planned on hearing so many stories of abuse, pain, rape, violence, murder, anguish, stress, strain, hard times and struggle. At the same time, I hadn't planned on feeling such warmth, seeing such happiness, or hearing such triumph. It was a lot to take at times.

My friend, Scott Miller, gave service with me at both the Foundation for Blind Children and the Mesilla Valley Hospice and discussed the feelings that these places tapped into while pedaling along with me in days that followed. Before leaving to fly back home, he asked how I was going to get through the rest of the trip and stopped me when I rambled on, only alluding to what I might encounter physically.

"I'm not worried about that," he said, referring to my body. "What are you going to do about that?" he said, pointing toward my heart.

All I could say was, "I don't know."

And I didn't know, though I did end up handling things the way I normally do when I underestimate things: I biked some, cried some, smiled some, cursed a lot, thought more, hugged more, felt more, wrote some, talked a lot about what I was experiencing, and opened my heart a little wider. It's the only way I know to deal with things.

V is for Volunteer.

I entered into each place that I volunteered the same way: unprepared to do anything specific but willing to do anything that needed to be done. My openness about my intent and actions, I believe, made my trip more interesting, because it opened the door for each executive director to give me a variety of things to do, and those tasks wound up preparing me for other things down the road.

In San Diego, I unloaded trucks and prepared meals at a homeless shelter. That prepared me to do the same thing at the hospice in Las Cruces. In Phoenix, I gave a talk to a blind audience, which prepared me for an audience of homeless men in Nashville who initially didn't see any value in me or anything I had to say. I walked dogs in Austin, which prepared me for walking more dogs in New Orleans.

Giving service for a few days at a domestic violence shelter in Mobile gave me credibility when I spent a half-day at an addiction center for women in Nashville. Having friends and family members who had passed away from cancer prepared me for conversations I had with people at a cancer treatment center in Austin. Each step I took helped me for another step or opened the door for another conversation.

Sometimes, though, it wasn't my past volunteering duties that opened up doors.

I had a bad fall on my bike in Virginia that left me scraped, bleeding, and badly bruised. I was still pretty banged up two days later when I went to give service at Walter Reed Army Hospital, so I took a nap while waiting to speak with a volunteer coordinator. With bandages on my forearms, a scrape on my face, three lumps on my head from where I'd been stung by a wasp three days prior, and wincing at every movement, I must have looked horrible.

After a few minutes, a vet limped over with a cane to sit in a chair across from me. We sat staring at each other for a few minutes, until he asked, "When did you get back?"

When I told him that I wasn't in the service, and was just biking and volunteering across the country he said, "Is that what that shit does to you?"

"It seems to be what it does to me," I said.

W is for Wonder.

I walked away from my day in the Walter Reed Army Medical Center's physical therapy unit wondering about the true cost of war.

Are the trillions of dollars that we are now spending worth the pain, the lost years, the lost limbs, disfigurement, displacement, dysfunction, anguish and glaring memories that our brave men and women will have to constantly pay throughout their lives? I don't know, but it makes me wonder.

I spoke with one patient who was doing recuperative therapy. He paid a steep price by losing an eye. He will continue to pay an even steeper price because there is still shrapnel in his body that can trigger severe muscle spasms and reduce him to kneeling and quivering.

We spoke while he was working with a physical therapist and I knew, from his gaze at the motivational posters of amputee athletes striking triumphant poses that adorned the unit's walls, that he wasn't listening to his therapist's plea to "take it easy."

He launched right into an exercise, overexerted himself and, within seconds, was writhing around on the floor in pain. He repeated this routine of ignoring, looking, overexerting, screaming and writhing with continuing diminished utility until I stopped him to ask why he was pushing so hard.

"I don't want to be a pussy," he said.

I will freely admit that from my civilian perspective it is easy for me to question things, but after walking the pristine grounds of Walter Reed and seeing and meeting so many wounded men and women, I wondered, *When is enough, enough?*

When will we know that we have won?

More importantly, when will we know that we may have lost too much?

X is for X-factor.

I endured my 2006 car accident because of my friends and expressed my appreciation for them by taping their pictures all over the bicycle that I took on my next trip from Istanbul to Beijing. Their images became the "X-factor" that turned my bicycle into something that looked odd but gave a clear message to even the most casual onlooker: these people meant something to me.

The kindness of humanity made this tour a success. So, to honor them, I took them into New York City with me.

On September 9, I bicycled into my hometown of Philadelphia and went straight to my favorite bike shop. From there, I walked down the street to a drugstore and printed up pictures of the people I'd encountered across the nation. I then went back to the bike shop, taped *those* pictures all over my bike, and turned my bike into a force.

"Me" became "we," and we then pedaled north, toward New York City.

Y is for hearing, "You matter."

On my first day of this tour, I met Bob Babbitt at a roadside diner in Pine Valley, California. He had just biked down a mountain pass that I was about to pedal up and asked me where I was going.

My casual reply, "New York," started a conversation about our lives that ended with an invitation to be interviewed on his "Competitor Radio" show, a radio program devoted to athletes.

Days had passed, and by the time we did the interview, I was in Gila Bend, Arizona, and Bob was in his San Diego studio. One of Bob's questions was what he or his audience could do to help me. Again, I answered casually, and said, "267-252-1974." He asked if I was sure that I wanted give my phone number out on the air, especially since his show was podcast worldwide.

"Sure," I said, telling him that I was energized and fueled by people, and that anyone inspired, motivated, or touched by my story should text or call me.

I told people that they mattered to me, and they told me "you matter" right back. In the weeks ahead, I received text messages and calls from Indonesia, Chicago, Los Angeles, Nashville, Europe, and other places around the world. The messages varied from a simple "Thank you" or "Pedal on, brother" to people telling me of weather systems I was about to go through.

Each message kept me connected, made me smile, and said "You matter" loud and clear.

Z is for Zenith.

September 11, 2008. I woke that morning in a Jersey City hotel feeling weird. I didn't oversleep, wasn't sick, or anything like that—I just felt a bit out of sync. The *weird* feeling I had made me stop a few times while cycling to catch the train that was going to take me across the bay and into New York to see if I had forgotten anything back at the motel. I hadn't, so I continued on.

Right after paying my fare at the station and lifting my bike over the turnstile, a transit police officer stopped me to say that it was not permitted to take a bicycle on the train during the morning rush hour. With the name reading ceremony due to begin in an hour or so and unaware of any other way to get into the city, I thought, *Please don't let some petty rule stop me when I'm this close.* I looked at the officer and started babbling about my friend Kevin's death, my reason for being there that day, my reason for traveling to Africa and Asia, my reason for everything. I listed every country, named most of the states, and even pulled a New Mexico newspaper clipping where I was featured out of my panniers. I did all of this along with saying "please" a dozen times.

The officer eventually let me pass, and though I was back on my way, I still felt off. I was content to ignore whatever I was feeling and made small talk with an African-American man in his early fifties standing on the platform. After talking about he train schedule and the weather that day, the man asked, "What's up with you today?"

I could have taken his question in a lot of ways, but I took it innocently and as confirmation that my "weird" feeling was real and visible. In order to explain what was "up" with me, I started to using the same words that I used with the officer minutes earlier. But, unlike when I was with officer, I took my time when speaking. Right then, I realized why I felt weird.

From the moment I woke up and heard the morning news reporters reliving the horrors of 2001 to riding through the quiet, almost somber, Jersey City streets to standing on a train where no one was grinning, I was smiling.

I was happy, but my personal feelings weren't in sync with the rest of the community. I was happy because something that was casually said to me on March 13, months earlier, had sparked an idea that morphed into giving charitable service, registering voters, hugging, high-fiving, and doing a lot of smiling across California, Arizona, New Mexico, Texas, Louisiana, Mississippi, Alabama, Tennessee, Virginia, Maryland, Washington DC, Delaware, Pennsylvania, New Jersey, and New York. I felt electrified by achievement.

Jimmy was the man's name. He was an elevator mechanic who worked in Manhattan on 9/11 and we continued our train-chat up from the subway to the street. As I stood listening to his every word about how his life had changed since that day, I found myself feeling guilty for feeling good.

Who was I to feel this way?

Who was I to feel this way on this day?

I imagine that just like many of the people who confided in me throughout my trip, I found great comfort in the presence of a stranger willing to stand there listening to what I was truly feeling. Almost cutting him off with eyes that were on the verge of being watery, I said, "Jim, I gotta tell you, right now I feel kind of shitty for feeling this good."

Jimmy told me not to feel guilty but to consider myself lucky, extremely lucky, for what I had experienced. He also noted that I looked more peaceful than happy, which was something he claimed he didn't seen often. His words felt like permission to fully accept what I was feeling. His accompanying hug was just what I needed and felt like a blessing. I wanted to talk longer, but Jimmy ushered me along by looking up the street and saying, "You got things to do."

And I did.

I bicycled away from Jimmy to meet Denise, Kevin's sister, and listened to her read her brother's name at the name reading ceremony. After the ceremony, I walked along with the thousands of family members, friends, and visitors down to the Ground Zero site to place flowers and then onto a memorial museum adjacent to a nearby firehouse. I slowly pecked my way through the crowded museum until I got to a wall that was filled with victims' pictures. Seeing the collage of faces and understanding that this was the closest any of us would come to feeling the warmth of their smiles again was overwhelming.

I stared at Kevin's face in a picture that was taken on his wedding day. I looked at the picture and had a quiet conversation with him, feeling a sense of loss and grief mixed with anger. I felt a lot of things but after being warmed by a tapestry of people, moved by revolutionaries, and meeting people like John Cooper, any negative feelings that I had about people only rested atop a bedrock of hope and passion for humanity. I stayed, staring at Kevin's picture, until my conversation was complete and then I left.

With my trip officially over, I spent the rest of the day walking around, calling friends, jotting trip notes down, reflecting, and admitting to myself that I had been wrong. 183 days earlier, I'd thought that thinking of and planning out this tour was as good as I could do—my apex. But the act of executing those plans and completing my earlier thoughts opened many doors to other ideas — and if I wanted to make any, or all them, tangible, I had to challenge myself to make them so. Realizing that there never really was an apex for me, nor any real zenith either, made me feel beautiful and boundless.

One man really can change the world.

State of Dave 2009

As soon as I finished my second ride across North America in 2008, I got right to work on writing *Traveling at the Speed of Life*. I knew what I wanted to say with my stories and believed that I could achieve it if just put the time in. That said, writing this book whittled my life down to two things:

- *Traveling at the Speed of Life*

- Everything else.

I didn't send out a "State of Dave" in 2008, but I believe that I ended up doing something much more meaningful.

By now, going in the ocean was a very personal New Year's Day tradition that I wasn't interested in breaking so I was up, out and at the beach by 5:30 in the morning. While driving there, I thought of the 365 days prior, the 365 days ahead and—as always—my friends. I raced into the ocean just as I had done before but afterward I dropped to my knees and began writing my wishes and the names of my friends in the sand, because I wanted them with me. Scrawling all of this into the shoreline while the first sunrise of 2009 warmed me felt great and I stood there to admire my work.

But I didn't stand long. I had to get home to write.

Faceless Angels

Traveling at the Speed of Life is a book about the simple encounters I had while bicycling around the world in order to detail a greater lesson (or lessons) that I may have learned. But some stories started right in my hometown of Philadelphia, long before I ventured onto my first biking adventure around the planet, and didn't reveal their deeper meaning until many miles and many years later. This is one of those stories.

Back in 1994, I was bored at my job and would often look for any excuse to take a break from it. When a coworker asked me to take a walk with him to the bank, I leapt at the chance. While we stood in line, one of the tellers caught my eye. She captured my attention so much that when my friend went up to one teller window, I went up to hers.

Nicola was her name, and we started talking—nothing deep or complicated. We just exchanged a few simple words between

"How do you do" and "Nice to meet you." But something special about her made me offer to walk with my coworker the next time he went to the bank. She was so special that I continued going back to that bank, day after day and without my coworker, just to stand in her line and talk to her. I didn't even have an account at that bank. I just wanted to see her.

Her pretty, smiling face and happy personality were enough to make me look right past the fact that she sometimes wore sunglasses indoors, and believe her when she said, "Oh these? I fell."

Nicola had a boyfriend and I had a girlfriend, but that was never an issue, because we never exchanged phone numbers or ever made plans to meet outside of her teller window. We were content with the brief bits of laughter and friendship we had through the bank's pane of bulletproof glass.

One sunny day, I went to the bank and asked Nicola to have lunch outside with me. She said that she had packed a lunch and was going to eat inside. When I said that it was too nice to eat inside, she flatly stated that she always ate in and never went outside. She never went anywhere, she said.

The day I asked Nicola to go outside just to share a meal was pivotal in our friendship, because that was the day she started sharing the details of her life. Over the next few days, Nicola and I spent our work hours chatting about her boyfriend's controlling ways. I sat on the other end of the line, listening to stirring revelations that had me going to the bank to beg for her permission to help. But she would always say "no" and leave me standing there, feeling helpless.

Nicola didn't speak about her life as much for a while, and when she finally agreed to meet me for lunch at a nearby food court, I thought that things were better. But as soon as I saw her walk up to me I knew they weren't. She stood out from the crowd, wearing a bright red coat, a black skirt, and a gorgeous hairstyle, but her eyes, covered with huge dark shades, told the real story.

When she saw me, she told me not to hug her or even act like I knew her. She just wanted me to get my food and then go sit down at one of two adjoining tables in a far corner of the food court. She followed and sat at the other table. We sat there, at these separate tables, speaking of her boyfriend's emotional, verbal, and physical abuse. The more she spoke, the more incensed I became. The more urgency she sensed from me, the less she spoke.

Nicola left me no choice: if I was to be her friend, I would have to just sit there and listen. I made the easy decision to be her friend. But it was a hard price to pay.

Over the next few days, while I should have been working, I sat on the phone listening to Nicola paint an excruciatingly vivid picture of her life. It was hard to idly listen to the jagged and ensnaring details of her relationship, which had most of her days starting off with "Wake up, bitch." It was even harder to hear her recount how her boyfriend's jealousy of her position and potential had eroded her will of even taking a promotion that might enable her to move on. Hearing all of this was all so difficult because I couldn't do anything; she was afraid and would not let me provide any assistance. We were both shackled.

But something happened within Nicola, and one day, she left him.

When Nicola did leave her boyfriend, she cut off contact with me. She needed time and space to "figure things out" and told me that she would contact me when she was ready. I gave her that space.

A few months passed before I stopped by the bank again and when I didn't see my friend at a teller window, I smiled and thought, *She's moved on*. I asked the bank manager where Nicola was and she said, "She's gone." But even though I didn't want to believe it, I knew from the manager's tone of the voice where my friend.

Nicola was dead.

By exercising her free will, Nicola was unaware that she had flipped a deadly switch in her ex-boyfriend's mind and put herself in the most vulnerable position of all. One morning, soon after moving out to a new apartment, Nicola was ambushed by her ex-boyfriend and killed.

I went to see her mother that day. By that time, Nicola had been buried for almost two weeks and her mother looked emotionally broken. Meeting any friend's parent can be awkward, but what do you say when the first time you meet that parent is after that friend's funeral and their killer is still on the loose? Her mother spoke to me directly as she told me that her daughter spoke fondly of me and referred to me as one of the "good ones." But her focus and gaze, through very still, puffy, and bloodshot eyes, never strayed too far from an array of pictures of Nicola on the mantle.

Sitting next to Nicola's mother as she held my hand in an effort to console me felt surreal. I heard myself telling her to call if she needed me, but I was telling a lie. I hoped that her mother would never pick up the phone to make that call. The circumstances surrounding Nicola's life and violent death were much more than I could handle. I was barely hanging in there and knew that there was nothing that I could do for her.

So, moments after bicycling away from her mother's home and hours from learning of her death, I unconsciously decided that I didn't want to even think about Nicola anymore and started to bury her in the depths of my mind. The year was 1995, and in less than a year, I had met, befriended, lost, and buried a very nice woman.

Sprinting ahead to 2008, I was now planning the *Let This Be the Moment Tour,* my service-oriented tour. The tour was my brain-child, a way of thanking the huge number of people who had read and responded to an article I wrote for ESPN. This tour was a part of my ongoing effort to change the world, one smile, one hug, one high-five, and one person at a time.

My plan to achieve all of this in the summer of 2008 was to bicycle from San Diego, California on July 4 and to arrive in New York City on September 11 with weekly stops of service at various charitable organizations. In an effort to try to touch every demographic possible, one of the places I contacted was Penelope House, a battered women's shelter in Mobile, Alabama.

I was totally unaware of just how pervasive and insidious domestic violence is in our society and was surprised by their evasive response to my initial call to make arrangements for my visit. When I was innocently trying to ask questions, I had no idea that the female switchboard operator believed that I might be a stalking husband looking for information about the location of the shelter.

Long before I flew to San Diego to start my journey and months before I'd pedaled one mile toward Mobile, Alabama's

Penelope House, the purity of my story, identity, and intentions were checked and re-checked again. Even after all of the vetting the administrators insisted on my bicycling to a Mobile parking lot where they would then drive me to Penelope House.

I hadn't set foot in the building or spent time with the women, and already domestic violence had grown beyond my comprehension.

Penelope House was a tough building to find and an even tougher one to get close to. As we approached the Penelope House property, the administrators stopped the van so they could give me an overview of the grounds. Standing atop a ridge, I looked down at a simple building surrounded by a deep gully. Minutes later, we drove under the watchful eye of a few cameras and through a series of automated gates. I got out of the van, and from that vantage point—looking up at the ridge and down at the gully—I felt secure, because it felt as though even Mother Nature herself was trying to shield these women from harm. But all of my suppositions of security were twisted into an extreme sense of vulnerability when one of the social workers casually told me that each of those safeguards was there because someone had tried to bypass them.

A man had tried to ram the single gate, so now a double one existed.

A man had tried to scale the ten-foot fence, so now it was topped by razor wire.

A man had even misused Mother Nature's serene ridge by turning it into a sniper's perch.

By the time that I actually stood outside the door, I had been screened, re-screened, and chaperoned past automated gates and electronic sensors. But before we actually entered the building, I was again reminded that strict anonymity was the primary means of safety for any domestic violence shelter, and that the Penelope House's residents had to remain anonymous in order to remain safe. Because of that, I

- Could not take pictures of the residents or their children.

- Could not reveal their location.

- Could not mention any names or specifics in articles or books.

I went to Penelope House with the clear and simple objective of presenting myself as a model of a good man. But as I stood behind a demarcated line on the floor and on the other side of a steel door, waiting for a facility-wide announcement that a sanctioned male was on the premises, and I thought about the underlying meaning behind all of these rules and safeguards, I knew this wasn't going to be easy.

While the words, "A male is on the premises" repeated again, it occurred to me that Penelope House was not like the many foreign countries I had visited on bicycle trips, where a language barrier or few custom differences or even a varied terrain might have slowed me down in getting to where I wanted to go. Here, I stood at the threshold of something much deeper: a culture created by violent men who did not know how to respect or treat women that went on to cast an intensely dark shadow where many of the children growing up in this culture would mimic the violent relationship patterns they'd seen. This was a place that might not have any use for my smile or hugs. Without my smile and hug, I openly wondered what I could really hope to achieve at Penelope House. But like so many other challenges that I found myself in throughout life, I was totally immersed, and there was nothing left to do but get oriented and move forward.

My tour of the one-floor haven for women and children was an exercise in contrasts, because these women could not have many of the things that I, as a male who has never suffered abuse, would need and desire if I were in need of healing.

When I am stressed, I find the sun healing. But the inside of the facility remained relatively dim, with small frosted glass windows, because plain glass provides a sightline and big openings can be trespassed. Where I would want to see a picture hanging on the wall, or look at a mirror, all I saw were red panic buttons. Where I would want to walk outside to get some air, I saw a door with a placard of warning on it.

Penelope House was a contrasting experience in other ways, too. I am a big, energetic man, and the people I had encountered on my tour had taken a lot of comfort and pleasure in my size and enthusiasm. The kids had loved hugging me at the YMCA in Galveston, Texas and the school for blind children in Phoenix, Arizona. In Las Cruces, New Mexico, many of the residents of the Mesilla Valley Hospice appreciated my size and energy. Even the animals at the New Orleans SPCA liked jumping all over me. But towering over everyone in a domestic violence shelter, where each person had had more than one harrowing experience with a male, my stature and unrestrained nature made both the women and children at least wary, if not frightened.

One of the most disturbing contrasts came when a clumsy bump on my part was interpreted as a threat by one of the women staying at the shelter. She was sleeping during the announcement and unaware that a man was on the premises. From my unenlightened male perspective, our bump was nothing more than an accident, no harm, no foul. But from her traumatized perspective, my clumsiness was an affront that made her recoil with a look of fear. I apologized, smiled, and extended my hand, but she refused it, even with the director standing next to me saying that I was okay.

Because domestic violence shelters are places that do not get much male traffic, by the time that my tour stopped in the library/TV/play room, many of the residents were there waiting for my arrival. I found myself standing before the executive director, two social workers, five residents, five little girls, and three little boys, but before I could say anything, someone asked, "Who are you?"

When I gave my answer to one individual, I tried to give as much information as possible to the whole room. I spoke about my friend Kevin, his death on September 11, and what prompted me to ride a bicycle across North America, Africa, and Asia. I also opened up about why my fourth cross-continental trip, and second across North America, was marked by weekly stops of service. As I continued to answer questions, I could feel some tension leave the room and noticed the softening of a few postures. Looking back, I think I might have resurrected the reputation of men, just a bit, because one of the women let me hold and rock her baby to sleep — the significance of which (me, a large, strange man being handed the newborn child of a severely abused woman) was lost on me until I started writing this book.

When a game of catch broke out between two girls, I felt obliged to return the baby to his mother and join in. Moments later, when one young boy started talking trash about beating me in video football, I felt obliged to play with him, too.

Between the laughter from the girls playing catch, the conversations among the residents and administrators, and the boy's friendly bravado, the mood of the room started to change. By video game kickoff, everything about the scene gave the room a more homey warmth that only friendly banter can produce. I hoped that it felt less like a shelter and more like a home to them, then, too.

By halftime of the video game, the trash-talking boy was beating me badly, and I was seated on a sofa with one little girl curled up in my lap and another girl making a big deal out of ignoring me.

By the third quarter, the score of the video game was close. The boy was talking even more trash. One girl was tossing a ball at me to see if she could mess up my game. Another girl was curled up in my lap.

I scored a touchdown and started a crazy touchdown dance. All of the kids decided to imitate me, except the girl in my lap, who refused to let go and just hung on tighter.

By the beginning of the fourth quarter, all of the adults were finding the whole scene quite funny. Trying to trip me up, they laughingly began to ask me more complicated questions, but I could barely hear them because one girl was playing cheerleader in my ear, and the girl in my lap, who had also taken my side, was clapping when I did well and yelling at the trash-talking boy whenever he scored.

Late in the fourth, the whole room was into the game, or at least what was taking place around the game. The cheerleader was still cheering, the trash-talking boy was still talking, laughing at me, and telling me that I was going to fold under his pressure, and the girl on my lap decided to move to a more comfortable position — around my neck.

When I scored and tied the game, the kids and I celebrated with another crazy touchdown dance. But our dance was premature, and the trash-talking boy was right: I folded under the pressure and blew the point that could have won me the game.

Penelope House's executive director knew that volunteering at a battered women's shelter could be stressful, so she limited my time inside the shelter by giving me a tour of the Mobile area. Joined by a social worker and a family therapist, I tried to take in all the history of the city, but it was hard to concentrate on anything but the enormity of domestic violence. I just listened, with my mouth wide open, as these professionals discussed how easily a slap could become a person's cultural norm and immerse them in a personal and private hell.

While I stared blankly at the city skyline, one of the social workers reached up from the back seat to touch my shoulder and *said*, "David, stop. Stop trying to make sense of senseless acts."

The brief, undiluted glimpse of domestic violence afforded me at Penelope House made me kind of leery of what I might learn during my full day there. Many of the assumptions I made, from my perspective, about the depth of domestic violence were way off, and I knew that if I were ever going to try and cogently speak about what I experienced to anyone, I needed some time to look over my notes.

I went to a bar near my hotel and quickly got lost in the amplifying quotes and details—such as the stress lines and prematurely gray hair on those young faces—that I had jotted down. My mental journey, though, from the comfort of a barstool back to Penelope House, sent an icy chill though my mind. When I openly looked at things, I saw just how easily, maybe too easily, individuals can find themselves painted into a horrifying corner.

Think about it: you meet someone who seems nice. You like this person's look. You like how they look at you. You like how he or she looks after you. You open up about your strengths, weaknesses, ambitions, family, and friends. You reveal intimate details of your life and open up your body. Even though this person may be nice, a line of proper decorum always seems to get massaged a bit. You can't quite put your finger on it and may not even realize it, but somehow your perspective on your own life gets blurred. A line eventually gets crossed. A caring, watchful eye slowly becomes a stalking, watching eye. Loving concern gnarls itself into petty jealousies. You think, *This is not happening. Not to me. Not him.* You are emotionally blindsided and find that your individual fiscal and physical powers have been leached, leaving you too embarrassed to talk and too confused to leave. Lines get erased. Off-handed remarks ramp up to open-handed slaps. Fingers that once caressed your body now always seem to be clenched into a bruise-delivering fist. Consensual lovemaking becomes forcible rape. You threaten to leave, but it's too late. He knows your thought patterns and thus where you are going to run. He tells you that he will hurt your friends. You never, ever, thought this would happen to you. You want to protect your friends, so you stay. You try to exercise your own free will, which only makes his behavior worse and leaves you more vulnerable. You can only run as fast or far as you can carry your children. Exhausted, you stay, thinking, *This cannot be real.*

But it is: you are trapped in your own life.

I got lost in thought so fast that I had no clue what the bartender was talking about when she asked, "Are you working there? Nodding toward a big purple Penelope House sticker that I forgot I was still wearing. I explained that I was volunteering there and gave her my whole story. After I was done, she told me she had once needed their services, and that my drinks were on the house.

"What happened?" I asked.

She pursed her lips, exhaled and said, "You don't want to know." Then quickly smiled and said, "But it's all better now."

I watched her walk away, thinking of every woman I knew, and became frightened as I wondered how many of them had ever said, "...but it's all better now." That turned to a chill as I realized that some of the women I knew might be saying, "You don't want to know," to me and to others right now.

On my second day at Penelope House, I encountered an unfortunate story of domestic violence that stood out from all the rest. The woman's age, race, looks, demeanor, countenance, intellect, and number of children do not give any particular shape to her story; she could be anyone you know. Anyone.

This "ordinary" woman was beaten, repeatedly, by her husband. The children of this every-woman suffered the trauma of hearing and seeing their mother get bruised.

She left her husband. She left her home. She left everything and took advantage of the adult therapy, children's therapy, education, refuge, camaraderie, and other services Penelope House offered. After a period of time, she left the shelter to take her family to dinner, and her abuser, who'd been searching the city for her, appeared. With nothing more than empty space and a restraining order separating them, an exchange took place between this man and his ex-wife and children. The exchange was brief, but it only takes a moment to feel fear.

There was an extra bit of tension in the air as he said, "Wow, the kids are growing fast," which made this woman quietly hope for the arrival of the police or divine intervention. Something about the way this male role model said the familiar promise that things "were going to be different this time" made his children want to believe him. The exchange was brief, but it only takes a moment to become terrified.

As this woman and her children sat there with strangulating lumps of fear building in their throats, watching every move this man made, this man, this husband, this father, pulled out a gun and shot himself in the face. The exchange was brief, but it only takes a moment to become permanently scarred.

This family was staying in a residence separate from Penelope House, receiving therapy. As a part of my service, the administrators wanted me to pay a special visit to this family with the hope that I could establish a positive male connection with the lone son of the family.

When I approached the apartment, I could see the family members smiling, laughing, and interacting with a female social worker through the window. Once I entered the room, though, the scene changed. The children got very quiet and rushed to occupy themselves with looking at coloring books. Even the mother's smile dimmed.

Despite my best efforts to engage all of the kids, but especially the boy, by taking out my laptop to show them pictures of some of the very animals that they were coloring and by telling them stories of riding my bicycle past those animals, the kids hardly spoke. Instead, they spoke volumes to each other with their eyes and facial expressions. When either one of them did speak to me, they never looked up from the coloring book and used the women in the room as a conduit, saying, "Ask him this," or "Tell him that." I didn't make much headway into their lives that day but can only hope that I made it easier for them to see that not all men bring pain and violence.

With a world's worth of material, I agreed to give the facility an entertaining, picture-packed and motivating slide show of my bicycle travels to each place I gave service on my North American tour. I entered into this knowing that public speaking is never my problem—public shutting-up is. So, it was not an issue when a computer glitch left me without visual aids. At least, it wasn't an issue until the women of Penelope House walked in.

Entering along with the residents, and quickly filling up the room, were the harrowing details of their derailed lives. There were plenty of chairs and physical space, but no room could contain these stories where each was more awful than the one prior — and the first one was plenty depraved.

As I scanned the room, the expression of a woman in the back of the room caught my eye. With folded arms and upturned lips, her expression screamed, "What the hell are you going to possibly tell me about life … *man?*" I quickly found the fullness of the room suffocating and forgot almost everything that I was thinking about saying.

But really, what was I going to tell her?

I mean, what on earth could I tell her?

When my video football-playing, trash-talking buddy entered the room and noticed that the TV was turned off, and even he gave me a deflated look, I found myself totally thoughtless. "Aww, man, I thought we were going to play football," he said, pausing as if resigning himself to a consolation prize. He followed with, "Well, then, what are you going to talk about?"

That was when my angel came to rescue me.

My angel was none other than the six-year-old girl who had first sat on my lap and later hung on my neck the day before, while I played video football. She walked up and stood between me and the boy and took my hand. She radiantly smiled "angelically" and said, "I don't know, but I know that it's gonna be good." She then dragged me toward her small chair, grabbed it, and then pushed me back up to the front of the room, asking, "Can I stand up here with you?"

I don't remember answering her, but I do remember holding her hand tighter simply because it felt better that way, and because, for some reason, I believed her—this was "gonna be good." I held onto my angel's hand and opened up my life to the women and children of Penelope House.

The first thing I did was acknowledge that I, like their attackers, "am a man." The next thing that I did was tell the women that I felt honored to be entrusted with their stories and apologized, on behalf of all men, for their suffered pain and humiliation.

I told the ladies that because I elected to travel the world on a bicycle, many had dubbed me a "hero" but, after speaking with them, doubted if I ever deserved that moniker. Heroism, as I always understood it, was always one masculine, life-saving, Superman-esque act, but my definition had been broadened.

Real heroes are those who endure and persevere every day. Perseverance is often not pretty. Endurance is not a short story. Both go unrewarded, unheralded, and most times overlooked. And sometimes the bravest act is to save yourself.

Bicycling all over the world is cool and different, and, yes, it requires a certain kind of endurance and perseverance, but it is not heroic. In contrast to the women in abusive relationships who are unable to exercise their freedom of choice and are in constant danger, I was rarely ever in danger. I doubted my ability to access their degree of strength and survivor's will. That they were able to endure and persevere to find their way to safety was a truly heroic act.

I shed tears and revealed a great deal about my life as I gave my presentation, but didn't reveal everything. I didn't tell the ladies about how it took listening to their struggle to shift almost fifteen years' worth of emotional earth that I had shoveled on top of my friend Nicola's memory. I didn't let onto how, after my first half-day at Penelope House, I went to sleep only to wake up in the middle of the night speaking her name to an empty hotel room.

I looked in those women's eyes and commended them for their strength but said nothing of being too weak to look Nicola's mother in the eye as she said, "He took my baby." As much as I revealed to the women of Penelope House, the combination of their painful stories, my guilt in not thinking of Nicola since the day I biked away from her mother's home, and the embarrassment I felt in suddenly remembering what I had forgotten of a past friendship had rubbed me too raw emotionally to say too much more.

My speech was not tight, but I knew that my point had gotten across when the woman whose skeptical facial expression had challenged me sat there smiling.

"Ladies," I ended, "if you can survive this, then you can thrive anywhere. Trust me, because I've been *everywhere*."

What became of my angel, you ask? She drifted off during the middle of my speech and crawled onto the sofa. She had done her job well.

The picture at the beginning of this chapter is not of my angel. That little girl, and everyone else at Penelope House, has to remain anonymous, and therefore safe.

The picture that I have chosen to represent this chapter is that of a Kenyan boy I encountered on my bicycle, just a few feet across the Ethiopian border. This boy ran over out of nowhere to shake my hand and initially I selected this picture for the chapter solely because he was a young child who grabbed my hand in a very similar manner to that of my angel, who came out of the blue to ease my fears before giving a speech. As I have revised this chapter, again and again, I have come to see so much more in this image.

Since I visited Penelope House, I realized that I carried a lot of guilt over Nicola. I don't carry guilt over her death—there was nothing that I could have done. I do carry the burden of guilt, though, for choosing to forget a friend and letting her stay buried in my memory for almost fifteen years until I heard, and chose to feel, the stories of those women who shared her predicament.

Since I visited Penelope House and chose to write this essay, many of my female friends have shared their harrowing stories of abuse with me—too many. I am honored that they trust me with their stories. But more than that, their vulnerability has given me permission to expose my own guilt and maybe do something good with it.

This picture represents me, stepping out of the shadow to extend my hand to any man reading this story.

Men, if you cherish and respect women, give service to them. Offer your time to a domestic violence shelter. Become a role model to an abused child. Become a big brother. Always look to step up.

I am also addressing men who disrespect women: get help, stop the cycle of abuse, and step away from your own shadow.

I dedicate this story to the nameless, faceless, but certainly not powerless victims of domestic abuse. Ladies: be strong, persevere, endure, and look for help. It is out there.

Shedding light on domestic violence is the most that I can do: I owe this to the women of the world.

Delving into and then revealing parts of my own life is the most intense thing that I can do: I owe this to you, the reader.

Rest in peace, Nicola. You were taken much too soon.

We Write Our Own Ending

When does the end of a story occur? I mean, after the good guy beats up the bad guy and gets the girl, then what?

Is that the end of the story? I don't know.

I wonder about stories and their endings now, because after my travels around the world, I haven't seen too many endings to too many stories out there. I believe that every story in life, truly, ends where you allow it to.

My life story did not start on a bicycle, but a spirit to make my life story even better grew with each pedal stroke that took me further across Africa, Asia, and North America. This book is full of those life stories and how my bicycling experiences awakened me in some way. My life stories are the powerful memories and vivid flashbacks that fuel me to continue on.

All I need to do in order to refocus on the pursuit of new experiences and eventual growth is to close my eyes and remember the beautiful sunrise I saw in Lake Langano, Ethiopia, the hug I felt in Texas, the peace I felt viewing a Kyrgyzstan mountain range, or the smell of the wildflowers where I camped in Turkey. The powerful feeling is instantaneous and always leaves me wanting more.

But as you read this, I am sure that you are wondering if I met bad people and had bad times that created bad memoires, and if I did, what did I do with them.

Yes, I had bad experiences that created bad memories all over the world. These memories are as pointed and detailed as my good memories, maybe even more so, and I remain powerless to will any of them away. Just like the good times, all I have to do is close my eyes and they are there. But where those particular stories end is solely up to me.

Let me explain.

As soon as I cycled into one small town, a fight broke out in the street. One lone man was surrounded by a group of others that were kicking and spitting at him. The violent scene looked barbaric and sounded even worse. Now, being the one who wasn't getting beat down did wonders for arousing my interest and my willingness to investigate things, and when I walked amid the orbiting gauntlet of ear-jarring jeering and open-handed smacks, I saw that only certain people stepped forward to strike this man. There did not seem to be any defined rhythm, but it felt as if each person who stepped forward was limited to the time and number of blows they could deliver.

Looking even deeper into the action, it seemed, from the amount of kicks to the man's behind, that the people stepping forward were not really trying to hurt this man but just trying to bruise him badly.

I never noticed an official signal, but soon the event was over. The encircling group parted for this man to limp out, but only just enough so that he flinched every time someone from the group whispered something or even breathed hard. As the man shuffled away, I learned that he had been caught stealing from a market and now must forcibly endure the humiliation and bear "the mark," or bruising, as a reminder/warning. This whole display was more of a highly public message to many, rather than a simple beating of one.

I stood and watched for as long as I could then got on my bike and pedaled on, thinking of the scene and the community's sense of justice.

In another place in the world, I was biking along on a hot day and got tired of the even hotter water in my bottles. Figuring that I could get some cool water at a one-floor building that I saw on an overlooking ridge, I pedaled up a path leading up to it. As I rode up, a man exited the building and began walking down to meet me. He introduced himself as a physician and explained that he was the administrator for the building, which was a hospital. He showed me where I could get some cold water and then offered me a tour of the facility.

While touring the hospital, which was apparently the only one in the region, the administrator and I compared our daily lives. Along the way, he made it a point to introduce me to each patient that we passed, most of whom were in sheeted beds, though some were on sheetless beds and still some others had to convalesce on the bare floor. The contrasts between our lives became more evident with each step we took around this place, which was light-years from any hospital that I was accustomed to. But overall, I was impressed by the amount of help that the administrator stated the facility was able to give. But I became truly amazed when I saw the lab.

The room was full of shelves lined with glass jars and canisters but empty of the contents that belonged in them. There were no cotton swabs, cotton balls, gauze, tongue depressors, bottles of alcohol, or any of the other items I expect to see in a hospital. All that was in the room was an antiquated microscope that sat on an island countertop with more empty canisters and boxes. The room was so full of stuff but barren of healing and necessary things that the light wasn't even turned on.

The rest of the tour was short, but the empty lab stayed in the forefront of my mind. I wanted to do something, but by the time my tour ended at the front door, I thought, "What could I, a lone guy on a bicycle who was just passing through, *really do* to effect change here?"

I felt even more powerless when, while shaking hands goodbye and enjoying my last bit of shade, I learned about the fate of a man I saw limping up the path. The limping man spoke about his injuries with the administrator, who apologetically expressed doubt in his ability to help him because the hospital was too full. There was nothing they could do for him. There was nothing I could do to help.

By the time my travels took me to a place that I now (affectionately) call Crazy Man Town, I had successfully camped with other cyclists in open farmlands, abandoned buildings, mountainsides, and other places without any nighttime visitors or incident. But that was all before 3 in the morning on one particular night.

On this night, a crazy man wandered into our campsite. I can comfortably say that he was crazy because he was yelling over a transistor radio that was blaring more static than anything, and because, quite honestly, crazy rambling sounds the same in any language—and sounds even crazier when it awakens you in the middle of the night. I lay in my tent getting annoyed as I pictured him with a self-satisfied grin, ambling and rambling about our tent city, yards away, while ignoring the shouts of "Shut up" and "Be quiet" from some of the other awakened riders. I started climbing out of my tent, ready to join in the chorus of yelling "Shut up," into the night, as well as to pee, but tent acoustics played a cruel trick on my sense of distance. Before I could finish setting one bare foot out of my tent into the pitch darkness and onto the dewy soil, he firmly grabbed my forearm. The crazy man had been standing by *my* tent the whole time.

Without shoes, a shirt or even the eyeglasses I need to see anything, I stood unnerved, bare, and defenseless. Scared doesn't even begin to cover how I felt. An enormous lump formed in my throat. I wanted to close my eyes to refocus on his strong, steady, and sweaty clutch, but I was too startled even to dare to blink. Acting on pure instinct, I wrenched my forearm away from his grasp and snapped, *"Don't you fuckin' touch me."*

His eyes widened as he took a step back, but I couldn't do the same. The night darkness and my pitiful eyesight left me with no other option than to stand only inches away from this man, which was more than close enough to smell his foul breath. The blurry vision I had was of a man with sweaty skin that looked glossy in the moonlight, with an unkempt beard and matted hair that was all over the place. But what struck me most were his eyes. His right eye piercingly looked at me while his left eye wandered a bit. But both of his eyes were vacant and let me know that this man was not in his right mind. So there I stood, in an eye-to-lazy-eye standoff with a crazy man wearing a transistor radio around his neck.

Now, the difficult thing about face-offs with a crazy person is that your depth, understanding, and control of a situation tends to go away. You have no idea what they will do and your concept of normal action and reaction has no bearing on their actions. All you see is their eyes.

This left me with two choices: 1) Get crazy—actually, that would mean getting even crazier, or 2) Get calm.

I was in no position to get crazy and had no inclination to get crazier, so I got calm—quick.

I was so tense that when I said, "Be easy, man. It's cool," my voice cracked and sounded prepubescent. I liltingly repeated the words over and over again but didn't know if they were registering. Truth be told, I didn't care. I was talking as much for my nerves as his.

Each time I said the words, "be cool," I moved in a deliberate manner. I slowly took one foot out of my tent, eased up my shorts, smoothly cinched up my belt and backed away. In doing this, I felt confident enough to exhale a bit and let my eyes drift away from his for a second, but that didn't make things better. In fact, that made things worse.

Knives and clubs are not scary by themselves; they are necessities in some regions around the globe. But a large bush knife is scary as hell when it is gripped in the right hand of a babbling man, and even scarier when that man is wearing a blaring transistor radio and has a club dangling from his waistband at his left hand.

My mellowing tone seemed to ease the pace and ferocity of the man's mumbling gibberish, so I felt it was the perfect time to take full advantage of the flickering moonlight. I backed even farther away, which seemed to make both of us a lot more comfortable.

I can only assume that he felt comfortable, because once we were about six feet away from each other, the crazy man sat down at a stool next to my tent. At first he seemed content just to take a load off, but he soon became very interested in what was inside my tent. He sat his bush knife and club on the ground and then casually started to root through all of my gear that was within his reach.

An integral part to both of my professions—as a personal trainer and, sometimes, a nightclub bouncer—is to watch people's movements and then read them. As I watched this man callously rifle through my stuff, something about him made me understand that he was harmless. Once I drew this conclusion, I felt myself getting bolder and angrier with each of his dismissive touches.

When he opened a bottle of spring water sitting outside the tent and started splashing his face with it, I lost it. Harmless or not, bush knife or not, this man had crossed my line. "Yo, motherfucker, it's time to jet," I yelled, thumbing the air.

It seemed that a stern tone of voice was all it took to change things, because at that point the man looked up, stood up, smoothed out his wrinkled clothes, turned up his radio, and ambled away into the pitch blackness. I stood there looking in the direction he walked, thinking, "Well, that was crazy."

I went to my tent and grabbed my glasses to see better — and · just when he was nothing more than a faint contrast to the night background, he turned and started running back to camp with his arm raised. Not knowing if he was wielding his club, his knife, or just raising his hand, I got ready to run, but the man stopped a few yards away from me, smacked another rider's tent with the club, and then walked off, amused. The tent belonged to Sandra, an Austrian rider, who yelled over the fading din of his transistor radio, "Stop playing and go to sleep."

"It's none of us (camping cyclists). So you better shut up," I yelled, walking toward her tent and straining to look ahead through the darkness.

All I heard from her tent next was a nervous utterance that was a mixture of maybe five languages at once, but once she focused on English, she blurted out, "What's going on? Where are the others? How come they didn't help?"

These were indeed very good questions. But believing that this was just a harmless guy with a startling bark, no bite, who was long gone, I leapt at the opportunity to be a smart-ass. In a macabre manner I said, "They can't help us because they're all dead."

This time she screamed something in about seven languages. But the joke was on me, because right after I spoke, the camp went silent. You could not hear a thing—not a snore, not a fart, not even a rippling breeze over a tent. Just silence.

This time, I got scared.

After a few moments, the silence broke and all of the common sounds of slumbering cyclists took over, and all was funny again. Assuming that the crazy man was off doing what crazy men do, my thoughts turned toward my tent and sleep. When a still-very-scared Sandra told me not to leave her tent, I, still in smart-ass mode, told her that there was no point in both of us getting killed and that I was leaving. Not finding my humor amusing at all, she scrambled through her gear to produce a can of pepper spray and a cell phone and asked, "What is the phone number of the police?"

"Zero," I said, "because they don't exist."

In yet another place that I biked, I went to a performance on my day off. I sat looking at a blank stage waiting for an event to begin and heard a voice yell, "I have to get ready for the fight."

"I must get ready," the voice yelled, louder and closer.

From stage right, a man emerged draped in a black oversized hooded robe. This vocal figure never raised his head to reveal his face but kept loudly talking. "My enemy never sleeps. It only gets stronger. It only gets bigger." The figure kept shouting this but then started shadowboxing. While gracefully dancing, ducking, weaving, jabbing, and counterpunching around the stage, the figure shouted, "I must prepare. I must be ready. I cannot weaken. I can only be strong."

With no other props or staging, your eyes had no choice but to focus on the figure who was dancing tighter and tighter circles toward center stage. Once there, he started moving even faster and more intensely to the point where his draping garment accentuated his every movement and transformed him into a more striking, compelling, and even more dramatic being. And then, the figure stopped.

With his head bowed, he stood motionless for one second, two seconds, three seconds. The moments ticked away until the figure quietly said, "And the opponent is ..." with hands that had just created so much drama, the figure pulled on his belt and quietly slid his hands up along the lapels. He opened his robe and revealed the face, or at least the name, of his tireless enemy.

So much happened in the one single and simple movement that it took a moment to really see and focus on the white letters A-I-D-S painted across his wiry torso. With the name of his foe revealed, and nothing more to say, the figure bowed his head and silently walked off the stage.

I was so taken with the dramatic power of this display that I almost didn't pay any attention to the following stage act. But I am glad that I did, because it dealt with a weighty issue that too many women the world over have to face: rape and sexual assault.

In this one-act play, a man sweet-talks a girl away from her group of friends and, once assured that they are alone, attempts to assault her but is beaten back into submission by a few self-defense moves. My overall feeling was that this production lacked the dramatic fire of the previous one but that only lasted until I spoke with the playwright and the cast members afterward. That is when I felt the heat.

I had only approached the playwright because I wanted to ask her a few questions about her play, but we got along right away. Before I knew it, a conversation about everything else in life started. We joked about a lot of things during our conversation, including her beating me up, but there was nothing funny about this woman. Only in her mid-twenties, she spoke with an entrancing sense of passion and sense of confidence that belied her age.

So affected by the region's high frequency of rape, she referred to her own rape as an inevitability, rather than a possibility, and said that it was this inevitable event that drove her. She said that educating women about the art of self-defense was her life's mission and was training her body and mind to be ready. "Because," she said, "whenever a man comes and tries to take what is mine... it will be the fight of *both* our lives."

I believed her, too. Every action of this woman said that she was powerful, confident, and capable. But because she joked about beating me up and because she kept repeating the rationale that one must be prepared at all times and because I am a smart-ass, I played a joke.

In the middle of speaking, I yelled loudly and raised my hand in the air. Surprised, the two female cast members screamed and cowered. But the joke was on me. The playwright had her fist balled up and right at my jaw.

Her face was smiling, but not her eyes—there was nothing but focused readiness there. She said "Thank you" as we both lowered our hands and then turned her gaze steely and said to the other women, "Be prepared, at all times."

On a day off in some other place in the world, a fellow female rider met some men not affiliated with our tour. Their heinous plan was to engage her in some conversation over lunch, drug her food, let her ride off, follow her to her hotel, wait for the drugs to take effect, and then assault and rob her. That was the plan, but the difference between that outcome and any other came down to nothing more than a rare decision on my part to be punctual for a lunch date. Being on time put me in the right place to see a lot of wrong being done.

The men were not in the room when I arrived but their drugs were inside of the rider and taking effect rather quickly. When she stumbled to the door and then mumbled that she met some men, I quickly deduced what happened. Though she really didn't want to believe what was happening to her, there was no stopping the drama that was beginning to unfold, piece by piece, in her body.

Her eyelids widened, pupils dilated, and skin glistened with a fear-induced sweat as the realization that she had been drugged took hold in her mind. I stared at her mouth to try and better understand her, but each word was slurred and bordered on incoherence. She stared at my face, which was unable to mask my extreme concern, and became frightened. Her chest heaved as her breathing became more panicked and made whatever drug she'd been given course through her bloodstream even faster. She was a mess.

As I watched her stare glaze over, I too became a mess.

I didn't know what was happening or what to do and was beginning to panic. I told her to stay put and left the room to get help, but the situation only worsened when she followed me. Stumbling, wild and wide-eyed, she yelled, "They're here! They're here."

"Who?" I asked, looking behind her and over my shoulders and seeing no one.

"Them," she said, providing no additional details.

We tried communicating, about who "them" were and just what "them" looked like, but she was losing her grasp on reality one finger at a time. Slumping forward she said, "Dave, right now, I barely know what you look like...help me."

The end.

Or maybe I should say, "That's it."

Mark Twain said, "Travel is fatal to prejudice, bigotry, and narrow-mindedness," and I can honestly say that I started these bike travels thinking like a tourist: I would fly one place, bike through another and fly back home, remaining somewhat detached. But somewhere, while riding through the many communities, cultures, and countries, I rode beyond my comfort zone and changed.

When I did, layers of me that I never knew existed were peeled back to unveil a new me who thought, acted, and, most importantly, reacted to things differently. I like to think this was the process of me evolving into Mark Twain's quintessential "traveler." Since becoming this "traveler," my individual sense of power has been enhanced, and I now believe that each life story ends where your own sensibilities allow them to end.

Some riders who were present during these stories took great relief in the belief that incursions like these and "trouble" in general lurked far away from their safe neighborhoods and homelands. For them, any bad experiences that occurred ended as soon as they set foot on their flights home. One rider took particular delight in the distance between his hometown and the environment we were cycling through as he almost gleefully said, "I would kill myself if I lived here."

Because each individual rider was on these cycling trips searching to discover something only they could see, I couldn't fault them for seeing the world through that particular lens. I have to even admit that I was a wee bit envious when I heard things like this, because their view was a luxury that I didn't have. I was there because of a bad experience.

At some point of every day that I biked through North America, Africa, and Asia, I thought of my friend, Kevin Bowser. When I really think about his last day, I picture him going to work early but taking the time to look out his 98th floor window in order to take in the spectacular morning view. I envision him smiling and thinking pleasant thoughts as the sunrise warmed his office. In my mind, he is doing all of these things and in a real good place right before his floor and whole world becomes engulfed in explosive flames from a jetliner flown into his building.

That is what I want to believe, because having Kevin's story end any other way hurts way too much.

My very presence in every place that I bicycled around the world was proof that trouble lurks everywhere. I was able to endure all of my bad experiences because I clung to the belief that everyone has the power to move forward and do something about those experiences, wherever they occur. Because of this, I removed "where" these occurrences happened and want to focus on "what was done" because of that occurrence. I don't want to stoke fear and maybe be responsible for stopping anyone from touring and possibly becoming a traveler.

There are certainly more details to each of these stories, but for me, none of these stories ended.

But I won't keep you in suspense, though, and will tell you that the drugged girl didn't get assaulted and the potential attackers didn't end up in jail. In fact, the only person who came dangerously close to getting harmed was an old hotel gatekeeper.

Shortly after my friend said "help me," I sat her down on a sofa in the corner of the hotel lobby and was able to figure out who the men were. There were three of them, and I didn't know what to do, so I started to follow them out of the hotel. As I kept an eye on my friend's deteriorating posture, seeing the gall of the men angered me more and more. As I passed the hotel manager's desk, I yelled out the barest details and kept walking behind the men.

The manager was a female, and she scurried around the desk and ran up beside me as I reach the hotel doorway. By this time, the men had walked down the hotel steps and were just starting through the enclosed hotel parking lot. The manager put her hand on my forearm to stop me and yelled at an old man that was working as a gatekeeper to do something.

From the steps of the hotel, we stood and watched the elderly man, armed with nothing more than an aged stare, step away from his post and get in the way of the men as they coolly walked toward their car. With the gatekeeper's presence just encouraging their arrogance, the men slowed their pace to a cocky stroll. I wondered just what the manager expected this gatekeeper to do against men young enough to be his grandsons, but she expected something. She yelled, "Do something!" at the top of her lungs.

What happened next was unbelievable. Forcibly thrust into this game of age vs. experience, the old gatekeeper seriously upped the ante. He looked up at his boss, turned to the men that were now in the car, shrugged his shoulders, and then lay down on the ground in front of their vehicle.

Even as the engine revved, he stayed there.

Even as I ran down the steps yelling "Whoa" to stop this madness, he lay there.

Once again, I will pause this story.

Watching a friend succumb to an unknown dosage of an unknown drug was an emotional rollercoaster that I don't want to soon ride again. I tell that story to tourists to remind them that wherever you go in the world, you always need a sense of awareness. Now, whenever I tell that story, I am always sure to highlight the gatekeeper's actions to remind myself that something can always be done, you just have to be willing to go to that end. But what I try to hang onto the most from that story is the feeling of warmth I felt later from the cyclist's parents' embrace and the tone in her father's voice as he tearfully whispered, "Thank you, you saved my daughter's life."

When I recount the "beating in the dusty street" story, some only see the brutality. But because I live in Philadelphia, I see another side altogether. Where I live, "snitches get stitches" is a phrase and mentality that has gripped and ripped apart some communities. The fear of reprisals from thugs has stopped people from talking to police or "snitching" to help them solve crimes. This ethos has emboldened a criminal culture that has suffocated neighborhoods with an air of lawlessness. So now, I speak about that scene at many Philadelphia area schools to compare and contrast the sense of community. I am not saying that the ways of those in that street is the answer, but I would rather live in a place with a strong sense of a community than a place that doesn't have one.

While coasting down the path away from the one-floor hospital, my mind was racing with thoughts of wanting to do something to help. I came up with a lot of ideas, but with extremely limited wealth and resources, my thoughts didn't race far. But once I thought beyond the power of a dollar, I started to come up with different ways to improve the healing that went on at that hospital. I remembered how, as a child, lollipops always stopped my crying whenever I got a needle. So, when I returned home I purchased a case of lollipops, perfect for the many empty jars I saw there, and mailed them to the hospital.

The morning after my Crazy Man Town standoff, I pedaled away from the campsite with more trepidation of my fellow cyclists than a random guy with a transistor radio, club, and knife. Over breakfast, I asked the group why no one had come to my aid when it had to have sounded obvious that I was in a distressful nighttime situation. The reply I received was, "Well, you're a big guy, and if you couldn't handle it, then what were we going to do?"

Being in trouble and not being seen by someone who can help is tragic, but being in trouble and ignored is terrifying.

I retell this story to tourists in order to remind them to pack a strong sense of self-reliance, self-confidence and a strong sense of calm before packing anything else. More than size, physical strength, mace, a gun or anything else, these important things that you can own will keep you safer anywhere in the world.

After watching the one-man AIDS play and the self-defense exposition, some riders sat at dinner dismissively tossing around words like, "disgusting," "awful" and "stupid" to describe the night's entertainment. But not me. I sat there aglow still feeling the unflinching energy from the two acts and artists. Their spirit and passion came across like an empowering beacon and left me remembering that whether the foe that you are battling is a global disease or the evil that lurks in the dark heart of mankind, we all, just like the playwright said, must "be prepared." Both of these performers left such an indelible imprint on me that I now give service at battered women's shelters, AIDS clinics, and have given a few self-defense classes.

I guess that's where those stories are, for now.

However, there is one more.

After one trip, I ran into a rider as I was leaving to catch my flight home. I asked him when he was leaving to go home, and he said that he was going to rent a car and backtrack along our cycling route and "see what I missed."

With eyes wide open, I looked at him and told him that it was too late. The best part of the trip was us changing as a group and changing as individuals, and there was no way for us to recapture it.

"We just have to move forward, man," I said.

As we parted, he looked at me like I was crazy. Maybe I didn't communicate my point well enough. Maybe I wasn't the right messenger. Maybe I am completely wrong about the message. I could be—I don't profess to have all of the answers.

All I know is that some of my experiences make me smile, some make me cringe, but all of my stories make me do something. That action is the best part of every one of my stories.

Don't let any of your stories end.

State of Dave 2010

With a publishing company expressing interest in *Traveling at the Speed of Life* and another company expressing interest in sponsoring me for a ride across Australia, 2009 ended on a high note. Though both eventually fell through by February 2010, I went to the ocean to do my Polar Bear—or Black Bear—thing as usual in January, feeling hopeful that something big was just around the corner.

"You were there the whole time" is my favorite line from *Forrest Gump*. Forrest said this referencing Jenny's being in his heart while he was experiencing special things around the world.

Like Forrest, I have kept you in my heart during my experiences around the globe. To hammer that point home, I took many of you with me across Asia and North America in the form of pictures taped on my bicycle.

But your energy has fueled me beyond my simple cycling trips and enabled me to live an even fuller life than I could have ever imagined. For that, I owe you greatly, though I was always at a loss as to how to convey my gratitude.

Today, January 1, 2010, I waded into the frosty ocean for the fourth straight time, but this year was different because you were there. Besides writing my own wishes in the sand—wishes of becoming a published success, bicycling Australia, better health, *much* better wealth, and stuff involving relationships—I wrote your name as well, in the hopes that maybe you can have your own great year, as well as share in my success.

So welcome to my Lone Black Bear club and may all of your wishes for 2010 and beyond come true.

"You have been with me the whole time."

Thanks and love.

DAVID

Maybe, Just Maybe

"Yo, are you gonna go to the nigger store?"

Of all of the questions that I expected Scott, my friend and fellow trans-African bike race participant, to ask, this was certainly not one of them.

But now that the question was out there, what in the world did he mean by that? I know that my sense of humor has few boundaries, but even Scott, a white American, had to know the history of that word and that this was pushing it. I ignored him, but then he asked me again. I gave a cursory nervous laugh, along with an eye roll, and kept putting my tent together, but then another rider came over to my tent and asked, essentially, the same thing. I had to address this.

"What are you taking about?" I asked.

As they began describing the store that was in an open-air market near our camp, my stomach started to knot up. I outwardly feigned disbelief but knew what they were saying was true and thought, "Not again." I also knew that while I had successfully ignored the word "nigger" before, there was not going be any denying this time.

The market was just like any of the open-air markets that I had now become accustomed to on the continent, where an open tract of land near the center of the city gets converted into a bazaar where local merchants sell their wares.

This market sat on a plot of land just a few yards off the main road and a few feet above street level. Judging from the number of tent stores and wheeled carts, it looked like each vendor came early in the morning to stake out the best spot and then set up. I wish that I could say that I really had to search for the store, but I didn't. There it stood, in a prime spot for all to see, just as they described.

I felt dirty and embarrassed as soon as I saw the dark blue tent storefront with the word NIGGERS painted in big white letters. I so wished that I were alone but Scott and another rider flanked me. Their stares, looking for some sort of reaction on my part, made each step closer to the store that sold the Malawian version of hip-hop clothing and a few mixed tapes feel like a weird dream. I wanted to run ahead of them, rip the sign down and say, "Let's forget this," but couldn't. By the time I reached the store, my feelings had formed a lump in my throat. "What's up with the sign?" I finally said, meekly.

Rather than give me a straightforward answer, one of the two men manning the store smiled and started doing a dance called the "Harlem Shake" and said, "P. Diddy, New York City, we are the niggers!"

Just what does one say to that?

Not much in my case; I stood there feeling inept for a few seconds. But even when I did say something, it wasn't that definitive: "This is wrong," I blurted.

I wanted to say more than ask the few questions that I did and do more than take the few pictures that I took, but I was aware that what I was experiencing was bigger than me. What was happening would require more strategic thought than just mindless action or reaction. I knew this because this was not the only time I'd had to deal with this word in Africa.

I went and ate some burgers with my friends and reminisced about the cycling day but was thinking about that store and that word the whole time. After lunch, I left my friends, telling them that I was going to find an Internet café, but instead I went back to the market and sat under a shady tree across from the store and just watched.

Our next day of riding was going to be another eighty-plus miles, and I decided that it was as good a time as any to think about the word.

I thought about the first time I'd ever encountered the word—it had been a question then, too. I was a 4th grader in Starkville, Mississippi and walking though a strip mall parking lot with my mother. In the middle of the lot, there was a table set up with a man recruiting for the Ku Klux Klan. I lingered back a few feet from my mother and stared at the man at the table who proudly wore a KKK button. He stared back and asked, "What are you looking at, nigger?"

I looked over both shoulders for whom he could possibly be speaking to. When I figured out that he was speaking to me and saw no hesitation in using what I had been taught was a bad word, I ran up and found my mother.

It was some years later, in high school, when I first uttered the word nigger myself. Or maybe it was earlier—I don't really remember that instance as vividly, because everyone within my circle was saying it.

By the time I reached college, recording artists and producers had latched onto the word. They said that it was a term of endearment, a source of strength, and that everything hinged on the syllable inflection and on how it was spelled: N-I-G-G-E-R was bad. N-I-G-G-A was good.

They didn't care about any negative images or perceptions attached to it; they embraced it. Nothing mattered as long as you were the nigger (or, more preferably, nigga) who got paid, and got paid handsomely. This opened a door, and all of a sudden, niggas were everywhere: on movie screens, on records, and especially in casual conversation. I fell right in line and used the word all the time.

Toward the end of college, I was still using the word but thought about saying it less, because the gatekeepers of the socio-economic circles I wanted to enter believed it was an ugly and disgusting term.

By the time I finished college, it seemed that the only thing that all black men and women agreed on was that "nigger" had some intangible, yet heavy, images attached to it and it all came down to an individual's era, perspective, and experience with the word.

Since I grew up with hip-hop as my main form of music, I was born at the right time to have a prime vantage point of both sides.

I saw the camaraderie of using the word with your friends along with the potential profit of shouting it during a song. But at the same time, I saw that there was an extreme lack of focus and a lot of confinement to any of the attached images and perceptions. In the end, I saw "nigger" being much more of a mindset than it ever was a simple word, no matter how you spelled it. For the most part, I was apathetic to the whole debate. *I am a man, and above this*, I believed.

I was more than sixty miles away from the Malawian store when I shifted my thoughts. I had to shift my focus, because all of my nigger and nigga thoughts were in America and I'd never heard the word on my 2002 North American trip, unless it was in some hip-hop music that I was listening to. But it was 2004 and I'd just seen that store in Malawi. I had to think about my African encounters with the word.

I hadn't heard the word in Egypt, unless it was in some hip-hop music that I was listening to. But while speaking with a group of men in a restaurant near Khartoum, Sudan, there it was, just like it was in Starkville, Mississippi. One of the Sudanese man casually referred to me as a nigger and though I acted like I didn't hear it, because I didn't want to deal with it, I most definitely did hear it.

Then, I heard it again while walking though a market near Gondar, Ethiopia. A man wanting to pick a fight yelled at me, "Nigger, son of slaves"—and those were his nicer words. His alcohol-infused vitriol didn't lead to the fight he was seeking, but it did get me thinking a bit.

I started thinking a lot more about what people saw in the word and saw in me, specifically, when dining at the home of an Ethiopian bike rider in Addis Ababa, Ethiopia. While joking around, he called me a nigger and when I asked him why he called me that, he said, "You are a nigger!" Looking around as if I was playing a joke on him, he added, "Isn't that what you want to be called?"

I didn't say anything but did point toward my friend Scott, a white American, and asked what he was.

"A man."

I then pointed to Pete, a white Canadian, and then to his friend, an Ethiopian male, and asked what they were. Both times, he said, "He is a man."

This was bad, real bad. I looked at everyone like I was the last person in on a very bad joke, and maybe I was. I piped up and boomed, "I am a man," but because the lyrics of the entertainment I had supported for years loudly yelled otherwise, my words were largely ineffectual.

By the time that I biked into Kenya and two schoolboys walked past me and tittered, "Hi, nigger," I began to think that I was wearing some sort of nigger suit or something that only others could see. Their greeting, though, prompted me to step outside myself and, when I did, I saw that I *was* wearing something.

My size, mannerisms, and speech was my "one size fits all" costume that marked me as a black American. This costume was woven of the powerful, marketable, and confusing images that had been projected from the Untied States and led to the distressing assumption that I was a nigger first and, only lastly, a man.

This "nigger" costume was way too confining and I desperately wanted to run away and break free from it. But I couldn't: the threads were too strong and the pants hung way too low. I was trapped.

But I started to feel a bit freer, or at least feel better about my potential to eventually rip the threads of this costume, after I met a guy named Peter in Iringa, Tanzania.

I met Peter in an empty bar where I'd I hung out until the wee hours before realizing it was too dark and I was too lost to find my way back to my campsite. I entered the establishment and asked the guy behind the bar if there was a cab I could catch. He laughingly pointed to a man who was passed out on the bar and said, "He's a cab driver."

"Fuck it, I'll walk," I said, and started to leave.

The guy behind the bar saw my size and heard my accent. He got a quick peek at my "costume" and asked if I was an American. When I said I was, he introduced himself to me as Peter and asked where I was going. When I told him the name of the campsite, he said that it wasn't far and that he would drive me after I had a drink with him. Peter didn't like drinking alone.

Over the drink, we started talking about my bicycle travels and reasons for being in Tanzania and Africa. From his questions and conversation, it was obvious that Peter knew a lot about American culture, but he wanted to know more. He wanted my opinion, as a black American, on what was happening in my country.

Did police target black men?

What did I think of the Kobe Bryant case?

Could a black man get a fair shot in America?

The conversation was too far ranging and I was too tired to get very deep into these issues, so I just said that we each play an important role in our rise and demise.

He said that sounded sensible to him, but what he really wanted to speak about most was how America's biggest export, entertainment, was affecting the minds, ideals, and actions of his countrymen. Speaking with an underscoring fire that indicated he had something important to get off of his chest, he started talking about lyrics, specifically hip-hop lyrics.

"What are you giving us?" he demanded. He went on to say that when he was younger, artists lyrically told him the only things worth fighting for were societal wrongs and the only thing worth dying for was injustice.

"But this shit!" he said, "this shit is crazy! You go get big money, big rims, big titties, big sex, big shit, and after all of that getting, you still have a shit day and are still so angry? I don't get it."

I sat there with nothing to say, because I'd never thought that way, and he was right. But he wasn't finished.

He then pointed to me and said that he held me responsible to do something about it all. Incredulous, I looked at him and asked what he expected me to do. "I'm just a biker, sitting in here with your drunk ass," I said.

He quietly sipped his drink, pointed his finger at me and said, "You told me that you have no money, and I believe you. But somehow, with nothing, you managed to figure it out here," pointing to his heart.

"…and here," pointing to his head.

"…to get here," pointing to the ground.

"So you have some power, and you have to figure out how to use it." With that, he slammed the rest of his drink, said, "Let's go" and drove me to my campsite.

We never spoke about the word nigger specifically during our conversation, but I felt that we were definitely speaking about the mindset that came with it. Maybe that is why seeing the store, one country later, in Malawi, affected me the way that it did.

Maybe that's why I left my fellow riders, just to go back to that Malawian store and watch it for a while.

I didn't hear the word anymore while I was in Africa, or maybe I did. I don't know.

All I know was that I was through with it.

Upon returning home to Philadelphia, I am sure that the word "nigger" was not said any more than it had been before I left, but I seemed to hear it a whole lot more often. Each time the word was used by comedians, actors, and individuals to spice up jokes, scripts, and coffee talk, it just ended up peppering my ears. No matter who said it, the word bothered me, but it especially hurt when it was levied at me after I gave a talk about my trip to a small group one rainy evening.

During the talk, I overtly stated that electing to bicycle Africa was the best decision I had made in my life. But I guess one of the attendees, an African-American male, never got that message because while giving me a ride to catch a train, he said, "Man, I don't know why you went to Africa…ain't nothing there but niggers and AIDS."

His words felt like a punch to my gut and left me sitting silently in his passenger seat. I wanted to change his opinion on many things but instead I just sat there looking at him with eyes that screamed, "Brother, why? Why did you say that—didn't you hear a word of what I just said?"

He kept talking and soon my passivity wasn't enough. I quickly made up an excuse, jumped out of his car at the next stoplight, and took a stand, in the rain. It felt good.

Goethe, the German philosopher, once said, "There is nothing more frightful than ignorance in action," and thus it took something that I felt was frightfully ignorant months later to make me take an even bigger stand.

During a break in a lecture series I was giving on critical thinking, a student was telling a story to others about her son. In the story, she referred to her son often — openly and endearingly — as "her nigger." Their casual use of the word frustrated me, but also started me thinking: Why am I so upset? What is a nigger? Is it different than a "nigga"? Is it still a term of endearment? Was it ever? What do I do? Where does a black man start and nigger begin? What can I do?

Feeling that the exchange could be a useful lecture tool, I took out my laptop, pulled up the picture of the Malawian store, and asked this woman what she would do if she saw a store named "Niggers." Would she shop there?

I told her not to answer right away, and then started to turn my laptop around to show her the picture. But before I could say or show anything, she answered, "It depends on what they're selling."

In an environment where I was teaching about making informed critical decisions based on the information that is at your disposal, I was now being schooled. Hers wasn't the answer I was angling for, but it was her answer, *from her experience*.

She hadn't biked anywhere with me and any image that *she* had of a nigger was more tangible than any of *my* stories. They were just pictures on a computer screen, just like fairytales. There was no connection.

I imagined that it was the same way for the black man that said there was nothing in Africa except for AIDS and niggers. He hadn't heard the Malawians say, "We are the niggers!" or felt a pang of embarrassment while watching them try and ingratiate themselves by doing some dance. He didn't see all of this and then feel like he was personally responsible for the sign because he had supported that image through CDs, movies, and other media. All of those stirring feelings were mine.

I went for a ride that night and thought a lot. I knew that I was going to continue traveling and wanted it assumed that if I went back to Africa—or anywhere on this planet—I would be thought of as a man, first and foremost.

I rode along and concluded that the word "nigger" may have been a galvanizing word at some point in time because the overriding image it called forth was that of an enduring, eternally-strong black man and woman. But that was very long ago, spoken by very different black people. I rode further and further concluded that this is not that time, and we are not those people.

My conclusions and experiences had me determined to do something, anything, to try and open some minds. I knew that this was going to be tough, because at another point in my life, I'd said "nigger" all the time, never thinking that the word would ever envelop or confine me. Back then, my thoughts about taking action to try and change anyone's mind about the use of any word would have been different. But I had experienced way too much and had come way too far in life to think so little of myself, or of the power I had to change things.

I was a very different David and this was a very different time.

I didn't think that it was much, but I wrote an email detailing my foolishness in believing that I was above it all and the circumstances that had led to my change of heart about the usage of the word. I pledged to stop using the word and stated that I was going to "keep it real" and be "about the Benjamins" by not buying this image anymore. I just couldn't. I attached the picture of the Malawian store to the email and sent it to thirty of my friends.

My email and picture must have been compelling, because it spread virally to the point where I received over 3,000 emails and eventually became published in *Essence* magazine. The email also seemed to put me right in the middle of the "N-word" debate.

Some people questioned the validity of my picture but it's authentic.

Some looked at my missive as waging a war on hip-hop but I wasn't. I love hip-hop.

Some called me foolish, but I don't think so.

Some even called me a dumb nigger. That's their opinion.

I did end up getting a lot of people to think differently, but wished that I could have done more. All of this got me thinking and searching for a shared experience and circumstance that we could all possibly learn and move forward from though.

There has to be something, because you were not on my 2007 bike trip across Asia when a Tajikistan man called me a "beeg neegah," and I was not with you throughout your life to get you to the point where you think the way you do. But I do believe that I've found that shared experience, maybe, just maybe.

Not long ago, Barack Obama stood on the steps of a Chicago memorial and got a lot of people excited with the word "change." Even though he said the same stuff that others before him had said, it looked and felt different coming from him. To me, it even sounded different, because, pointing to us, he reminded each individual of his or her own power to provide that change. He was speaking about change in politics and government, but maybe, I thought, he could change even more.

Generations of black men and women have endured a lot of pressure and unneeded heat that has made many of us think less of ourselves and our individual rights and abilities. We have read so many headlines about innocent individuals getting killed, jailed or discriminated against that each newsflash erodes our faith in any governmental system more and more. Our spirit has been undermined to the point where we, culturally, suffer from posttraumatic stress disorder and so I understand why some boys grow up believing all they can ever be is a "nigger."

I remember sitting with friends at Temple University and hearing the Rodney King verdict announced in legalese. Stacy, a former classmate, said, "I may not be smart and all, but it sure sounded like we didn't get shit." How many times did we sit around the TV to see or hear a verdict that went the other way?

How many times did we not get "it," whatever we were hoping for or whatever we knew was just?

We got to the point at which we cheered for things that meant nothing — or even worse, cheered for reprehensible outcomes simply to feel like we got a "win."

Diamonds are nothing more than pieces of coal, forged under extreme pressure and heat, and maybe generations of black men and women had to endure what we have to enter this, our possible diamond era. Maybe this is our time of alchemy. Barack Obama is not perfect — no man is — but maybe clearly watching his ascension will make us see the diamonds that reside within us all.

Maybe seeing his circumstances, reading about my experiences, and being reminded of your own individual power will make you think differently.

Maybe, just maybe, Barack Obama's Kenyan roots will make us think more of Africa and Africans.

Maybe his becoming President will make us, here, think more of ourselves as well as what we are capable of achieving.

Maybe Peter will see that his words eventually affected me so much that I dedicated this book to him.

Maybe P. Diddy, Diddy, Sean, Puff, Puffy, or whatever he is calling himself these days will read this and be humiliated that some Africans would use his name to legitimize the embarrassing name of their store. But maybe it won't stop there. Maybe he and other record executives will promote acts that make us strive to be more, and not settle for some placating bullshit.

On November 4, 2008, we got a lot more than a new administration. On that fall Chicago evening, our nation got a new portrait of the first family. In addition to shedding a shared prideful tear, we also gained a common experience that can be used as an opportunity to shed a shared burdening image. I thought of Stacy that night and wished I knew where she was to say, "Baby, we got some *big* shit tonight!"

I know that I am hanging a lot on the election of one man, but maybe some changes, well beyond politics, can happen. I certainly hope so, because I still have a lot more countries and continents to bicycle and I want it assumed that I am just like the 44th leader of my nation—a black man, and damn sure not some "nigger."

"I freed a thousand slaves. I could have freed a thousand more if only they knew they were slaves."

—*Harriet Tubman*

State of Dave 2011

Last year, I wrote the names of my friends and my wishes in the Brigantine, New Jersey sand and then ran into the ocean as the sun broke the horizon on a new day and a new year.

Yes, I know that I am crazy for doing this, but this ritual is my thing and I am cool with my crazy.

But maybe I'm not that crazy, because my sand wishes came true and my friends are still with me.

The first decade of the 2000s were tough, emotionally-wrenching years that were scarred by 9/11, 2 wars, recessions, rampant downsizing, record winters, feisty elections, floods, hurricanes, tsunamis, high gas prices, *Glitter* starring Mariah Carey, death, and *Pluto Nash* starring Eddie Murphy. But, they're over, and if you are reading this, then we did the hardest part: we endured.

We survived the tough times, which means that we can, and will, thrive in the times that lie ahead.

I went back to Brigantine again on 1/1/11 and traipsed through a few feet of snow to get to the shoreline again. Again, I wrote more wishes and more names in the sand, and again I look forward to my wishes coming true and to you still being in my life. Thank you for being my friend and here is to thriving in the next ten years.

Love,

DAVID

A Final Word, Before We Part...

"Sylvester, you never know where life takes you."

Mr. Byrne, my seventh-grade English teacher, said this to me in reply to a question I had regarding whether he thought that I would ever do anything of enough note to be a part of the world-renowned Explorers Club, an organization that promotes the scientific exploration of the earth and beyond. Mr. Byrne sticks out in my memory as one of my best teachers ever because he introduced me to new things, new literature, and new organizations like The Explorers Club and then afterward would challenge me to try and feel things from the author's perspective and then write about it.

His answer to my question was perfect, because I was (and still am) a big daydreamer who constantly dwells on the possibilities. Around that time in my life, I wanted to be an ambassador—or was it a congressman, or maybe it was a senator? In any case, a moment later, I wanted to be a professional athlete. Later on, it was a photographer. Then it was a writer, and later still, it was a professional speaker. Then there was the next day when I wanted to be a_____.

Almost all of the teachers and coaches I have had in my lifetime, except for Mr. Byrne and a few others, wanted me to settle down, focus on just one thing, and just "color inside the lines," but that wasn't me. I was an independent-minded kid that was fast becoming an independent-minded adult and was all over the place, all of the time.

One of the things that Mr. Byrne shared with our class was Robert Frost's poem, *The Road Less Traveled*. Poems and lyrics had never struck a chord with me, but even at an early age, this one did. In one of Frost's most famous verses, he wrote:

I shall be telling this with a sigh

somewhere ages and ages hence:

Two roads diverged in a wood, and I—

I took the one less traveled by,

and that has made all the difference.

To me, the poem said: getting on any road less traveled was fairly easy, as long as you had passion, but staying on the road long enough to feel the difference was the tough part.

Mr. Byrne had no idea what challenges I would face in life and how I would think, feel and then act upon them. He didn't know that the events of one day in 2001 would stir my passions enough to get on my bike and go. He was just teaching his class and conditioning the mind of a big afroed kid who sat daydreaming in the back row.

Some of you may have read my stories and wondered at my actions, thinking them something extraordinary, but I can tell you that I am nothing special. The only thing that may be special about me is that I now have a better idea of where my limits are. I say this because, on September 10, 2001, I believed that I knew all there was to know about me. I thought that my capacity and limit for achieving, pain, work, sweat, pleasure, and other things was "right here."

But once I elected to venture down the road less traveled, I had to search for abilities within me that would have otherwise remained overlooked and dormant. After discovering those abilities, I had to dig even deeper to then cultivate them into talents. And in doing all of this, I discovered that my limit for pain, pleasure, work, hugs, smiles, achievement, sweat, tears, everything, and anything was somewhere "..way...........out............... there."

And that is really all there is to my story.

Once stripped of the names, specific locales, and even the bicycle and broken down to its most basic kernel, all you have is a man crossing a void.

Crossing my void's distance between what I thought I could do and bear - "right here"- and what I actually could endure and achieve- "..way...........out...............there"- was the "all the difference" Frost so beautifully wrote about.

Crossing my void's distance is the difference between who I was as a kid and who I am now as a man.

I won't lie to you: a lot of effort has been put into planning and riding on these trips, writing this book, and everything else that I have done. But all of the effort that I have put forth can pale in comparison to the amount of effort that one puts into not drinking for a day, not doing drugs for an hour, writing a love letter, responding to a love letter, apologizing, believing, moving forward, battling depression, or a myriad of other things that happen during our days.

It has been a long time since seventh grade, but after having paid the price long enough to feel the life-affirming difference, I can tell you I feel even more deeply about Frost's ode. I also feel stronger about Mr. Byrne as a teacher because life is a lot like his English classes: the lessons learned all depend on how you feel, think, and react to the material given.

While crossing my void, I learned that none of what is gained and lost on the road will ever exactly match up; it is up to you to fill in those gaps between. For instance, I lost a lot when Kevin died, and nowhere I bike or anything I do will ever bring back my friend but the fact that on every September 11 since 2002 I receive beautiful messages like "I am thinking of friendship today" from people all over the planet who never knew Kevin other than through me brings me solace. It also brings me comfort to know that his passing triggered the Kevin Bowser Memorial Scholarship which assists Philadelphia's urban youths in proceeding to the next level of life.

But as much as I have achieved, I hope that I have done enough.

In the Bowser household, there is going to be a day when Kevin's children are going to need their father to navigate dilemmas that only he could compass. Sadly, they will not be able to benefit from the man who I was fortunate enough to befriend and admire. When that time comes, I hope that this tapestry of travels, encounters, lessons, and experiences that was prompted by his death will be enough to keep them warm and will help instill them with a confidence to know that they came from a very special individual.

So after all of that: "What's next," you ask?

I don't know, but I think I'll keep daydreaming- it's worked for me thus far.

Each time that I have dreamt of something and achieved it, or even attempted it, the main byproduct was a stronger passion for life and living along with a healthier belief in my own ability to make my next dream possible. That belief and passion combined to make my next dream possible, and the next dream, and the next, to the point that I believe that I can do anything.

If my life had followed a traditional track, I might only have been able to achieve one or maybe two of my envisioned possibilities. But, in the process of riding a bicycle with an open heart and an open mind with my focus being only on attaining the next smile and next high-five, I became everything I ever wanted to be.

In addition to being a personal trainer, I now make a living by cycling the world and motivating others through my story in words and pictures. When I travel to foreign lands, I proudly represent my country, my race, and, most especially, my family. Within all of those things, I am the professional athlete, photographer, writer, ambassador, and professional speaker that I always wanted to be.

And it gets even better, because I am something that I never overtly wished for but needed so much: I am happy.

But let me really answer your question of what's next with another quote from Mr. Byrne who, when I asked him what I had to do to get an "A" on an essay, said, "Sylvester, if you lead from your heart, you'll never be wrong."

Thank you, Mr. Byrne. You shaped my life. (And thanks for telling me about the Explorers Club—I got in!)

Thank you to all of my friends. You drove me more than you'll ever know.

And thank you, reader, for reading this book.

At the end of my documentary, "Contribute 2 the Experience," I asked viewers to find their bike. Not their actual bike, but their proverbial, poetic, artistic, and "passionate" bike that is vital to their being and makes their heart sing. I requested that each viewer "find their bike," and when they find it, to ride it. So, after reading my book, I ask you dear reader: find your bike, please.

Find your bike and ride it across your own void, and when you do, it will make all the difference.

Have faith in yourself, lead with your heart, and always remember to inspire responsibly.

Ride on.

Shout Outs

It has taken me well over two years to write about the last ten years of my life and, while I have lived all of the experiences and written all of the words, this book and the quality of my life would not have been possible without my friends.

My friends have fed, hugged, listened to, and loved me. My friends have given me money, advice, support and encouragement. They have given me so much and only asked me to do one thing in return: "Keep moving forward Dave."

Here are just a few that have helped me along the way:

All of the strong black men that I have been most fortunate to know: you honor me.

Aimee Glocke: the revolution is being televised.

Dr. Alan Branson: a little dose of evil ain't so bad.

Alma Qualli: thanks for your will and snatching the want-ads from my hands.

Alyson Silver: you're gonna make a great mom.

Amy Hooper: your warmth kept me from giving up.

Amy Saggiamo: let's go get a sippy cup of vodka.

Anne Burke: thanks for helping me read the map.

Andrea Nass: your half ass is a great ass.

Andrea Zak: you always find a way to help me.

Aunt Elaine: thank you for showing me that one can push through pain.

Aunt Paula: thank you for showing me the amazing power within one hug.

Avelina Espelita: food, friendship and years of laughter go a long way.

Ben Seal: thanks for not charging me- it's not like I could have afforded you anyway.

Brian Rodgers: thank you for making Austin, Texas feel like home.

Brandon, Thaon and Laila: be ever confident and always remember that you are a Sylvester, which means that you can do everything and anything.

Carline Raphael: thank you for showing me the nobility within enduring.

Catriona Kennedy: thanks for seeing past my volume.

Carnell 'Caveman' Baugh: you kept me floating.

Charlie Davidson: thanks for getting me home.

Cedric, Mark, Stephan and Wayne: employees of the month-every month!

Chris Gabello: your talent behind the camera is unmatched.

Dr. Christa Heyward: thanks for visiting me.

Cyndi Kwan: thanks for reading my first draft—it was so rough but you still saw promise.

Dana Robinson-Melendez and Trixie: thanks for the rides, the food and the sunscreen…but what do I do with these tampons?

Daniel Bennett: your description of me meant more than you'll ever know.

David Sims and John Lindsay: thank you for showing what art and artists are all about.

Denise Sistrunk: so many would be lost without you—including me.

Don Johnson: thanks for teaching me that yoga without the spirituality is just posturing.

Ed Highsmith: thanks for making lifting fun.

Frank Schinchirimini: thanks for believing in me when other bike shops wouldn't.

Greg Perry: nothing in the gym has been as much fun since you left- you really did cover the ground that you stood on.

Ingrid Vanderveldt: thanks for letting me talk.

Jim Caple: more than making me look cool, you made me *be* cool.

Jill Widra: your gift helped me get out of my own way.

James Turner: always calm, always cool, always there.

Jarrod Lewis: you called it all from the beginning— thanks for helping me see it too.

John Moser and Delco Development: your input made my rides come full circle.

Johnny Cash: thanks for showing me that the hardest decisions are sometimes the best decisions.

Joe Lee: thanks for nothing:)

Kallan Resnick: when it comes to raw strength and determination, you are unrivaled.

Kedrick Johnson: thanks for your brotherhood, the rides, Scarface movie trivia and your beautiful letter- but don't think for a minute that I'm gonna forget you making me push a car with the emergency brake on.

Kellen Carter: you're a special man and the world is lucky to have you.

Kelvin Bowser: thank you for being my brother.

Korinna Shaw: thanks for reading my profile.

Kristen Sullivan: your story is badass and deserved more: earthcycle.org

Leigh, Elizabeth, Benny, Amelia and Chico: thank you for showing me what Billy Clyde Tuggle would do.

Lynne Hernandez: thanks for reminding me to get to the point.

Malini Sekhar: your presence and patience were a godsend.

Malinda Daniel: for 70 bucks we can go all the way.

Mary Porter: thanks for your courage.

Dr. Matthew S. Johnson: always remember the 3 B's.

Matthew Siembeda, your support got this whole ball rolling.

Mark Wallace: thank you for showing me that it's never too late to pick up a skill, and that passion can make up for any amount of lost time.

Maurice Baynard: shit don't stop, brother, shit don't stop.

Dr. Merida Grant: thanks for showing me what focus is all about- by the way, Kobe Bryant is the best ever.

Melina Bell: thanks for showing me what discipline can achieve.

Miia Melkoniemi: thanks for accepting my apology.

Mike Perkins: my hero.

Michelle Price and Price Communications: the knowledge I gained from just hanging around you has been immeasurable.

Mike Vitez: the response to your story changed the direction of my life.

Nancy, Dennis and Ziva: we are family. Sake and Simon: RIP.

Natalie Martin: thanks for always sounding excited to hear my voice.

Natalie Panaia: thanks for opening your heart and your stores to me.

Otis Ivy: you are the best bike mechanic on the planet, by far.

Pat Marshall: thank you for a wonderful party.

Pete Madden and Agile Cat: you don't just do things—you do things right.

Priscilla Coblentz: red is everyone's favorite color.

Rachel Gans: always moving forward- always inspiring.

Ramith Nukrumah: we are a lot more than mentor and mentee now—we are brothers and I love it.

Sandra Simon: Dongala still touches me.

Sara Trohaugh: you are my human ray of sunshine.

Scott Brookens and Steve Ebersole: long live "The Room of Doom."

Scott Miller: life aint nothing but big ballin' and Uigher yes, yes yall'n.

Shelley Meaney: thanks for getting to know me though my writing.

Sherri Franklin: your words and vision still keep me thinking and evolving.

Sheryl and Larry: thank you for looking after me. Santos: RIP.

Stan Wilkes: thanks for the offer, but I'm good.

Stephanie Falkenstein: getting lost with you wasn't so fun but finding a fabulous friend has been great.

Sue Prant: New Year's Eve in Topeka was fun.

Suzy Q: thanks for the birthday cake.

Thomas Puleo: music, photography, coffee: is there anything that you can't do?

Tracy Sylvester: being in your big-sister shadow made me stronger.

WSB: you remain the prime directive.

Wendy Laurijssens: thanks for the pictures- they still motivate me☺

Wheeler del Toro: you are peerless when it comes to hustling.

Zoe Bisk: thanks for seeing my movie.

Waldron Academy, Central High School and Temple University: thank you for molding my mind.

The employees of Café Loftus: thank you for starting off so many of my days with a smile and a high five.

The members and staff of the Union League of Philadelphia: thanks for reinforcing the tenet that people with ideas earn acknowledgment, and that people who move to actualize their ideas earn respect.

Essence Magazine, *Philadelphia City Paper*, *Philadelphia Inquirer*, and *Philadelphia Daily News*: you made me believe I had talent as a writer.

SunRims Big Mammoth Fat rim: 2 continents, 18 countries, countless miles and NEVER needed truing. These rims are badass.

The Philadelphia Foundation and the Kevin Bowser Memorial Scholarship

My 'Wife', my 'Girlfriend', my 'Sidepiece' and my 'Baby': thanks for holding up under my weight.

Neighborhood Bike Works of Philadelphia

Bike Coalition of Philadelphia

My apologies to those I've missed: I'll give you a shout out in the next book.

Made in the USA
Lexington, KY
11 October 2012